Preface

In the everyday life of a busy business, with the overriding need to secure contracts of sale or purchase, attention to the contract itself can often be overlooked. This can have disastrous consequences; an imprecise or non-existent written contract can often leave the rights and obligations of the parties uncertain. As a consequence, businesses can be held up from running their usual operations, and – in many cases – expensive and protracted litigation results.

It is, of course, sometimes the case that entirely informal contracts are embarked on and work themselves out to the complete satisfaction of the parties. All too often, however, this is does not occur.

It can be time-consuming and costly, particularly if the business has no immediate access to legal advice, for contracts to be drafted in the required form. This book, therefore, sets out model contracts for use in the type of agreements in which businesses will generally become involved. While the specimen contracts will no doubt often need amending to suit the facts of the individual contract, we have prepared models which can serve as the basis, sometimes without any change at all, for a properly set out contract.

We have also been mindful of the type of contracts most often made by modern businesses. The sale and purchase of goods will remain the most common, but new technology has become of increasing importance, and hence we have included specimen contracts dealing with software and with on-line agreements.

This purports to be a handy tool for businesses, rather than a legal text book. It was, however, necessary to explain the background to the contracts which we have prepared, and so the relevant legal principles lying behind them have also been set out.

Dr Richard Lawson LLM PhD
Partner, Lawmark

Contents

Contents

Contents

Contents

Contents

Section A:
Commentary

Chapter A1
Forming and Concluding a Contract

At a glance A1.1

- Ideally, though not essentially, a contractual arrangement should be expressed in a formal document (that is to say in writing and signed by both parties).

- An agreement which is not formally expressed will still be binding but since the parties may have a different recollection of what exactly was agreed, there should always be a document setting out, if only in the form of bullet points, the heads of agreement.

- A binding agreement will normally be reached between parties if they have agreed on the essential points of the contract. Such items as the precise subject matter of the agreement and the price to be paid should usually be definitely agreed.

- The relevant contract terms must be adequately brought to the attention of the other side. The terms themselves do not have to be presented to the other side; it is enough if reference is made to them, e.g. by stating in a letter that copies are available on request.

- If the parties have formed contracts between themselves in the past, terms can be incorporated as a result of this normal course of dealing. It will be a matter of fact dependent on the circumstances of each case as to how many previous contracts need to have been made between the parties.

- A relatively new development has been the decision by the courts to strike down clauses which are harsh or onerous. It will be a matter of fact for the individual case whether a clause is in this category.

- Contract terms are categorised as 'conditions', 'warranties' or 'intermediate terms'. The remedies for breach depend on which category of term has been broken.

- When parties send their own terms and conditions to each other, this is often called the 'battle of the forms'. In broad terms, the victor is the person who presents his terms last of all.

- For most contracts a signature is not required to make it binding. Provision has been made by statute for the treatment of electronic signatures.

- Any description applied to the goods in the contract must be very closely complied with. The courts generally assume that businessmen want goods exactly as described in the contract.

- Statute requires goods supplied under a contract to be of satisfactory quality and reasonably fit for their purpose. Under certain circumstances, and separately from any issue as to exclusion clauses, these provisions will not apply.

- Where the contract for sale is made by reference to a sample, similar provisions to those described apply in relation to description, fitness and quality.

- One of the most important issues in a contract of sale is when the risk of damage to the goods has passed to the buyer. Statute sets out basic rules, but these can be displaced by the specific terms of the contract.

- The passing of property is no less important than issues of risk. Again, statute sets out certain rules, but the parties in this case can displace them with the express terms of the contract.

- Sellers often seek security for payment by retaining title to the goods. This requires great care in the drafting of the specific terms.

- Parties are well advised to use exclusion or limitation clauses to ensure that they do not face open-ended liability in the event of breach. At the same time, statute significantly restricts the effect of such clause, making it particularly difficult to exclude or limit liability in the case of a consumer contract. The use of such clauses can give rise to a criminal offence.

- An alternative approach to the use of exclusion clauses is to use a clause setting out just how much will be paid by the guilty party in the event of a breach. Care must be taken in the drafting of such clauses to avoid them being categorised as unenforceable penalty clauses.

- Damages for breach of contract are, by long-established principles, assessed on the basis of what the guilty party contemplated as the probable result of the breach. Principles have also been developed by the courts concerning the reimbursement of expenditure incurred by the innocent party.

- The basic rule laid down by statute is that no action for breach of contract can be brought after six years, though there are many exceptions to this rule. This can be addressed by the parties in the contract.

- A party can enter into a contract on the basis of a mistake or because of a misrepresentation which the other party might have made in the course of negotiation. A considerable body of law has developed as to the remedies available in such circumstances.

- There are strictly limited circumstances where a contract becomes void due to supervening circumstances.

- The so-called doctrine of privity of contract means that only the actual parties to the contract acquire rights and duties under it. This rule remains intact but has been considerably affected by recent legislation.

- Parties will often wish to protect their intellectual property. This can happen where the buyer is heavily involved in the development of the contract goods. Likewise, there will be matters which neither party may wish to be disclosed. These issues should be catered for in the contract when appropriate.

- To ensure correct delivery of documents, the contract should provide for the service of notices on each other.

- If the contract is made with a party overseas, care should be taken for the contract to have a term specifying which legal system applies.

- When drafting a contract, the parties should always bear in mind that certain aspects of the agreement, such as pricing, can fall foul of both EU and UK competition law.

Whether agreement has been reached   A1.2

Negotiations between the parties can often be a long, drawn out process, before being concluded by one side or the other. In such a case, there will often be a dispute as to whether a contract had been concluded, or whether the parties had simply been engaged in negotiations which had, in the end, achieved no result. For example, the parties may reach agreement on essential points of principle, but still leave some important points unsettled, so that the agreement is incomplete and no contract has arisen.

Where there is no binding agreement

Case Example: *Harvey v Pratt [1995] 1 WLR 1025.*

In this case, there was no agreement as negotiations for a lease failed to specify the date on which it was to commence.

Case Example: *Bushwell Properties Ltd v Vortex Properties [1976] 1 WLR 591*. An agreement for the sale of land by instalments was not a binding contract when it provided for the conveyance of a 'proportionate part' of the land as each instalment of the price was paid, but which failed to specify which part was to be conveyed on each payment.

Case Example: *Baird Textile Holdings Ltd v Marks & Spencer (Court of Appeal; 28 February 2001)*.

Baird had been one of the principal suppliers of clothing to Marks & Spencer (M&S) for 30 years. This ended when, on 19 October 1999, M&S determined all supply arrangements between them with effect from the end of the then current production season, without warning.

In their claim that a binding contract had materialised between the parties, Baird emphasised specific aspects of the commercial relationship between the parties. Such aspects included:

- close relationships between the senior executives;
- regular consultations on strategy, sales, design, technology, quality and logistics;
- the appointment by Baird of managers selected by M&S to monitor the relationships between the parties;
- co-operation by Baird working to seasonal timetables laid down by M&S;
- carrying out procurement policies in a manner designed to benefit M&S;
- the implementation of an umbrella arrangement of an unusual sort whereby substantial advantages were conferred on M&S;
- acceptance by Baird of M&S requirements as to place and standards of production, approval of sub-contractors and other commercial associations both in relation to specific acquisitions, investment, and generally; and
- the provision to M&S of confidential information. The Court of Appeal, however, decided that the alleged obligation on M&S to acquire garments from Baird was 'insufficiently certain to found any contractual obligation because there are no objective criteria by which the court could assess what would be reasonable either as to quantity or price'.

Additionally, it is not enough for the parties simply to agree that the price is to be agreed by them at a later date (*Courtney and Fairbairn Ltd v Tolaini Bros (Hotels) Ltd [1975] 1 WLR 297*).

Where there is a binding agreement

Case Example: *DMA Financial Solutions Ltd v BaaN UK Ltd (Chancery Division; 28 March 2000).*

In this case, the court held that an agreement had given rise to a binding contract, even though not contained in a formal written document. The parties had negotiated for DMA to become BaaN's authorised computer trainer. Negotiations to this effect had started in October 1998, and included a meeting, faxed and oral communications. In December, BaaN contacted DMA and agreed one minor change to the terms settled at the earlier meeting. DMA contended that a binding agreement had come into being at that time, despite BaaN not producing a formal written agreement, as expected, by 1 January 1999.

The court held that it was not necessary for there to be a formal agreement before there could be said to be a binding contract. In particular, the court stressed that there was no or little disagreement between the parties on the following issues:

- training;
- the territory to be covered by the contract;
- its duration;
- the price and payment terms;
- accreditation;
- access to and use of BaaN staff;
- the passing on of customer queries;
- promotion; and
- the endorsement of training courses.

The incorporation of contract terms   A1.3

It is always open for the parties to agree expressly on a set of written terms. If this is the case, then those terms will be incorporated into the contract, and form the basis of the agreement between them. Many situations are not so clear-cut, and a number of issues can arise, as follows.

Notification of the relevant terms   A1.4

Generally, unless one party notifies the other of the particular terms before a contract is concluded between them, those terms will not apply. It is for a court, as a matter of law, to decide whether there is evidence for holding that the notice is reasonably sufficient.

Cases in which notice has been held to be insufficient have been those where the conditions were printed on the back of a document without any reference to them on the face, or where the conditions have been obliterated by a date stamp (*White v Blackmore [1972] 2 QB 651; Richardson v Spence & Co v Rowntree [1894] AC 217*). It is important to understand, however, that it is not necessary for the documents themselves to be set out in the document which is tendered.

Where there is sufficient notice

Case Example: *Lacey's Footwear v Bowler International [1997] 2 Lloyd's Rep 369.*

The defendant carriers had been soliciting work from the claimants by sending them mailshots and visiting them at their place of work. The first approach had been by telephone in May 1986, and this had been followed by a letter, the bottom of which bore a reference to the defendants' terms and conditions. These were on the reverse of the letter and in print 'so small and so faint as to be legible only to one of such tender years that he or she would be far to young to comprehend the meaning of them'. The reverse of the letter, in large print, indicated that a large print version was available. No contract was made at that stage.

Two years later a letter was tendered to the claimants which contained terms and conditions on the reverse. Still no contract materialised, nor did an approach in 1991 result in a contract being formed. In October 1992, however, the claimants sought quotations from a number of carriers, including the defendants. The latter prepared a document which referred to the terms of trading, and they telephoned the claimants. In the proceedings which followed, the managing director of the claimants did not dispute that the letters from the defendants did have the terms and conditions on the back though – as a matter of practice – he never read them. The court concluded that reasonable notice of the contract terms had not been given.

The opening move had been the call from the claimants, followed by the defendants' brief covering letter, which had small print at the foot of the page reading: 'Trading Conditions – See Reverse'. No other effort had been made to bring the defendants' conditions to the claimants' notice. The defendants' rate proposal specifically referred to the terms of trading in block capitals, but that reference specifically detailed 'from FOB Alicante to delivered London E2. Excluding customs clearance'. There was nothing in the proposal to refer back to the small print on the reverse of the covering letter. In reaching its decision, the Court said that it had borne in mind that this was an oral contract negotiated over the telephone, and made in a hurry. The rate proposals, which formed the basis of the contract, did not refer to the conditions of contract; it made no reference to the conditions set out on the reverse side of the accompanying letter.

It is possible to incorporate contract terms by reference, i.e. by giving proper notice of them without setting them out in full. It is also the case, using this fact as a principle, that a written document can incorporate terms by referring to a website address where those terms are to be found, and vice versa. For examples, see *Parker v South Eastern Ry (1877) 2 CPD 416*; *Hood v Anchor Line (Henderson Bros) Ltd [1918] AC 837.*

The course of dealing   A1.5

There is an important qualification to the principle that advance notice must be given of the terms of a contract in that, where the parties have habitually dealt on the basis of certain terms in the past, they will be assumed to do so in the instant case, even though those terms were not specifically referred to. For this qualification to apply, a course of dealing must be established, and that depends on the circumstances of the particular case. The following cases are instructive.

Where there is a course of dealing

Case Example: *Henry Kendall & Sons v William Lillico & Sons [1969] 2 AC 31*

The contract in dispute had been preceded by a verbal contract, followed the next day by a contract setting out the relevant terms and conditions. There had been more than 100 similar contract notes in the course of dealing stretching back over the previous three years. This was held to constitute a course of dealing, the result being that, in the instant case, the terms of the contract received the day after the contract was made were incorporated into it.

Case Example: *Petrograde Inc v Texaco Ltd 1998 Folio 1348, QBD.*

There was no dispute that, over the 13 months or so prior to the contract in question, there were five other contracts for the sale of similar if not of the same products on the same terms and effected in the same manner. That was held to be enough to establish a course of trading.

Where there is not a course of dealing

Case Example: *McCutcheon v MacBrayne [1964] 1 WLR 125.*

The claimant's agent had dealt with the defendants on a number of occasions, yet he had not always signed a note containing the contract terms. He had not signed the note on the relevant occasions to the case. It was held that no course of dealing had been established in this case which allowed the terms to be incorporated by course of dealing.

Case Example: *Hollier v Rambler Motors Ltd [1972] 2 QB 71.*

There had been three or four contracts between the parties over a period of five years. On the last two of these occasions, but not when the contract in dispute was made, a note had been signed by the claimant. It was held that no course of dealing had been established.

Unusual or onerous terms   A1.6

Clauses should not be unusual or onerous and a court will strike out such clauses from a contract unless the clause is highlighted or special prominence is given to it.

Clauses which are unusual or onerous

Case Example: *Interfoto Picture Library Ltd v Stilleto Visual Programmes Ltd [1989] QB 433.*

One of the provisions in a contract for the hire of transparencies provided for a holding fee of £5 a day to be charged if the transparencies were returned late. This was well above the industry norm, and was regarded by the court as an unreasonable and extortionate clause. Given that no effort had been made to bring the other side's attention to this clause, it was held not to be part of the contract, even though the relevant provision would, under the rules discussed above, have been incorporated into the contract.

Case Example: *AEG (UK) Ltd v Logic Resources Ltd [1996] CLC 265.*

In this case a clause stated that: 'The purchaser shall return the defective parts at his own expense to the suppliers immediately on request of the latter'. This was a sub-clause in what was called a 'warranty'. Other sub-clauses contained a guarantee that the goods were free from defects caused by faulty materials and bad workmanship, adding that if the supplier were not the manufacturer, the warranty would extend only to the extent of any warranty provided by the manufacturer. The buyer was also required to notify the supplier of any defect within seven days of discovery and to tender proof of purchase and guarantee. Once goods had been returned, the buyer was to allow the supplier 'the time and opportunity requested as estimated' by the supplier. The buyer was also required to pay the costs of any tests on the goods should the supplier deny liability. This whole clause was held to be extremely onerous and, since no special effort had been made to draw the attention of the buyer to its content, it did not form part of the contract.

It will be a matter of evidence and of all the surrounding circumstances as to whether a term is onerous. In the AEG case, it was a majority decision that the clause in dispute was onerous, the dissenting judge ruling that it was 'in no way unusual for standard conditions to qualify obligations for sellers under a contract of sale. The clauses deal with a topic one would expect to be dealt with in the Conditions of Sale and they cover the type of points which would be commonly dealt with'.

For further information see *Thornton v Shoe Lane Parking Ltd [1971] 2 QB 163*.

Steps to be taken with possibly onerous clauses

The precise steps to be taken by a party when seeking to incorporate an onerous or unusual clause depend on all the circumstances of the case. A useful point of reference is provided in *J Spurling Ltd v Bradshaw [1956] 1 WLR 461* when it was stated there was need for a clause to be in red ink, with a 'red' hand pointing to the particular clause.

Clauses which are not unusual or onerous

Case Example: *Lease Management Services Ltd v Purnell Secretarial Services Ltd [1994] CCLR 127.*

The following clause, in a contract for the lease of a photocopier was held not to be onerous.

'Our Exclusion and Limitation.

The equipment and the supplier have been selected by you relying entirely on your own judgement. If you require any warranties or guarantees in respect of the equipment, its maintenance or suitability for any purpose, you must obtain them from the supplier. We exclude all express or implied warranties, conditions or guarantees from this agreement, and in no event will our liability under this agreement exceed the aggregate of the rentals paid by you at the time the liability arises. In no event will we be liable to you in contract, tort, or otherwise including any liability for negligence:

● for any loss of revenue, business, anticipated savings or profits, or any loss of use or value; or

- for any indirect or consequential loss however arising. "Anticipated savings" means any expense which you expect to avoid incurring or to incur in a lesser amount than would otherwise have been the case.'

A clause of such a nature was 'plainly to be expected...in equipment leasing contracts with finance companies'.

Case Example: *O'Brien v MGN Ltd (Court of Appeal; 1 August 2001).*

One of the terms in a scratchcard promotion provided that: 'Should more prizes be claimed than are available in any prize category for any reason, a simple draw will take place for the prize'. It was held that this was neither 'onerous' nor 'outlandish'.

The 'battle of the forms' A1.7

This is a shorthand expression which is often used to describe the occurrence when one party notifies the other that their terms apply to the contract they are negotiating, but the other responds by saying their terms will apply. 'Battle of the forms' issues tend to arise in cases involving retention of title and exclusion clauses. Neither clause is likely to feature in the buyer's terms. A court may be called on to decide whether the retention or exclusion clause has been incorporated into the contract prior to ruling on the validity of the particular clause.

The basic rule is that the person who refers to his terms and conditions last of all is the one whose terms and conditions prevail.

Case Example: *Butler Machine Tools Ltd v Ex-Cell-O Corporation (England) Ltd [1979] 1 WLR 401.*

The sellers offered to supply goods subject to their terms and conditions, whereupon the buyers placed an order, but making it subject to their terms and conditions. This order contained a tear-off slip, to be signed and returned by the sellers, stating that the sellers accepted the order 'on the terms and conditions stated therein'. The sellers signed and returned the slip with a letter saying that they were 'entering the order' in accordance with the offer.

It was held that the buyer's terms prevailed since the sellers, in the reference to the offer, were only identifying the goods and the letter was not made for the purpose of reiterating the seller's terms. It should be noted that a clause in the seller's terms and conditions providing that these terms and conditions would prevail over any others was ineffective in light of the circumstances.

Case Example: *BRS v Arthur V Crutchley Ltd [1968] 1 All ER 811.*

The claimants delivered a consignment of whisky to the defendants for storage. Their driver handed the defendants a delivery note purporting to incorporate the claimants' 'conditions of carriage'. The defendants stamped the note: 'Received under [our] conditions'. It was held that this amounted to a counter-offer which the claimants had accepted by handing over the goods, thus incorporating the defendants' own terms and conditions.

Cases for further information

A Davies & Co (Shopfitters) v William Old (1969) 113 SJ 262; *OTM Ltd v Hydranautics [1981] 2 Lloyd's Rep 211*; *Muirhead v Industrial Tank Specialities Ltd [1986] QB 507*; *Souter Association v Goodman Mechanical Services (1984) 34 Build. LR 81.*

The relative importance of the contract terms   A1.8

The rights and remedies available to the victim of a breach of contract will depend on the importance of a contract term. It has become traditional to classify the terms or conditions of a contract as 'conditions' in the strict sense; or as 'warranties'.

Essentially, a term is a 'condition' if it is a major term of the contract, whereas a term is a 'warranty' if it is of minor importance (*Wallis, Son & Wells v Pratt & Haynes [1910] 2 KB 1003*). The fact that a contract term might be described in the contract as a 'condition' does not mean that, on analysis, it is properly classified as a warranty (*Schuler v Wickman Machine Tool Sales Ltd [1974] AC 235*).

In some cases, it is provided by statute into which category a term falls. The *Sale of Goods Act 1979* (*SGA 1979*) provides that terms relating to description, quality and fitness for purpose are conditions. Terms as to title are also conditions, while terms as to quiet possession and freedom from encumbrances are warranties. Corresponding provisions are contained in the *Supply of Goods (Implied Terms) Act 1973* (*SG(IT)A 1973*) and the *Supply of Goods and Services Act 1982* (*SGSA 1982*).

In the absence of any statutory provision as above, or where the parties have not themselves clearly identified terms as falling into one category or the other, it will be for the courts to decide on the facts of the particular case.

Case Examples: Mercantile Contracts

In mercantile contracts, stipulations as to time are of the essence – for example:

- as to the time in which a ship must be ready to load (*The Mihail Angelos [1971] 1 QB 164*);

- as to when goods must be delivered under a contract of sale (*Hartley v Hymans [1920] 3 KB 475*).

- as to the time in which certain oil company approvals should be obtained (60 days was stipulated) (*BS&N (BVI) v Micado Shipping Ltd (Malta) [2000] 2 All ER (Comm) 169*); and

- as to the time frames within which any *force majeure* (i.e. events outside the parties' control) should be notified, extensions of the shipping period could be claimed, and the option to cancel the contract (*Bremer Handelsgesellschaft v Vanden Avenne-Izegem [1978] 2 Lloyd's Rep 109*).

Cases for Further Information

Glaholm v Hays (1841) 2 M&G 257; Bentsen v Taylor, Sons & Co [1893] 2 QB 274; Re Comptoir Commercial Anversois and Power, Son & Co [1920] 1 KB 868; Astley Industrial Trust v Grimley [1963] 1 WLR 584; Bunge Cpn New York v Tradax Export SA Panama [1981] 1 WLR 711; State Corp of India Ltd v M Golodetz Ltd [1989] 2 Lloyd's Rep 277; Compagnie Commerciale Sucres et Denrees v Czarnikow Ltd [1990] 1 WLR 1337; Torvald Klaveness A/S v Arni Maritime Corp [1993] 2 Lloyd's Rep 335.

Intermediate terms   A1.9

In recent years, the courts have moved away from a rigid classification of contract terms into conditions and warranties, and have recognised instead the category of 'intermediate' or 'innominate' terms.

Where a term falls into this category, the courts will instead look to the gravity of the breach and apply the appropriate remedies accordingly. A term is most likely to be classified as intermediate if it is capable of being broken either in a manner which is trivial and capable of remedy by an award of damages, or in a way which is so fundamental as to undermine the whole contract. For instance, a shipowner's obligation in a charter-party to:

- provide a seaworthy vessel (*Hongkong Fir Shipping Co Ltd v Kawasaki Kisen Kaisha [1962] 2 QB 26*);

- load containers without any stability problem (*Compagnie Generale Maritime v Diakan Spirit SA [1982] 2 Lloyd's Rep 574*); or

- commence any carriage out the voyage agreed on with reasonable despatch (*Freeman v Taylor (1831) 8 Bing 124*),

have all been classified as intermediate terms, the breach of which does not allow for discharge of the contract unless the consequences of breach are such as to deprive the charterer of substantially the whole benefit of the contract or to frustrate the object of the charterer in chartering the ship.

The uncertainty which can arise as to the classification of a contract is to be avoided. If the matter is not specifically decided by statute, the contract itself should clearly state that a term is to be regarded as of the essence, and hence a condition; or should spell out the consequences of a breach.

Signing a contract   A1.10

There is no general requirement in the law of contract that contracts have to be in some special form or signed. If the parties do stipulate that a contract will have no effect until signed, then, of course, there will be no contract until signature has been applied. If a contract is signed, then the party signing will be bound by the contract whether or not he has read the terms or even understood them (*L'Estrange v Graucob [1934] 2 KB 394*).

Electronic signatures   **A1.11**

The *Electronic Communications Act 2000 (ECA 2000)* provides that an electronic signature incorporated, or logically associated, with a particular electronic communication or data, and the certification by any person of such signature, shall be admissible in evidence in relation to any question as to the authenticity of the communication or its integrity. There is, though, no presumption as to the validity of such signature. This will allow contractual documents and negotiations to be exchanged by e-mail, and for any electronic signature to be used to confirm the authenticity of the transmission. For these purposes, an electronic signature is associated with or incorporated into a communication, and also purports to establish the validity of the communication.

ECA 2000 also provides for any legislation requiring documents to be in writing to be amended to allow for electronic communication. This power has been exercised in the *Unsolicited Goods and Services Act 1971 (Electronic Communications) Order 2001 (SI 2001/2778)*. This allows for the electronic communication of entries for directories, where before such entries had to be requested in writing.

Checklist   A1.12

- Have you agreed on the important aspects of the intended contract, such as

  - the subject matter;

  - the price and terms of payment; and

15

      o   the duration of the contract, if appropriate, including start date and end date?

- Have you ensured that your terms and conditions have been adequately brought to the attention of the other party?

- Have you made sure that you are the 'winner' in the 'battle of the forms'?

- Does the contract clearly spell out which terms are considered fundamental and which are considered to be of a more minor nature?

- Have you taken care to ensure that proper attention has been brought to any unusual or onerous terms?

- Have you considered the necessity for signature and made proper provision for securing it?

- Have you made sure that copies of the agreement are safely stored away?

Chapter A2
Common and Specific
Clauses

At a glance

- When the contract describes the goods, the description then becomes a major term of the contract. This description, once established, must be closely complied with by the seller.

- Statute requires all goods supplied under a contract to be of satisfactory quality and reasonably fit for their purpose.

- There is scope, subject to restrictions, on the use of exclusion and limitation clauses. Careful note should be taken of possible criminal offences arising from the use of exclusion clauses in consumer contracts.

- It is not just the contract goods which are covered by the above obligations, but also all goods supplied under the contract.

- Obligations as to fitness and quality apply to contracts made by reference to a sample.

- A central feature of the contract is the passing of risk. There are statutory presumptions as to when risk passes but parties can provide in the contract for when risk is to pass.

- Equally important is the passing of property. Again, there are statutory presumptions which can be displaced by the terms of the contract.

- Suppliers should always consider retention of title clauses to secure their position in the event of a buyer's non payment.

- The *Unfair Contract Terms Act 1977* (*UCTA 1977*) can apply to business and consumer contracts, while the *Unfair Terms in Consumer Contracts Regulations 1999* (*SI 1999/2083*) only apply to persons acting in a private capacity.

- An alternative to an exclusion or limitation clause is the liquidated damages clause.

- Penalty clauses cannot be enforced.

- Damages for breaches of contract are assessed on the basis of what the wrongdoer contemplated would be the probable result of any breach. Recovery for loss of profits generally requires advance disclosure to the other side of the relevant facts.

- The victim of a breach of contract must do all that is reasonable to limit the loss which arises from the breach.

- Actions for breach of contract must generally be brought within six years, but there are exceptions to the rule. The parties can provide for their own limitation periods.

- If a contract has been included by mistake or by a misrepresentation, much depends on the nature of the mistake or misrepresentation. A contract may be automatically void, or voidable, or it may be unaffected.

- Clauses excluding or limiting liability for misrepresentation are subject to statutory control.

- In strictly defined and limited circumstances, a contract affected by supervening events will be void for frustration. Special rules deal with the perishing of goods.

- There may be scope for contracting out of the rules relating to frustration and perishing.

- The consequences of frustration are spelled out by both common law and statute. Scope exists for the contract itself to deal with potential frustrating events.

- It is a fundamental rule of law that those who are not contracting parties have no rights under the contract. This principle has, however, been modified by statute.

- The parties are free to use contract terms protecting their intellectual property rights and securing that all necessary confidences are maintained.

- Provision can be made for the serving of notices on each party to the contract.

- Quite often, signature is not a pre-requisite to a binding contract. The provision of a signature does, however, commit the party to the full terms of the contract.

- Parties making overseas contracts can provide for which jurisdiction is to govern the contract. Certain restrictions are imposed on the parties' choice.

- Both domestic and European law impose restrictions on anti-competitive behaviour. Fines can be imposed.

Describing the goods or services   **A2.2**

Section 13 of the *Sale of Goods Act 1979* (*SGA 1979*) provides that any description applied to the contract goods is a condition. Comparable provisions are to be found in the *Supply of Goods (Implied Terms) Act 1973* (*SG(IT)A 1973*) and the *Supply of Goods and Services Act 1982* (*SGSA 1982*).

Key to description   **A2.3**

The key to description is identification. Statements in the contract as to the quality of the goods do not normally identify a product and hence are not part of its description. In the case of *Ashington Piggeries Ltd v Christopher Hill Ltd [1972] AC 441* it was explained that:

> '. . . ultimately the test is whether the buyer could fairly and reasonably refuse to accept the physical goods proffered to him on the ground that their failure to correspond with that part of what was said about them in the contract makes them goods of a different kind from those he had agreed to buy'.

Terms held to be part of description

Case Example: *Varley v Whipp [1900] 1 QB 513.*

Statements as to the location, age and use of goods were all part of the description.

Case Example: *Arcos Ltd v EA Ronaasen and Son [1933] AC 470.*

Stipulations as to the dimensions of wooden staves were held to be part of the contract description.

Case Example: *MacPherson Train & Co Ltd v Howard Ross & Co Ltd [1955] 1 WLR 640.*

A statement that goods sold were 'afloat per SS Morton Bay due London approximately 8 June' was also held to be part of the description since it enabled the goods to be identified.

Terms held not to be part of description

Case Example: *T&J Harrison v Knowles and Foster [1918] 1 KB 608.*

Two ships were sold, each of which was stated in particulars supplied to the buyers to have a deadweight capacity of 460 tons. The capacity of each was, in fact, 360 tons. It was held that these statements were not part of the description.

Case Example: *Harlingdon & Leinster Enterprises Ltd v Christopher Hull Fine Arts Ltd [1991] 1 QB 564.*

The statement that a painting was the work of a certain artist was held not to be part of the description. This was because the description was not, on the facts, an essential part of the sale. It was said that, for all practical purposes 'there cannot be a contract for the sale of goods by description where it is not within the reasonable contemplation of the parties that the buyer is relying on that description'. In this case, the claimants were specialists in the particular work of art, while the defendants were not.

Compliance with description   A2.4

Once it is established that a statement is part of the description, strict compliance with that description is required.

Case Example: *Arcos Ltd v EA Ronaasen & Son [1933] AC 470.*

The contract required wooden staves to be half an inch thick. Only 5% of the total delivered matched this description. A large proportion were over half an inch, but not more than 9/10 of an inch, in thickness; some were larger but less than 5/8 of an inch in thickness, and a very small proportion larger than that. It was found as a fact that all the goods could be used for their intended purpose. It was also found that they did not correspond to their description.

Case Example: *Re Moore & Co Ltd and Landauer & Co Ltd [1921] 2 KB 519.*

The contract was for 3000 tins of fruit packed in cases of 30 tins. When the goods were delivered, it was found that about half the cases contained 24 tins, though the correct quantity was delivered. It was found that the goods did not conform to their description.

The effect of these rulings has been mitigated in business-to-business contracts by *s 15A* of the *SGA 1979*, which restricts a buyer's right to reject goods where the breach of the term as to description is so slight that rejection would be unreasonable.

Since the *SGA 1979* does imply a term as to description, there is no particular need for a contract of purchase to contain any specific clause as to description. A contract of sale could state: 'The description of the goods has been given by way of identification only and the use of such description shall not constitute a sale by description'. It should be said, however, that such a clause might well be unsuccessful in its aim of avoiding the impact of the implied term, but, in certain circumstances, it might be enough to tip an argument in favour of the seller.

Quality and fitness for purpose   **A2.5**

Just as with matters of description, the *SGA 1979* implies into contracts of sale conditions that the goods supplied under the contract will be of satisfactory quality and reasonably fit for their purpose. There are corresponding provisions in the *SG(IT)A 1973* and the *SGSA 1982*. It should always be borne in mind that, in business to-business-contracts, s 15A of the *SGA 1979* prevents a buyer from rejecting for a breach of these conditions where breach is so slight that rejection would be unreasonable.

Satisfactory quality   **A2.6**

When it comes to deciding if goods are of satisfactory quality, the *SGA 1979* says that this is a matter of what a reasonable person would regard as satisfactory, taking into account any description applied to the goods, the price (if relevant) and all other relevant circumstances. The following are stated in the *SGA 1979* to be aspects of quality in appropriate cases:

* fitness for all the purposes for which goods of the kind in question are commonly supplied;
* appearance and finish;
* freedom from minor defects;
* safety; and
* durability.

Where goods are of satisfactory quality

Case Example: *Thain v Anniesland Trade Centre 1997 SLT (Sh.Ct) 102.*

The buyer purchased a six year old car for £2995.00, which had 80,000 miles on the clock. A fortnight later, the buyer noticed a droning noise, and after six weeks, the car could no longer be driven. It was found that the cause of the trouble was the failure of a bearing in the automatic gearbox, which could have failed at any time. The court held that the car was of satisfactory quality and, because of the car's age, the buyer had no rights as to durability.

Where goods are not of satisfactory quality

Case Example: *Bernstein v Pamson Motors (Golders Green) Ltd [1987] 2 All ER 220.*

A new car was purchased for £8000, but it broke down within three weeks having travelled a mere 140 miles. The fault was a minor defect in a piece of sealant, but this led to the engine seizing up, which meant that the car was unsafe. The court held that the car was 'unmerchantable' which was the test before the criterion of 'satisfactory quality' replaced it. The ruling would be the same under the new test.

Cases for Further Information

Sumner Permain and Company v Webb and Company [1922] 1 KB 55; Niblett Ltd v Confectioners' Materials Co Ltd [1921] 3 KB 387; Mash & Murrell Ltd v Joseph I Emanuel Ltd [1961] 1 WLR 862; Lee v York Coach and Marine [1977] RTR 35; Rogers v Parish (Scarborough) Ltd [1987] QB 933.

Avoiding the obligation as to satisfactory quality   A2.7

A distinction is to be drawn between contracts between businesses, and contracts made with a consumer. In the former case, a seller can always try to exclude liability for any breach, but the test of reasonableness imposed by the *UCTA 1977*, and the onus of proof being on the seller to show that it is a reasonable exclusion, makes it difficult, though not impossible, for the seller to succeed. In the case of a consumer contract, any such clause is rendered void by *UCTA 1977*, and its use was actually made a criminal offence under the *Consumer Transactions (Restrictions on Statements) Order 1976 (SI 1976/1813).*

Since the term regarding satisfactory quality applies automatically, it does not need to be spelled out in a contract.

Business and consumer contracts

Since an exclusion clause can be simply invalid when used in a business contract, but a criminal offence can result when present in a consumer contract, care must be taken when such clauses are used in contracts supplied to businesses and consumers alike. Where this is so, the contract should contain the clause:

> 'Terms in this contract excluding or limiting liability in relation to breach of the terms implied by the *Supply of Goods*

(Implied Terms) Act 1973 or the *Sale of Goods Act 1979* do not apply when this contract is made with a consumer'.

Circumstances disapplying the implied obligation

The *SGA 1979* (and the other appropriate enactments) do, however, identify certain circumstances where, irrespective of the presence of any exclusion clauses, there will be no implied term as to satisfactory quality. This will be when:

- the defect is specifically drawn to the buyer's attention;

- the buyer examines the goods beforehand and that examination should reveal the defect; or

- where the sale was by sample, a reasonable examination of the sample would have revealed the defect.

Reasonable fitness for purpose   A2.8

The *SGA 1979* provides that where a buyer, expressly or by implication, makes known any particular purpose for which the goods are wanted, there is a condition that the goods must be reasonably fit for that purpose.

Meaning of 'purpose'

If the goods have only one normal purpose or purposes, there is no need for the seller to spell these out, since the seller will be automatically taken to know what the purpose is.

Case Example: *Priest v Last [1903] 2 KB 148.*

The seller was assumed to know what a hot-water bottle was bought for even though this had not been mentioned by the buyer. This case demonstrated that the seller will not be liable, however, even if the goods are not fit for the purpose if there was something special, or unique, about the purpose for which the buyer wanted the goods, and he had not disclosed this to the seller.

Case Example: *Slater v Finning Ltd [1996] 3 All ER 1997.*

The House of Lords ruled against the buyer where camshafts were supplied for an engine which suffered an abnormality which created excessive torsion resonance in the shafts. The suppliers had not been made aware of the engine abnormality.

Case Example: *Griffith v Peter Conway Ltd [1939] 1 All ER 685.*

The seller of a fur coat was not liable when the buyer contracted dermatitis since this was due to an abnormal skin condition not disclosed to the seller.

Securing the benefit of this provision   **A2.9**

To overcome such problems, the buyer should always take care to disclose all the relevant facts to the seller prior to contract and to make sure that these are provided in written form. It is, of course, always possible that the buyer himself is unaware of the relevant special factor. To avoid this further problem, the buyer should write into the contract a provision to this effect:

> 'The seller will provide goods which are in all respects fit for the buyer's intended use, whether or not such use, and any factors relevant to that use, have been disclosed, expressly or by implication, to the seller'.

Avoiding the obligation as to fitness for purpose   **A2.10**

A seller can always try to exclude liability for any breach, but the test of reasonableness imposed by the *UCTA 1977*, and the onus of proof being on him to show that it is a reasonable exclusion, makes it difficult, though not impossible, for the seller to succeed. In the case of a consumer contract, any such clause would be illegal under the *Consumer Transactions (Restrictions on Statements) Order 1976 (SI 1976/1813)*.

Business and consumer contracts

Since an exclusion clause can be simply invalid when used in a business contract, but a criminal offence can occur when used in a consumer contract, care must be taken when such clauses are used in contracts supplied to businesses and consumers alike. Where this is so, the contract should contain the following clause:

> 'Terms in this contract excluding or limiting liability in relation to breach of the terms implied by the *Supply of Goods (Implied Terms) Act 1973* or the *Sale of Goods Act 1979* do not apply when this contract is made with a consumer'.

Circumstances disapplying the implied obligation

The *SGA 1979* (and the *SG(IT)A 1973* and *SGSA 1982*) do, however, themselves provide for the obligation as to reasonable fitness not to apply when:

- the buyer did not rely on the seller's skill and judgement;
- it was unreasonable for the buyer to rely on the seller's skill and judgement.

Where there has been no relevant reliance

Case Example: *Wren v Holt [1903] 1 KB 610.*

The claimant bought beer in a public house which he knew was a tied house. It was held that this meant there was no evidence as to the buyer having relied on the seller's skill and judgement.

Case Example: *Phoenix Distributors Ltd v LB Clarke Ltd [1967] 1 Lloyd's Rep 518.*

The sellers sold potatoes for export from Northern Ireland to Poland. It was shown that a clearance certificate was from required from the Northern Ireland Ministry of Agriculture. It was held that the buyers relied on the certificate rather than on the sellers in respect of matters covered by the certificate.

Case Example: *Knight v Mason (1912) 15 GLR 300.*

The defendant was an ordinary small farmer, while the claimant was an experienced dealer in seeds. The latter asked for and received from the defendant a quotation for seed potatoes. He was shown a heap of mixed potatoes which he bought. The defendant had told the claimant that the potatoes were not blind, when, in fact, a large proportion were and hence were not reasonably fit for their purpose. The court stressed that the defendant was 'an ordinary farmer', while the claimant was a 'skilled dealer'. The claimant had completed the purchase after a 'very slight conversation'. In these circumstances, there was no evidence 'that the [claimant] relied on the judgement of the defendant'.

Case Example: *Henderson Ltd v AEF Electric Ltd (1962) 10 MCD 290.*

The claimant, a wholesaler of photographic goods, ordered a number of plastic screens from the defendant. These were not reasonably fit for their purpose. It appeared that the claimant had some experience in importing screens, and – when it became difficult to import them – he discussed with the defendant the possibility of the latter producing screens similar to those in the claimant's possession. The defendant had no experience in making such equipment. The claimant approved the material to be used, and discussed modifications with the defendant on many occasions. The court held that this was more in the nature of a joint venture; in any case, if anything, the defendant relied on the claimant's skill and judgement rather than the other way round.

Cases for further information

Manchester Liners Ltd v Rea [1922] 2 AC 74; Ashford Shire Council v Dependable Motors Pty Ltd [1961] AC 336; Young & Marten Ltd v McManus Childs Ltd [1968] 2 All ER 1169; Gloucestershire County Council v Richardson [1968] 2 All ER 1181; Hardwick v SAPPA [1969] AC 31; Corbett Construction Ltd v Simplot Chemical Co Ltd [1971] 2 WWR 332; Aswan Engineering Establishment Co v Lupdine Ltd [1987] 1 WLR 1.

Goods supplied under the contract   A2.11

In relation both to the requirement as to satisfactory quality and fitness for purpose, the obligations laid down by the *SGA 1979* apply to the goods supplied under the contract. The implied conditions therefore apply, not just to the goods directly the subject–matter of the contract, but also to the goods supplied with them.

Where goods are supplied under the contract

Case Example: *Wilson v Rickett Cockerell & Co Ltd [1954] 1 QB 598.*

A product called Coalite was supplied which, unknown to the parties, contained an explosive. It was held that the *SGA 1979* applied to all products supplied under the contract, and not merely to the Coalite alone.

Case Example: *Geddling v Marsh [1920] 1 KB 668.*

It was held that the *SGA 1979* applied to the bottle in which a drink was supplied, even though the bottle remained the property of the seller.

Sales by sample   A2.12

Section 15 of the *SGA 1979* implies into contracts for sale by sample an implied condition that the bulk corresponds with the sample in quality, and that the goods will be free from any defect, rendering the quality unsatisfactory, not apparent on a reasonable examination of the sample.

When a contract is a sale by sample   A2.13

SGA 1979 provides that a contract is a contract for sale by sample when there is an express or implied term to that effect. There seems no reason why a seller cannot avoid this implication by the use of the following:

> 'notwithstanding that a sample of the goods has been exhibited to and inspected by the buyer, it is hereby declared that such sample was so exhibited and inspected solely to enable the buyer to judge for himself the quality of the bulk, and not so as to constitute a sale by sample'.

Such a provision would, though, not affect the general duties as to the supply of goods of satisfactory quality and of reasonable fitness. At the same time, such a clause could well be within the jurisdiction of the *UCTA 1977* and hence valid only if reasonable. In the case of a consumer contract, and if held to be an exclusion clause, any such clause would be illegal under the *Consumer Transactions (Restrictions on Statements) Order 1976 (SI 1976/1813)*.

Where a breach of the provisions of *s 15, SGA 1979* is so slight that rejection would be unreasonable, *s 15A, SGA 1979* prevents a business from rejecting.

Passing of risk   A2.14

The time at which risk in the goods passes to the buyer is crucial. If the risk of loss or damage is with the buyer, then he will still have to pay for them, however useless the goods might be. If the risk was on the seller at the time when the goods were damaged or destroyed, he cannot sue for the price.

Differing approaches of parties as to who bears risk   A2.15

The position as to who bears the risk is set down in *s 20(1), SGA 1979* which provides that risk passes with property unless the parties agree otherwise. The parties obviously have divergent views on this, and the buyer should always ensure that the contract provides for risk to pass only on delivery of goods in conformity with the contract; while the seller should, of course, seek to provide that risk passes as soon as possible. The law imposes no restraints in this context on what the contract may say. Thus, the conditions of purchase need simply say:

'The goods will be at the seller's risk until such time as goods in conformity with the contract are delivered to and received by the buyer or his authorised agent'.

The conditions of sale would say:

'The risk in the goods will pass to the buyer at the time the goods are allocated to the contract and will remain at the buyer's risk thereafter'.

Passing of property   A2.16

There are two reasons why it is important to know when property (which can perhaps be better understood as title) passes to the buyer. As we saw in A2.14, it can, unless the contract states otherwise, determine where risk lies. Importantly, it is only when the buyer obtains property that they effectively becomes owner and can assert the normal rights of ownership. *Section 17* of the *SGA 1979* provides that the parties can settle in the contract when property is to pass. If the contract says nothing on this point, then *s 18, SGA 1979* lays down a number of rules as to when property (and potentially risk) passes to the buyer.

The five rules   A2.17

Rule 1

If the contract is for the sale of specific goods in a deliverable state, and the contract is unconditional, then property passes when the contract is made, regardless of payment time or delivery time. Unconditional in this context means that there are no pre-conditions to the passing of property, such as payment, while deliverable means, according to *s 61(5), SGA 1979*, goods which are in such a condition that the buyer would be bound to take delivery of them.

> **Case Example**: *Underwood Ltd v Burgh Castle Brick and Cement Syndicate [1922] 1 KB 343.*
>
> Machinery was not in a deliverable state when still attached to the factory floor, and it had to be dismantled prior to delivery.

Rule 2

This concerns specific goods not yet in a deliverable state. Where it is the seller's duty to do something to the goods in order to put the goods into a deliverable state, property passes when he has made the goods deliverable and informed the buyer.

Rule 3

This concerns specific goods in a deliverable state, but where the seller has to do something to the goods, such as weigh or measure them, in order to work out the price. Property passes to the buyer when whatever is required has been done, and the buyer has been notified.

Rule 4

This deals with the situation where goods are delivered to the buyer on approval, or on sale or return or similar terms. Property will pass when the buyer indicates acceptance or performs any act adopting the transaction. If he does neither, and fails to indicate rejection, then property will pass after the lapse of a reasonable time, or the expiry of a date set for the return of the goods.

Case Examples: *Kirkham v Attenborough [1897] 1 QB 201*; *London Jewellers Ltd v Attenborough [1934] 2 KB 206.*

These illustrate the point that if a buyer pledges or sells the goods, this will constitute approval or acceptance and property will pass under Rule 4.

Case Examples: *Elphick v Barnes (1880) 5 CPD 321*; *Re Ferrier [1944] Ch 295.*

These cases demonstrate that if the buyer is unable to return the goods through no fault of his own, as for example in the case of theft or seizure by a third party, this is not acceptance and Rule 4 will not apply.

Case Example: *Atari Corporation (UK) Ltd v Electronics Boutique Stores (UK) Ltd [1998] QB 539.*

Unless the parties specify otherwise, a buyer can reject the goods by any indication to the seller which clearly shows that he does not wish to exercise the option to purchase. In this case, the Court of Appeal held that, in the absence of contrary indications, the notice rejecting the goods did not need to be in writing, nor did it need to identify with certainty the goods to which it related (as long as the generic description enabled them to be identified with certainty), and nor did the goods have to be physically capable of collection when the notice was issued (so long as they were available within a reasonable period).

Rule 5

This is the one rule which relates to unascertained goods; that is to say goods which have not been agreed on and identified at the time of sale. It also applies to future goods. *Section 61(1), SGA 1979* defines these as 'goods to be manufactured or acquired by the seller after the making of the contract of sale'.

> **Case Example**: *Healy v Howlett & Sons [1917] 1 KB 337.*
>
> Where Rule 5 applies, *s 17, SGA 1979* provides that property cannot pass until the contract goods are first ascertained. In this case, the buyer instructed the seller to send him 20 boxes of mackerel. The seller consigned 190 boxes to a railway company, instructing it to deliver 20 to the buyer, and the remaining boxes to other consignees. The train was delayed and the fish went off before reaching the train's destination. The court held that the goods had not been ascertained vis-a-vis the buyer since no specific boxes had been ear-marked for him.

Once ascertained, Rule 5(1) provides for property to pass when the goods are unconditionally appropriated to the contract, by either party with the assent of the other, and such assent can be express or implied.

> **Case Example**: *Aldridge v Johnson (1857) 7 E&B 885.*
>
> The claimant buyer agreed to buy 100 quarters of barley out of 200 which he had seen in bulk and approved. It was arranged that he would send 200 sacks for the barley, which the seller would fill and send to the buyer by rail. The seller filled 155 sacks, leaving 45 unfilled. On the eve of his bankruptcy, the seller emptied the barley from the sacks back into the bulk. It was held that the property in the 155 sacks had passed the instant they were filled.

Rule 5(2) provides that there can be unconditional appropriation where, acting under the contract, the seller delivers the goods to the buyer, or hands them over to a third party for transmission to the buyer.

If the facts show, however, that the carrier is the seller's agent, or his employee, then this rule will not apply (*Badische Anilin und Soda Fabrik v Basle Chemical Works [1898] AC 200*).

Goods in bulk   A2.18

Rule 5(3) deals with goods which form part of an identified bulk. Where the bulk is reduced to the same (or a smaller) quantity ordered by the buyer, and he is the only buyer left with goods in the bulk, then the remaining quantity is taken as appropriated to the contract, and the property passes to the buyer. Rule 5(4) applies the foregoing rule to cases where, again, the amount left in the bulk is the same as or smaller than the agreed quantity, but are due to a single buyer under separate contracts.

Undivided shares in bulk   A2.19

Section 20A of the *SGA 1979* was added to cater for the fact that property in goods forming part of an identified bulk cannot pass until the goods have been separated from the bulk, including by consolidation or exhaustion as demonstrated by Rules 5(3) and 5(4) above.

Where the buyer has paid for some or all of the goods, the buyer acquires ownership in common with others of a proportionate share of the bulk. This share is determined according to the ratio that the quantity of goods already paid for but not received bears to the entire bulk existing at that time.

Section 20B of the *SGA 1979* makes it clear that each co-owner can deal with goods within his share without needing the consent of the other co-owners. It is also made clear that these provisions:

* do not impose any obligation on a buyer who takes delivery out of a bulk to compensate others who receive short delivery as a result;
* do not affect any contractual arrangement between the buyers for adjustments among themselves; or
* alter or diminish any contractual rights of the buyer against the seller.

Differing approaches of parties as to passing of property   A2.20

It should again be remembered that all the foregoing rules as to when property is to pass apply only if the parties have made no separate arrangement as to this. It will always be in the seller's interest to delay passing of property until the last minute (usually until he has been paid) and for the buyer to stipulate that property is to pass the moment the contract is made. Bearing in mind the presumption that risk passes with property unless the parties agree otherwise the buyer should draft the relevant term on these lines:

'Property, but not risk, in the contract goods shall pass to the buyer on the making of this contract'.

The corresponding seller's term is discussed in A2.21 below

Retention of title   A2.21

It is, of course, always in the seller's best interests to postpone the passing of title for as long as possible. While property remains vested in the seller, the goods remain as a security against default by the buyer, and can thus always be repossessed. The importance of using a retention clause was indicated by Templeman LJ in *Borden (UK) Ltd v Scottish Timber Products Ltd [1981] Ch 25*, who stated: 'Unsecured creditors rank after preferential creditors, mortgagees and holders of floating charges, and they receive a raw deal'.

This right to reserve or retain title is expressly preserved in *s 19, SGA 1979*. Although retention clauses are common in continental Europe; it was not until relatively recently that they became common in this country.

> **Case Example**: *Aluminium Industries Vassen BV v Romalpa Aluminium Ltd [1976] 1 WLR 676.*
>
> The clause before the court was an English translation of the original Dutch:
>
> > 'The ownership of the material to be delivered by AIV will only be transferred to the purchaser when he has met all that is owing to AIV, no matter on what grounds. Until the date of payment, purchaser, if AIV so desires, is required to store the material in such a way that it is clearly the property of AIV.
> >
> > AIV and purchaser agree that, if purchaser should make (a) new object(s) from the material, mixes this material with (an)other object(s) or if this material in any way whatsoever becomes a constituent of (an)other object(s), AIV will be given the ownership of this (these) new object(s) as surety of the full payment of what purchaser owes AIV.
> >
> > To this end AIV and purchaser now agree that the ownership of the article(s) in question, whether finished or not, are to be transferred to AIV, and that this transfer of ownership will be considered to have taken place through and at the moment of the single operation or event by which the material is converted into (a) a new object(s), or is mixed with or becomes a constituent of (an) other object(s). Until the moment of full payment of what purchaser owes AIV, the purchaser shall keep the object(s) in question for AIV in his capacity of fiduciary owner and, if required, shall store this (these) object(s) in such a way that it (they) can be recognised a such.
> >
> > Nevertheless, purchaser will be entitled to sell these objects to a third party within the framework of their normal carrying on of his business and to deliver them on condition that if AIV so reqires purchaser, as long as he has not fully discharged his debt to AIV shall hand over to AIV the claims he has against his buyer emanating from this transaction'.

The subject matter of this contract was aluminium foil. The seller, on the buyer going into receivership, successfully claimed to be entitled, as against the receiver, to foil worth £50,000 and to £35,000 held in a separate account which represented the proceeds of sub-sales of the unused foil. The Court held that the unused foil was held by the buyer as bailee, and in a fiduciary capacity, and that, as a result, the seller was entitled to trade and claim the proceeds of any sub-sales in priority to both the bank appointing the receiver and the buyer's general creditors.

Case Example: *Borden (UK) Ltd v Scottish Timber Products Ltd [1981] Ch 25.*

The relevant clause ran:

> 'Risk and property.
>
> Goods supplied by the Company shall be at the purchaser's risk immediately on delivery to the purchaser or into custody on the purchaser's behalf (whichever is the sooner) and the purchaser should therefore be insured accordingly. Property in the goods supplied hereunder will pass to the customer when (a) the goods the subject of the contract (b) all other goods the subject of any other contract between the company and the customer which at the time of payment of the full price of the goods sold under the contract, have been delivered to the customer but not paid for in full, have been paid for in full'.

The contract was for the supply of resin. This was supplied but a receiver was appointed to the buyer's affairs. When required for use, the resin was transferred to a separate tank where it was mixed with wax emulsion and hardeners to form a glue mix. It was then blended with desiccated timber and pressed to form chipboard. Of the final chipboard, the timber components comprised 24% by value, and the resin 17%. The Court held that once the buyers had used the resin in the manufacture of chipboard, the resin ceased to exist and there was nothing which the seller could trace.

The effect of the reservation of title clause was merely to reserve to the sellers the property in the resin so long as it remained unused. When the resin ceased to exist when incorporated into the chipboard, the seller's title also ceased to exist. Furthermore, there was no express agreement and no ground to imply an agreement in the contract that the buyers were to provide substantial security for the resin used in the chipboard. The court questioned whether a tracing remedy could ever be applied where goods have been mixed and also queried how, if tracing were available, the proportion of the value of the manufactured product which the tracer could claim as property was attributable to his ingredient.

Case Example: *Re Bond Worth [1980] Ch 228.*

The relevant terms were:

'(a)   The risk in the goods passes to the buyer upon delivery, but equitable and beneficial ownership shall remain with us until full payment has been received (each order being considered as a whole), or until prior resale, in which case our beneficial entitlement shall attach to the proceeds of resale or to the claim for such proceeds.

(b)   Should the goods become constituents of or be converted into other products while subject to our equitable and beneficial ownership we shall have the equitable and beneficial ownership in such other products as if they were solely and simply the goods and accordingly sub-clause (a) shall as appropriate apply to such other products.'

The court interpreted this as creating a security interest rather than an ownership interest. The seller had not reserved equitable ownership at all, and the buyer had created a charge rather than a trust.

Cases for Further Information

Hendy Lennox Industrial Engineers Ltd v Grahame Puttick Ltd [1984] 1 WLR 485; Re Peachdart Ltd [1984] Ch 131; Clough Mill Ltd v Martin [1985] 1 WLR 111; Stroud Architectural Systems Ltd v John Laing Construction Ltd [1994] 2 BCLC 276.

Such clauses are most useful when dealing with easily identifiable goods. In such a case, a simple clause such as the following will suffice:

'Property in the goods will remain with the seller and shall not pass until payment in full for the goods has been received by the seller'.

The clause should also specify that risk has passed even though property has not; it should also give the seller the right to enter the buyer's premises to repossess and should stipulate that the buyer must have full insurance cover for the goods. The seller must always take care to reserve the whole title in the goods. A major problem with the use of such clauses arises from the fact that under the *SGA 1979*, the *Factors Act 1889* and the *Hire-Purchase Act 1964*, and also under established principles of agency and estoppel, the buyer of goods – notwithstanding the presence of a retention clause – is still able to pass a valid title to a third party. Problems will also arise where the buyer mixes or uses the goods in the normal course of business. In such cases, the seller will want to be able to trace the proceeds of sale or the goods in their new form.

Varieties of retention clause A2.22

To help deal with these and other problems, more elaborate retention clauses have been devised. These need expert drafting and will usually need to consider factors such as whether the buyer:

- will hold the goods as the seller's bailee and fiduciary agent;

- will store the goods separately so that they can be identified as the seller's property;

- may resell the goods to a third party, (although the buyer shall act as the seller's agent when sub-selling);

- is to be accountable for the entire proceeds of sale, not merely the sums owing to the seller, and will keep the proceeds in a separate, identified fund.

It should be noted that, under *section 30* of the *Insolvency Act 1986 (IA 1986)*, the seller may not enforce his rights under a retention clause once the court has made an administration order, without the consent of the administrator or by leave of the court. *IA 1986* also provides that an administrator may dispose of the goods free of the seller's rights if authorised by the court, but the proceeds of sale must be applied towards discharging the sums due to the seller.

Examples of retention clauses A2.23

Sellers could consider the use of one or more of the clauses below as might fit their own circumstances. Expert guidance should always be taken.

- The intending purchaser acknowledges that before entering into an agreement for the purchase of goods from the company, he has expressly warranted and represented that he is not insolvent and has not committed any act of bankruptcy, or being a company with limited or unlimited liability, knows of no circumstances which would entitle any debenture holder or secured creditor to appoint a receiver, to petition for the winding up of the company or exercise any other rights over or against the company's assets.

- Goods the subject of any agreement by the company to sell shall be at the risk of the intending purchaser as soon as they are delivered by the company to his vehicles or his premises or otherwise to his order.

- Such goods shall remain the sole and absolute property of the company as legal and equitable owner until such time as the intending purchaser shall have paid to the company the agreed price.

- ○ (together with the full price of any other goods the subject of any other contract with the company).

- The intending purchaser acknowledges that he is in possession of goods solely as bailee for the company until such time as the full price thereof is paid to the company.

- ○ (together with the full price of any other goods the subject of any other contract with the company).

- Until such a time as the intending purchaser becomes the owner of the goods, he will store them on his premises separately from his own goods or those of any other person and in a manner which makes them readily identifiable as the goods of the company.

- The intending purchaser's right to possession of the goods shall cease if he, not being a company, commits an available act of bankruptcy or if he, being a company, does anything or fails to do anything which would entitle a receiver to take possession of any assets or which would entitle any person to present a petition for winding up. The company may for the purpose of recovery of its goods enter upon any premises where they are stored or where they are reasonably thought to be stored and may repossess the same.

- In the case of any purchaser who is not a company, the purchase price shall be payable in two instalments, namely 10% on receipt of the goods and the balance at the end of such time as may be separately agreed or in default of agreement 30 days after the delivery of the goods.

- Subject to the terms hereof, the intending purchaser is licensed by the company to process the said goods in such fashion as he may wish and/or incorporate them in or with any other product(s) subject to the express condition that the new product(s) or any other chattel whatsoever containing any part of the said goods shall be separately stored and marked so as to be identifiable as being made from or with the goods the property of the company; or

  Subject to the terms hereof the intending purchaser is licensed by the company to agree to sell on the company's goods, subject to the express condition that such an agreement to sell shall take place as agents, (save that the intending buyer shall not hold himself out as such), and bailees for the company, whether the intending buyer sells on his own account or not and that the entire proceeds thereof are held in trust for the company and are not mingled with other monies or paid into any overdrawn account and shall be at all times identifiable as the company's monies.

- If goods the property of the company are admixed with goods the property of the intending purchaser or are processed with or incorporated therein, the product thereof shall become and/or shall be deemed to be the sole and exclusive property of the company. If goods the property of the company are admixed with goods the property of any person other than the intending purchaser or are processed with or incorporated therein, the product thereof shall become or shall be deemed to be owned in common with that other person.

- The intending purchaser shall be at liberty to agree to sell on any product produced from or with the company's goods on the express condition that such an agreement to sell shall take place as agents and bailees for the company whether the intending buyer sells on his own account or not and that the entire proceeds therefore are held in trust for the company and are not mingled with any other monies and shall at all times be identifiable as the company's monies.

- If the intending purchaser has not received the proceeds of any such sale he will, if called upon to do so by the company, within seven days thereof assign to the company all rights against the person(s) to whom he has supplied any product or chattel made from or with the company's goods; or

  If the intending purchaser has not received the proceeds of any such sale, he will, if called on to do so by the company, within seven days thereof assign to the company all rights against the person(s) to whom he has supplied any product or chattel made from or with the company's goods.

The registration of retention clauses A2.24

A clause which only retains a beneficial or equitable interest creates an equitable charge. In order for this to be valid it must be registered under *s 395* of the *Companies Act 1985 (CA 1985)* (*Re Bond Worth [1980] Ch 228* and *Stroud Architectural Systems Ltd v John Laing Construction plc [1994] 2 BCLC 276*). *CA 1985* provides that a charge created by a company registered in England and Wales, if of the type described in the Act, – so far as any security on the company's property or undertaking is conferred by the charge – is void as against the liquidator, administrator and any creditor of the company unless the charge is properly registered. The most important categories of registrable charges for present purposes are floating charges, charges on book debts and charges which, if executed by an individual, would require registration as a bill of sale (see further below).

Where the buyer is not a company, *CA 1985* will not apply. The consequences in respect of purported retention clauses over products and proceeds are similar, however, because of the operation of the *Bills of Sale Act 1878* and the *Bills of Sale Act 1882*, and of the *Insolvency Act 1986*. The provisions of these Acts effectively render void, as against the buyer's creditors, any unregistered attempt by the buyer to assign by way of security any interest in either the buyer's goods or his book debts.

Exclusion clauses and unfair terms A2.25

The supplier of goods or services will typically wish to exclude altogether any liability, or at any rate restrict the level of any potential liability. In recent years, the validity of such clauses has been considerably affected by the controls imposed by the *Unfair Contract Terms Act 1977*, and the *Unfair Terms in Consumer Contracts Regulations 1999 (SI 1999/2083)*. The following clause may be regarded as typical of this category of clause:

- No liability whatsoever shall be incurred by the seller in respect of any representation made by the seller or his agents before the contract was made where such representation related or referred in any way to (a) the correspondence of the goods to any description or (b) the fitness of the goods for any purpose whatsoever.

- No liability whatsoever shall be incurred by the seller to the buyer in respect of any express term of the contract whether a condition, warranty or intermediate stipulation (including any liability arising from the breach of such term) where the said term relates or refers in any way to (a) the correspondence of the goods to any description or (b) the quality of the goods or (c) the fitness of the goods for any purpose whatsoever.

- All implied terms, conditions or warranties – statutory, common law or otherwise – as to (a) the correspondence of the goods to any description or (b) the satisfactory quality of the goods, or (c) the fitness of the goods for any purpose whatsoever (whether made known to the seller or not) are hereby excluded from the contract.

As indicated above, an alternative approach is for the seller to accept some responsibility rather than to exclude it altogether. For example, liability may be limited to the contract price, to a percentage of that price, or simply to a specific figure. It has been said that a person who limits his liability takes a 'very ordinary business precaution' (*Cellulose Acetate Silk Co v Widnes Foundry (1925) Ltd [1933] AC 20*).

The Unfair Contract Terms Act 1977   A2.26

The *Unfair Contract Terms Act 1977 (UCTA 1977)* applies to both business and consumer contracts, but in differing ways.

Negligence liability   A2.27

UCTA 1977 makes it impossible for any contract term or notice to avoid or exclude liability for death or personal injury resulting from negligence. Where any other form of loss, such as damage to property, is caused by negligence, liability can be excluded or restricted if the clause is reasonable. It is common to see contract terms which state:

'The supplier hereby altogether excludes liability for any loss or damage, howsoever arising, from any act of negligence on his part, except where such negligence results in death or personal injury'.

38

General exclusion clauses   A2.28

Where the contract is on written standard terms, or is made with a consumer, then the following categories of contract term or notice are valid only if shown to be reasonable:

- clauses seeking to exclude or restrict liability; and

- clauses seeking to allow a substantially different performance from that which was reasonably expected, or clauses seeking to allow no performance at all.

Meaning of 'written standard terms'

No definition is given of 'written standard terms', but it has been considered on occasions by the courts.

Case Example: *St Alban's City and District Council v International Computers Ltd [1995] FSR 686.*

It was accepted that a contract can be subject to some negotiation between the parties and yet be on written standard terms (see too *McCrone v Boots Farm Sales Ltd 1981 SLT 103*).

Case Example: *British Fermentation Products Ltd v Compair Reavell Ltd [1999] BLR 351.*

It was said that a contract made on the terms and conditions of a trade association is not on one party's written standard terms except, perhaps, where these are adopted either by practice or by express statement as a party's own standard terms.

Meaning of a performance which is 'substantially different' or 'no performance'

Case Example: *Timeload Ltd v British Telecommunications plc [1995] EMLR 459.*

BT made certain phone numbers available in a contract containing the following clause:

'Termination of service by notice. At any time after service has been provided this contract or the provision of any service under it can be ended:

(1)   by one month's notice by us; or

(2)   by seven days' notice by you'.

No final decision was reached on whether this clause was one allowing a contractual performance from that which was reasonably expected, but the court said that: 'If a customer reasonably expects a service to continue until BT has substantial reasons to terminate it, it seems...at least arguable that a clause purporting to authorise BT to terminate without reason purports to permit partial or different performance from that which the customer expected'. Reference should also be made to *Zockoll Group Ltd v Mercury Communications [1999] EMLR 385.*

Case Example: *Brigden v American Express Bank Ltd [2000] IRLR 94*

In this case a clause in an employment contract allowing for dismissal during the first two years of employment without recourse to the disciplinary procedure was held not to be a term allowing the employer to render a performance substantially different from that which was reasonably expected.

It was also stated that the clause under consideration was not one allowing the employer not to perform the contract at all.

In practice, the parties to a contract of sale will often reserve the right not to perform upon the happening of certain events. For example, the seller may refuse to deliver until payment has been received, or the buyer may refuse to pay until the seller has delivered. Such a clause is one that seeks to allow no performance at all.

Excluding implied terms   A2.29

UCTA 1977 provides that no contract term can exclude or restrict the term as to title implied into contracts for the sale or supply of goods by the *SGA 1979* or the *SGSA 1982*. This is true whether the other contracting party is a business or a consumer. Where, however, any term as to title is implied at common law, the reasonableness test applies regardless of the status of the other contracting party.

In the case of the implied terms as to fitness for purpose and satisfactory quality, however, any clause seeking to exclude or restrict liability is automatically void against a consumer, and the inclusion of any such term is also a criminal offence under the *Consumer Transactions (Restrictions on Statements) Order 1976 (SI 1976/1813)*. In the case of a contract with a business, however, these implied terms can be excluded or restricted subject to the test of reasonableness.

Indemnity clauses   A2.30

UCTA 1977 provides that a consumer can only be required to indemnify another in respect of liability for the negligence of the other if the indemnity clause is reasonable. For instance, a clause in a contract for tree-felling on a consumer's property might seek to make the consumer liable to indemnify the tree-feller for any damage which he incurs to a neighbour while felling the trees. Such a clause is valid if reasonable.

Misrepresentation   A2.31

The *Misrepresentation Act 1967*, as amended by *UCTA 1977*, provides that any clause seeking to exclude or restrict liability for misrepresentation, or to exclude or restrict any right or remedy available on a misrepresentation, is valid only if reasonable. This applies to business and consumer contracts alike.

Guarantees   A2.32

A consumer cannot be deprived of any right against a negligent manufacturer or distributor by anything contained in a written guarantee.

Anti-avoidance measures

Normally, the disputed clause will be in the contract between the parties. *UCTA 1977*, however, also covers those cases where a contracting party seeks to rely on a clause contained in another contract, if that clause would be caught by the Act had it been contained in the contract between the parties.

Limiting liability to a specific sum
                                                                  A2.33

If liability is limited to a specific sum, a court must also consider:

- the resources which the relevant party could expect to be available for the purposes of meeting the liability should it arise; and
- how far it was open to that party to obtain insurance cover.

Case Example: *Overseas Medical Supplies Ltd v Orient Transport Services Ltd [1999] 1 All ER (Comm) 981.*

A contract of carriage limited liability for loss or damage to approximately £600. The contract also stated that, by special agreement in writing, the carrier would accept a greater degree of liability 'upon the customer agreeing to pay the company's additional charges for accepting such increased liability. Details of the company's additional charges will be provided on request'. There was also a clause which provided for insurance cover to be effected if written instructions were given, and that, when effecting such insurance, the carrier would act as agent for the customer using its best endeavours to arrange such insurance. Instructions were given to take out insurance, but these were ignored.

The Court of Appeal held that the clause was unreasonable. The Court pointed in particular to the fact that there was no equality of bargaining power; the contract failed to make it clear that the £600 limit would apply if the other party failed to take out insurance, so that there was 'no "reality of consent" to the effect of the clause'; and that limit was in any event 'derisory'.

The reasonableness test   **A2.34**

Central to the application of *UCTA 1977* is the reasonableness test. A clause challenged under the Act must prove that it is reasonable. A number of precedents are set out below, but it must always be remembered that each case must be judged on its individual facts and 'has to be considered in the light of the particular circumstances of the parties in question at the time the contract was made' (*British Fermentation Products Ltd v Compair Reavell Ltd [1999] 2 All ER (Comm) 389*). It is always possible that a clause found reasonable in one case will, because of the different contractual context, be found unreasonable in another.

In applying the reasonableness test, the courts are required by *UCTA 1977* to consider:

- the strength of the bargaining position of the parties relative to each other, taking into account (among other things) alternative means by which the customer's requirements could have been met;

- whether the customer received an inducement to agree to the term, or in accepting it had an opportunity of entering into a similar contract with other persons, but without having to accept similar terms;

- whether the customer knew or ought reasonably to have known of the existence and extent of the term (having regard, among other things, to any custom of the trade and any previous course of dealing between the parties);

- where the term excludes or restricts any relevant liability if some condition is not complied with, whether it was reasonable at the time to expect that compliance with the condition would be practicable; and

- whether the goods were manufactured, processed or adapted to the special order of the customer.

The reasonableness test (business contracts) – clause reasonable

In assessing the reasonableness test in business contracts, the starting point must be the observations in *Photo Production Ltd v Securicor Transport Ltd [1980] 1 All ER 556* that 'in commercial matters generally, when the parties are not of unequal bargaining power, and when risks are normally borne by insurance, not only is the case for judicial intervention undemonstrated, but there is everything to be said...for leaving the parties free to apportion the risk as they think fit and for respecting their decisions'.

Case Example: *W Photoprint Ltd v Forward Trust Group Ltd [1993] 12 Tr LR 21.*

A clause in a hire purchase contract contained a term to the effect that the customer had examined the goods and accepted that 'they are in every respect satisfactory and suitable for the purpose for which they are required and that he has relied on his own skill and judgement in choosing the goods'. The agreement also stated that, subject to the requirement of reasonableness, the defendants did 'not let the goods subject to any undertaking express or implied whether statutory or otherwise save the condition as to title...'. These clauses were considered to be reasonable in all the circumstances of the case.

Case Example: *British Fermentation Products Ltd v Compair Reavell Ltd [1999] 2 All ER (Comm) 389.*

The contract contained these terms:

- If within twelve months after delivery there shall appear in the goods any defect which shall arise under proper use from faulty materials, workmanship, or design (other than a design made, furnished, or specified by the purchaser for which the vendor had disclaimed responsibility), and the purchaser shall give notice thereof in writing to the vendor, the vendor shall, provided that the defective goods or defective parts thereof have been returned to the vendor if he shall have so required, make good the defects either by repair or, at the option of the vendor, by the supply of a replacement. The vendor shall refund the cost of carriage on the return of the defective goods or parts and shall deliver any repaired or replacement goods or parts as if [the contract terms as to delivery] applied.

- The vendor's liability under this Condition or under Condition 5 (Rejection and Replacement) shall be

> accepted by the purchaser in lieu of any warranty or
> condition implied by law as to the quality or fitness for
> any particular purpose of the goods and save as pro-
> vided in this Condition the vendor shall not be under
> any liability to the purchaser (whether in contract, tort
> or otherwise) for any defects in the goods or for any
> damage, loss, death or injury (other than death or per-
> sonal injury caused by the negligence of the vendor as
> defined in *section 1* of the *Unfair Contract Terms Act
> 1977*) resulting from such defects or from any work
> done in connection therewith.'

The court upheld these clauses, referring to their 'good business sense'.

Case Example: *BTE Auto Repairs v H&H Finance Factors Ltd (unreported, 26 January 1990).*

This involved a contract for the lease of machinery. The relevant clause
ran:

> 'The lessee has satisfied himself as to the condition of the
> goods and acknowledges that no condition or warranty
> whatsoever has been or is given by the lessor as to their fit-
> ness for any purpose and all conditions or warranties express
> or implied and whether by statute or otherwise are expressly
> excluded and delivery of the goods to the lessor shall be con-
> clusive evidence that the lessee has examined them and
> found them to be completely in accordance with the descrip-
> tion overleaf, in good order and condition, fit for any pur-
> pose for which they may be required and in every way
> satisfactory. The lessee shall not be entitled to any remission
> of rental in respect of any period during which the goods or
> any of them are unserviceable and the lessor shall not be liable
> to provide the lessee with any replacement goods during any
> such period or at all. The lessor shall use all reasonable efforts
> to obtain for the lessee the benefit of the manufacturers guar-
> antees and warranties (if any) given to the lessor'.

The Court of Appeal upheld the clauses.

Trade association terms   A2.35

It has been said that when a clause is in common use, and is well known
in the trade following comprehensive discussions between reputable and
representative bodies 'mindful of the considerations involved, the likelihood is that a clause will be held to be reasonable', because the clause
'reflects a general view as to what is reasonable in the trade concerned'
(*Overland Shoes Ltd v Schenker Ltd [1998] 1 Lloyd's Rep 498*).

The reasonableness test (business contracts) – clause not reasonable

It should always be remembered that the observation made in the Photo Production case (see A2.34 above) does no more than raise a presumption, at most, that a clause in a business-to-business contract will be upheld. Every case must be judged on its own facts.

Case Example: *Edmund Murray Ltd v BSP International Foundations Ltd [1992] Con LR 1.*

A contract for the supply of a rig was subject to a term providing that, while the supplier would make available to the buyer any rights afforded by his own supplier, this was to be in place of 'any other conditions, guarantees, liabilities or warranties expressed or implied statutory or otherwise and in no event shall the seller be liable for any loss, injury or damage however caused...'. The Court of Appeal held this was not reasonable.

A further clause in the contract excluded liability for loss of profit or for any other category of loss however caused, and also provided that the suppliers were not to be liable for damage arising from any 'stoppage or breakdown of the goods or in any other way from the performance of the goods in operation or any damage to the plant'. This too was held to be unreasonable.

The provision in the contract whereby the suppliers agreed to repair or replace the goods was made subject to certain conditions, such as notification to the suppliers and to the return of the 'defective goods or part or parts thereof...satisfactorily packed, at the risk of the buyers, carriage paid, to the sellers' works, or to such other place as the sellers may direct'. This too was unreasonable.

Case Example: *The Salvage Association v CAP Financial Services Ltd [1995] FSR 654.*

A limitation clause put a limit on liability, in a contract relating to the supply of computer software, at £25,000. This limit was arbitrary and there had been suggestions of raising it to £1m (these suggestions were not acted on). It was also the case that the service to be provided was relatively straightforward. The recipient of the service could not obtain insurance cover, while the supplier could. The clause was held to be unreasonable.

Case Example: *Lease Management Services Ltd v Purnell Secretarial Services Ltd [1994] CCLR 127.*

A contract for the lease of a photocopier contained a clause which offered to obtain for the lessee the benefits of any manufacturer's guarantee, but which excluded all liability:

'. . . in respect of any conditions, warranties or representations relating to the condition of the equipment or to its merchantability or suitability or fitness for the particular purpose for which it may be required whether such conditions, warranties or representations are express or implied and whether arising under the agreement or under any prior agreement or in oral or written statements made by or on behalf of the lessor or its agents in the course of negotiations in which the lessee or its representatives may have been concerned prior to the agreement'.

Finding the clause unreasonable, the Court said:

'We would like to think that the days of such blanket clauses, daunting to anyone and incomprehensible to an ordinary customer are passed. One would hope that finance companies and suppliers of expensive equipment no longer use pre-printed standard conditions as a means to avoid liabilities otherwise attaching to them for breach of pre-sale representations or breach of implied warranties'.

Cases for Further Information

Green (RW) Ltd v Cade Bros Farms [1978] 1 Lloyd's Rep 602; Walker v Boyle [1982] 1 WLR 495; Josef Marton v Southwestern General Property (unreported, 6 May 1982); George Mitchell (Chesterhall) Ltd v Finney Lock Seeds Ltd [1983] 2 AC 803; Fillite (Runcorn) Ltd v APV Pasilac Ltd (The Buyer, July 1995); Flamar Interocean v Denmac Ltd [1990] 1 Lloyd's Rep 434; AEG (IK) Ltd v Logic Resources [1996] CLC 265; McCullagh v Lane Fox & Partners Ltd [1996] PNLR 205; Danka Rentals Ltd v Xi Software (1998) 17 TrLR 74; Nippon Yusen Kaisha Ltd v Scandia Steam Navigation Ltd [2000] 1 All ER (Comm) 700; Messer UK Ltd v Britvic Soft Drinks Ltd (Court of Appeal, 30 April 2002).

While businesses might generally be able to care for themselves, the same cannot always be said with regard to consumer contracts. The tendency of the courts is to find against exclusion or limitation clauses in consumer contracts, although this is not always the case.

The reasonableness test (consumer contracts) – clause reasonable

Case Example: *Spencer v Cosmos Air Holidays Ltd (The Times, December 6 1989).*

A clause in a contract between holidaymakers and a company acting as a travel and holiday organiser, but which did not run or administer the hotel central to the dispute, disclaimed liability for any loss 'caused by any negligence of the management or employees of an independent contractor arising outside our normal selection and inspection process'. The County Court upheld this clause, and the Court of Appeal agreed if the clause was read as excluding any vicarious liability of the tour operator for a sub-contractor's wrongful act unless the operator was personally at fault. It added, however, that the clause would probably be regarded as unreasonable if what it really meant was that the tour operator was not to be liable if, through the mistake of a sub-contractor, a customer was to be without remedy even though deprived of all or part of the service contracted for.

Case Example: *Brigden v American Express Bank Ltd [2000] IRLR 94*.

A clause in a contract of employment stated that 'an employee may be dismissed by notice and/or payment in lieu of notice during the first two years of employment without implementation of the disciplinary procedure'. The Court said that this was not, in fact, an exclusion clause, but, had it been one, it was likely that it would have been upheld.

The reasonableness test (consumer contracts) – clause not reasonable

Case Example: *Lally v Bird (unreported, 23 May 1980)*.

Furniture was moved subject to a clause limiting liability to a specific sum per article, and also requiring claims to be made within a specific period. The night before delivery, the defendant's driver left the furniture outside his house, from where it was stolen. The clause was held not to be reasonable.

Case Example: *Waldron-Kelly v Marshall (unreported, 17 March 1981)*.

A case was delivered to one British Rail station for transmission to another. The contract was made at the owner's risk and provided for damages to be assessed on the weight of the goods. This was held not to be reasonable.

Case Example: *Smith v Eric S Bush*; *Harris v Wyre Forest District Council [1989] 2 All ER 514*.

A form used by a surveyor contained a disclaimer to the effect that neither the building society which instructed the surveyors, nor the surveyors themselves warranted that the report or valuation would be accurate, and that the report and valuation were to be supplied without any acceptance of responsibility. The House of Lords held that, having regard to the high cost of houses and the high interest rates, it would not be fair and reasonable for mortgagees and valuers to impose on purchasers the risk of loss arising as a result of the incompetence or carelessness on the part of the valuers. The Court did add, though, that when a surveyor was asked to survey industrial property, large blocks of flats or very expensive houses for mortgage purposes, where prudence would seem to dictate that a purchaser obtain his own survey, it may be reasonable for the surveyor to limit his liability or to exclude it altogether.

The Unfair Terms in Consumer Contracts Regulations 1999   A2.36

As the title to *The Unfair Terms in Consumer Contract Regulations 1999* (*SI 1999/2083*) implies, they go beyond simply controlling exclusion clauses. Instead, the Regulations (which apply only where the seller or supplier is a business and the other party a consumer), apply to consumer contracts which have not been individually negotiated and deem unfair – and hence unenforceable – any terms which 'contrary to the requirements of good faith...causes a significant imbalance in the parties' rights and obligations arising under the contract, to the detriment of the consumer'.

Meaning of 'good faith'   A2.37

In *Director General of Fair Trading v First National Bank [2002] 1 All ER 97*, the House of Lords interpreted 'good faith' to mean a duty to deal fairly and openly. Openness required that the terms should be expressed fully, clearly and legibly, containing no concealed pitfalls or traps. Appropriate prominence should be given to terms which might operate disadvantageously to the customer. Fair dealing required that a supplier should not, whether deliberately or unconsciously, take advantage of the consumer's necessity, indigence, lack of experience, unfamiliarity with the subject matter of the contract, weak bargaining position or any other factors listed in or analogous to those listed in *Schedule 2* of the Regulations (see A2.38 below).

The indicative list   A2.38

Schedule 2 of the Regulations contains an indicative and non-exhaustive list of terms which may be regarded as unfair. Not surprisingly, the list is headed by examples of exclusion clauses. Other clauses include requiring a consumer who fails to fulfil his obligation to pay a disproportionately high sum in compensation; irrevocably binding the consumer to terms with which he had no real opportunity of becoming acquainted before the conclusion of the contract; and enabling the seller or supplier to alter unilaterally without a valid reason any characteristics of the product or service to be provided.

Fairness

In applying the test of fairness, the Regulations require the court to take into account the 'nature of the goods or services for which the contract was concluded', and 'at the time of conclusion of the contract...all the circumstances attending the conclusion of the contract and...all the other terms of the contract or another contract on which it is dependent'.

> **Case Example**: *Director General of Fair Trading v First National Bank [2002] 1 All ER 97.*
>
> A credit agreement provided that the lender was entitled, on default of an instalment, to demand payment of the balance and interest outstanding. It further provided that interest on the amount that became payable would be charged at the contract rate until payment, after as well as before judgment, and that such obligation was to be independent of and not to merge with the judgment. In the absence of such a provision, a lender seeking to enforce an agreement in the County Court would have been unable to recover post-judgment interest.
>
> The House of Lords, reversing the Court of Appeal, held that this term was not unfair. The essential bargain was that the bank would make funds available to the borrower which the latter would repay, with interest, over time. Neither party could suppose that the bank would willingly forgo any part of the principal money or interest. If the bank thought that this was the likely outcome, it would not lend. The House of Lords also said that the borrower's obligation to repay the principal money in full with interest was very clearly and unambiguously expressed in the conditions of the contract.
>
> **Cases for Further Information**
>
> *Falco Finance Ltd v Michael Gough [1999] CCLR 16; Murphy v Kindlance (Consumer Law Today, November 1996); Gosling v Burrard-Lucas (unreported, 4 November 1998); Broadwater Manor School v Davis (unreported, 8 January 1999).*

Core terms

The Regulations provide that, if expressed in 'plain and intelligible language', the test of fairness is not to apply to terms which relate:

- to the definition of the main subject matter of the contract, or

- to the adequacy of the price or remuneration, as against the goods or services supplied in exchange.

Case Example: *Director General of Fair Trading v First National Bank [2002] 1 All ER 97.*

It was held that the terms referred to above were not a core provision. It did not concern the adequacy of the interest earned by the bank as its remuneration, but was designed instead to ensure that its entitlement to interest did not come to an end on the entry of judgment. It was an ancillary provision, not one concerned with the adequacy of the bank's remuneration for the services supplied.

Plain, intelligible language

The Regulations provides that if a term is not expressed in plain, intelligible language, any doubt as to the meaning of the term will be interpreted in favour of the consumer.

Enforcement   A2.39

It is the duty of the Office of Fair Trading (OFT) to consider any complaint made to it that a contract term drawn for general use is unfair, other than those complaints it considers frivolous or vexatious. The OFT can then seek a court injunction against any person appearing to be using or recommending an unfair term drawn up for general use in consumer contracts. The OFT also produces bulletins as part of its duty to publish details of steps taken under the Regulations. These can be found on www.oft.gov.uk/index.htm and copies can be supplied free of charge.

Qualifying bodies   A2.40

The Regulations list a number of 'qualifying bodies' who may apply for injunctions against the use of unfair terms. These bodies are:

- The Information Commissioner;
- The Gas and Electricity Market Authority;
- The Director General of Electricity Supply for Northern Ireland;
- The Director General of Gas for Northern Ireland;
- The Director General of Telecommunications;
- The Director General of Water Services;
- The Rail Regulator;

- The Department of Enterprise, Trade and Investment in Northern Ireland

- The Financial Services Authority; and

- every weights and measures authority in Great Britain;

Liquidated damages clauses   A2.41

A contract will frequently contain a clause which spells out the amount payable by the other party in the event of a breach. This has the practical value that such a clause could avoid litigation over the precise amount due in the event of a breach. Care must be taken in the drafting of such a clause, however, since the courts will only uphold a clause which is properly regarded as a 'liquidated damages' clause and which is not in fact a 'penalty clause'.

Determining whether a clause is a penalty clause or a liquidated damages clause

Case Example: *Dunlop Pneumatic Tyre Co v New Garage & Motor Co Ltd [1915] AC 79.*

The House of Lords stressed that the description given to the clause by the parties was not relevant to the test, so a clause described in the contract as a penalty clause could well, on analysis, prove to be a liquidated damages clause (and vice versa).

In this case, the company had supplied tyres subject to a price maintenance agreement which was then lawful. If there was any breach of the agreement, £5 was payable in respect of every tyre sold in breach of the agreement. This was held to be a valid liquidated damages clause because, while the sum itself might seem excessive, news of any undercutting would spread and the damage to Dunlop's selling organisation would be impossible to estimate.

Case Example: *Ford Motor Co v Armstrong (1915) 31 TLR 267.*

The defendant retailer agreed not to sell supplies obtained from Ford below the list price, not to sell Ford cars to other dealer, nor to exhibit any Ford car without permission. He agreed to pay £250, for 'the agreed damage which the manufacturer will sustain'. This was held to be an unenforceable penalty; it was made payable for various breaches differing in kind, and its very size prevented it from being a reasonable pre-estimate of the probable damage.

The test for determining the category into which a clause fell was: 'The essence of a penalty is a payment of money stipulated' in such a way as effectively to coerce a party to perform the contract, while a liquidated damages clause is one which is a 'genuine covenanted pre-estimate of damage'.

See also *Lombard North Central plc v Butterworth [1987] QB 527.*

It was stated in the *Dunlop* case that there will be a presumption that a clause is a penalty when 'a single lump sum is payable by way of compensation, on the occurrence of one or more or all of several events, some of which may occasion serious and others but trifling damage'. This rule has caught out a number of contract draftsmen and clauses have been held to be penal because they failed to distinguish between serious and trifling breaches of the agreement.

The fact that, in many cases, precise pre-estimation is almost impossible will not be a bar to a clause still being a valid liquidated damages clause. This was stated by the House of Lords in the *Dunlop* case. This is likely to be of more significance where the obligation of the party in breach is to perform a particular obligation other than payment. In such a case, it may be very difficult to calculate the financial consequences of breach, and the courts take the view that the parties are in a better position to assess the consequences of breach than the courts themselves. The courts are unwilling to second-guess the parties in such cases, as explained in *Clydebank Engineering and Shipbuilding Co v Don Jose Ramos [1905] AC 6)*. The same case also shows that the courts have generally insisted for there to be a large disproportion before the clause is classified as a penalty clause.

Interpreting a liquidated damages clause

Case Example: *Cenargo Ltd v Empresa Nacional Bazan de Construcciones Navales Militares SA (unreported, 26 March 2002).*

A clause in a contract for the building of a line of ferries provided that:

> 'if the actual trailer-carrying capacity of the Vessel is less that 146 Units of 13 metres each the Builder shall pay to the Buyer as liquidated damages One hundred and fifty thousand United States Dollars ($150,000) for each trailer unit by which the Vessel is deficient but excluding the first one (1) in respect of which deficiency no liquidated damages shall be payable. If the deficiency in trailer carrying capacity is ten (10) or more the Buyer as an alternative to receiving the aforementioned liquidated damages may rescind the contract'.

The particular deficiencies in the vessels as delivered were minor in that they could have been rectified in a matter of hours at little cost. The Court of Appeal held that where a substantial sum was payable in respect of deficiencies, a court should 'lean naturally to the conclusion that the clause was intended to apply only to major breaches'. Presumably, a clause drafted to cover minor breaches, but providing for payment of the same sum as for major breaches, would in any event be construed as penal and hence unenforceable (see A2.42 below).

Avoiding penalty clauses   **A2.42**

There are three main ways by which a party can avoid a contract term being a penalty clause.

- The first is to draft an 'acceleration clause'. This can be used where the buyer wishes to pay for the goods in instalments. The crucial ingredient in such a clause is the creation of a present debt ('the entire price shall be payable on the signing of this agreement') followed by what is sometimes called 'an indulgence', which provides that the buyer may make payments in instalments. Should the buyer fail to make any payment on the due date, an indulgence also provides that the entire balance becomes immediately payable (*Protector Loan Company v Grice (1880) 5 QBD 592; Wallingford v Mutual Society (1880) 5 App Cas 685*). The reason why such a clause is not a penalty clause is because it does not create any new liability. It simply accelerates an existing liability.

- A clause cannot be a penalty clause where the relevant sum is payable on the happening of an event which does not constitute a breach of contract. If, for example, the sum becomes payable on the buyer becoming insolvent, being jailed, or leaving the country, then the sum is not payable on a breach and does not constitute a penalty clause (*Associated Distributors Ltd v Hall [1938] 2 KB 83*). It should be noted, though, that the House of Lords was divided on this point in *Campbell Discount Co Ltd v Bridge [1962] AC 600*.

- The contract may be drafted in such a way so as to elevate the obligations of the buyer into conditions.

Case Example: *Lombard North Central plc v Butterworth [1987] QB 527*

The contract provided that 'punctual payment of each instalment was of the essence of the agreement'. The Court of Appeal held that the effect of this clause was that any failure to pay an instalment punctually was a breach going to the heart of the contract, giving a right to terminate the contract at law, and not simply a right to terminate under a power given by the contract itself. It followed that the creditor was entitled to compensation for loss of future instalments, making due allowance for accelerated payments, since the loss flowed from the buyer's fundamental breach and not from the creditor's election to terminate.

Prepayments and forfeitures

A2.43

A seller will be in a much stronger position if he requires the buyer to make a payment to him in advance. Should the buyer default, the seller's right to recover depends on the nature of the prepayment. Where the sum has been paid as part of the purchase price, the buyer can recover what he has paid. Where the sum, however, has been paid as a deposit, it is generally irrecoverable unless the deposit is an unreasonable one, or unless the court thinks that it has jurisdiction to grant relief against forfeiture (that is to say, relief against the buyer having to forfeit or lose his deposit) (*Stockloser v Johnson [1954] 1 QB 476*).

Damages

A2.44

The measure of damages in an action for breach of contract is governed by the rules laid down in *Hadley v Baxendale*.

Case Example: *Hadley v Baxendale (1854) 9 Ex 341.*

A mill-owner had sent a broken crankshaft for repair by carrier. The carrier delayed in delivering the crankshaft for repair, during which times the mill was out of action and hence not generating profits. The carrier was held not to be liable for these profits since he had not been told that the mill-owner had no spare crankshaft and that the mill was currently at a standstill. The rule laid down in the case is that the party in breach is liable only for the probable consequences of the breach. This is defined to mean the loss he contemplated would arise in the event of breach on the basis of the facts known or disclosed to him at the time the contract was made.

Case Example: *Victoria Laundry (Windsor) Ltd v Newman Industries Ltd [1949] 2 KB 528.*

The claimants agreed to buy a large boiler from the defendants, and a date was fixed for delivery. When the boiler was delayed, the claimant sought to recover for:

- the large number of new customers that could have been taken on had the boiler been installed; and

- the amount which they could have earned under special government contracts.

The defendants knew that the claimants were launderers, and that the boiler was wanted for immediate use. The Court of Appeal held that, with such knowledge, the reasonable man could have foreseen that delay would lead to some loss of profits, though he would not have foreseen the special government contracts since these were not within the defendants' actual knowledge. The defendants were, therefore, only liable for the normal loss of business profits to be reasonably expected.

Case Example: *Re R&H Hall Ltd and W H Pim (Junior) & Co's Arbitration [1928] All ER Rep 763.*

The sellers sold 7,000 tons of wheat. As a result of a rise in the market price of the wheat after the conclusion of the contract, the buyers sold it on at a profit. The sellers failed to deliver, however, and, at the time of failure to deliver the price of wheat had slipped back. The House of Lords held that the buyers could recover for their loss of profit. On the facts, the sellers knew, or should have known, that the buyers were buying for resale; the sellers also knew that the buyers had contracted to re-sell the very goods being purchased. The contract itself recognised the possibility of 'string' sales.

Recovery of expenditure   A2.45

A claimant might incur expenditure in the belief that the defendant will perform the contract as promised. Such expenditure is usually referred to as 'reliance expenditure'. Where the claimant terminates the contract on the grounds of the breach, he may claim damages to cover his expenditure towards his own performance, but only to the extent that it has been wasted as a result of the breach. The claimant cannot, however, recover more than he would have obtained had the contract been properly performed.

Cases for Further Information

C & P Haulage v Middleton [1983] 1 WLR 1461; CCC Films (London) Ltd v Impact Quadrant Films [1985] QB 16; Molling & Co v Dean & Sons Ltd (1908) 18 TLR 217; Mason v Burningham [1949] 2 KB 545.

Claims for expenditure and loss of profit   A2.46

In principle, a claimant should be entitled to claim damages both for wasted expenditure and for loss of net profit. There can be no valid objection to this provided the calculations show that there is no overlapping; that is to say, the net profit is determined by deducting from the expected gross return the expenditure incurred.

Case Example: *Cullinane v British 'Rema' Manufacturing Co Ltd [1954] 1 QB 292.*

The Court of Appeal indicated that a claimant had to choose between a claim for expenditure and a claim for profit, but this can only be so if there is an element of overlap in the claims.

Mitigation of loss   A2.47

Lord Haldane stated in *British Westinghouse Electric Co Ltd v Underground Electric Rys [1912] AC 673, 689* the victim of a breach of contract must take 'all reasonable steps to mitigate the loss consequent on the breach [and cannot claim] any part of the damage which is due to his neglect to take such steps'.

The standard of the duty to mitigate is not high, since the other party is, of course, the wrongdoer.

> 'The law is satisfied if the party placed in a difficult situation by reason of the breach of a duty owed to him has acted reasonably in the adoption of remedial measures, and he will not be held disentitled to recover the cost of such measures merely because the party in breach can suggest that other measures less burdensome to him might have been taken' (*Banco de Portugal v Waterlow [1932] AC 452, 506*).

Case Example: *Jewelowski v Propp [1944] KB 510.*

It was held that the duty to mitigate did not require a claimant to take risks with his money.

Case Example: *Finlay & Co v NV Kwik Hoo Tong HM [1929] 1 KB 400.*

A claimant need not take steps which might endanger his commercial reputation, as by enforcing sub-contracts.

Case Example: *Pilkington v Wood [1953] Ch 770.*

A claimant is not under a duty, even if the defendant offers an indemnity, to embark on difficult and complicated litigation against a third party.

Where the claimant has failed to take reasonable steps to mitigate

Case Example: *Payzu v Saunders [1919] 2 KB 581.*

The seller – in breach of contract – declined to deliver goods on the agreed credit terms, but offered to do so on 'cash on delivery'. The refusal of the buyer to accept that offer was judged unreasonable in the circumstances.

Case Example: *The Solholt [1983] 1 Lloyd's Rep 605.*

Similarly, where the claimant bought a ship from the defendant, who could not deliver it on the agreed date, it was held that it would have been reasonable for the claimant to have mitigated his loss by accepting late delivery (for which he could have claimed damages).

Case Example: *Wilson v United Counties Bank [1920] AC 102.*

A claimant is entitled to recover damages for loss or expense incurred by him in reasonably attempting to mitigate his loss following the breach, even when the mitigating steps were unsuccessful or in fact made matters worse.

Limitation periods   A2.48

Section 5 of the *Limitation Act 1980 (LA 1980)* provides that no action on a simple contract 'can be brought once six years have passed from the date when the cause of action accrued'. A 'simple contract' is, essentially, one not made by deed. A contract made by deed is a 'specialty contract', for which *LA 1980, s 8* prescribes a limitation period of twelve years. In the case of any action for breach of contract where the damages claimed consist of or include damages for personal injuries, *ss 11* and *14* of *LA 1980* specify that the limitation period is three years from:

- the date on which the cause of action accrued, or
- the date of the claimant's knowledge (if later) of certain facts relevant to his right of action.

The general rule in contract is that the cause of action accrues when the breach takes place. As a result, time begins to run from the moment the contract is broken, and not from the time when any damage is actually sustained. For example, in an action for breach of warranty or condition against a seller, the cause of action accrues when the goods are delivered, and not when the damage is discovered.

LA 1980 also contains a number of provisions which extend the limitation period.

Fraud, concealment, mistake   A2.49

Section 32 of *LA 1980* applies:

- if the action is based on the fraud of the defendant;

- if a fact relevant to his cause of action has been deliberately concealed;

- or if the action relates to mistake.

The limitation period in these cases does not run until the claimant discovers, or should have discovered, the fraud, concealment or mistake.

> **Case Example**: *Cave v Robinson Jarvis & Rolf [2002] 2 All ER 641.*
>
> The House of Lords laid down the following principles for the application of *LA 1980, s 32*. It deprived a party of a limitation defence:
>
> - where that party took active steps to conceal his own breach of duty after he had become aware of it; and
>
> - where he was guilty of deliberate wrongdoing and concealed or failed to disclose it in circumstances where it was unlikely to be discovered for some time.

Latent damage   A2.50

Section 14A of *LA 1980* provides for a limitation period running from:

- six years from the date on which the cause of action first started to accrue; or

- three years from the earliest date on which the claimant first had both the knowledge required for bringing an action and a right to bring the action (if that three year period expires later than the six year period). This provision only applies, however, to actions in negligence, and even then does not cover actions involving personal injuries (see A2.48 above). It does not apply to contract actions, and will be of use only to contracting parties who have a concurrent or independent cause of action in negligence.

Acknowledgement and part payment   A2.51

Section 29 of *LA 1980* lays down a uniform rule applicable to both simple and specialty contracts by providing that where a person acknowledges the claim, or makes any payment in respect of it, the right is to be treated as accruing on the date of acknowledgement or payment.

Section 30 says that an acknowledgement must be in writing and signed by the person making it.

What counts as writing

Case Examples:

- *Re River Steamer Co (1871) LR 6 Ch App. 822* (correspondence (unless written 'without prejudice')).
- *Hony v Hony (1824) 1 Sim & S 568* (an account rendered).
- *Howcutt v Bonsor (1849) 3 Exch. 491* (a recital in a deed).
- *Re Gee & Co (Woolwich) Ltd [1975] Ch 52* (a company's balance sheet).
- *Goode v Job (1858) 1 E&E 6* (a pleading).

Acknowledgement is a question of construction, to be decided on the facts of the instant case, and it has been said that the decided cases are of little value as precedents (*Spencer v Hemmerde [1922] 2 AC 507*). Under the present law, all that is needed from the debtor is an admission that there is a debt or other liquidated pecuniary claim outstanding, and of his legal liability to pay it.

Guidelines for determining acknowledgement

Case Example: *Jones v Bellgrove Properties Ltd [1949] 2 KB 700*.

This case explained that it is not necessary for the acknowledgement to specify the amount of the debt if it can be ascertained by other means.

Case Example: *Howcutt v Bonsor, Re Gee & Co (Woolwich) Ltd [1975] Ch 52*.

The acknowledgement must, though, acknowledge a claim, and not merely that there might be a claim, and it must further acknowledge that the claim exists at the date of acknowledgement or that it existed on a date which falls within the appropriate period of limitation next before action is brought.

Case Example: *Consolidated Agencies Ltd v Bertram Ltd [1965] AC 470*.

This case showed that acknowledgement of past liability, however, is ineffective.

Shortening the limitation period   A2.52

The parties to a contract can always agree on a shorter period than allowed for by *LA 1980*. Such provisions are not uncommon in commercial agreements and their effect may be, depending on the exact wording, to bar or extinguish a right of action, or deprive a party of their right to recourse to particular proceedings after the expiry of the agreed time limit. It should be realised though that such clauses, if contained in a contract made on written standard terms, will be valid only if they can be shown to be reasonable.

Remedy itself barred not the right   A2.53

If time has lapsed under *LA 1980*, this means that the *remedy* of court action has gone, but not the particular *right*. If, for example, a buyer pays a debt which is time-barred, he cannot subsequently recover that payment on the ground that it was no longer due.

Effect of mistake and misrepresentation   A2.54

Generally a mistake made by one or both parties as to the terms of the contract has no effect on the validity of the contract. There are, however, exceptional and limited types of mistake which will render a contract void. In addition, contracts which are not void for mistake under common law may be held voidable in equity.

If a contract is declared void it is as though it had never existed. Thus neither party can enforce the agreement, and any property transferred can usually be recovered because the transferee can have no legal title to it. A voidable contract, on the other hand, is one which is binding until the innocent party seeks to rescind (cancel) it.

A representation is a statement made during pre-contractual negotiations which induces a person to enter into a contract. If the statement proves to be false or misleading then it is a misrepresentation, which gives rise to a remedy under the *Misrepresentation Act 1967* (*MA 1967*). The contract is voidable at the option of the innocent party. They can choose to affirm (carry on with the contract) or rescind, and they may also be able to claim damages.

Types of mistake   A2.55

It is usual to divide mistake into three types; common, mutual, and unilateral. A common mistake is where both parties are under the same misconception. In mutual mistake, both parties are mistaken but do not make the same mistake. In unilateral mistake, only one party is mistaken and the other party is aware of that misapprehension.

Common mistake

If the parties have made the same mistake about a fundamental element of the contract the court may find it void. For example, if two parties agree to the supply and purchase of goods but, unknown to them, the goods do not exist when the contract is made, then the court may declare the contract void. In deciding whether the contract should be made void for mistake in these circumstances, the court first has to be sure that neither party had accepted responsibility for the existence of the goods. That is, could a term be implied into the contract which encompassed that obligation? In the majority of disputes this is usually the case.

Case Example: *Associated Japanese Bank (International) v Credit du Nord SA [1988] 3 All ER 902.*

The bank, in a £1m loan arrangement, agreed to buy four business machines from a client, B, and lease them back to him. The arrangement was guaranteed by the defendants. B paid one quarterly payment, then was adjudged bankrupt. The bank sued the defendants on the guarantee. It was discovered that the whole arrangement was a fraud by B and the machines had never existed. The court held that the existence of the machines was fundamental to the contract of guarantee, therefore the contract was void. The court emphasised that common law would only hold a contract void for common mistake if the mistake was made by both parties and it rendered the subject matter of the contract radically different from that which the parties believed to exist.

The court also emphasised that the rules on mistake were for exceptional circumstances, so mistake is not an excuse to get out of a bad bargain. Consequently, a mistake as to the quality of the subject matter of the contract will not affect the validity of the contract.

Case Example: *Leaf v International Galleries [1950] 2 KB 86.*

Leaf bought a painting of Salisbury Cathedral from the defendant. Both parties believed it to be by the artist John Constable. Five years later, when Leaf tried to sell it, he discovered it was not by Constable. The court said the contract was unaffected. Both parties had made a mistake about the quality and value of the painting but there was still a valid contract for a painting.

Case Example: *Solle v Butcher [1950] 1 KB 671.*

Both parties to a lease thought that a recently refurbished flat was no longer subject to the various Rent Acts and agreed a rent of £250 a year. However, they were mistaken, and the maximum rent under the Acts, at that time, was £140. The tenant claimed repayment of the excess rent and the landlord served notice on the lessee. The Court of Appeal held the mistake was not sufficiently fundamental for the contract to be void, however, it was voidable in equity. The tenant had the choice of giving up the lease or accepting a new one at an increased maximum rent under the Rent Acts.

Where a common mistake is not sufficiently fundamental to render the contract void at common law, equity may hold that the contract is voidable in order to achieve a fair result.

Mutual mistake

This involves situations where the parties are at cross purposes. For example, A, when buying a house, thinks that carpets are included in the sale, but B, the seller, believes the carpets are excluded. The sale goes ahead, then the mistake is discovered. Clearly there is no consensus, but rarely is the contract held to be void at common law. Usually the court resolves the contract in favour of one of the parties by deciding what a reasonable onlooker would understand the terms of the contract to be.

Case Example: *Smith v Hughes (1871) LR 6 QB 597.*

A racehorse owner bought a quantity of oats after inspecting a sample. When the bulk of the order was delivered, he discovered the oats were 'this season's' not 'last season's' oats, which were of no use to him. He claimed the contract was void for mistake. The seller had not misrepresented the oats as being last season's, neither was he aware of the buyer's impression. Taking an objective view, the court held that there was a valid contract. The buyer had been careless and merely misled himself as to the type of oats.

If, however, from the standpoint of the reasonable onlooker, the parties have clearly failed to reach any agreement, the contract will be void for mistake.

Case Example: *Raffles v Wichelhaus (1864) 2 Hurl & C 906.*

The parties agreed, in London, on a contract of sale for a cargo of cotton 'Ex Peerless from Bombay'. There were, in fact, two ships called Peerless sailing from Bombay with cotton, one departing in October, the other in December. The buyer intended to buy the October shipment, the seller intended to sell the December shipment. It was held there was no agreement, offer and acceptance did not coincide, and the contract was void for mistake.

Unilateral mistake

A unilateral mistake arises when only one of the parties is mistaken and the other is aware of that mistake. This may occur in two situations; a mistake as to the terms of the contract or a mistake as to the identity of one of the parties.

> **Case Example**: *Harthog v Colin and Shields [1939] 3 All ER 566.*
>
> The defendants offered to sell animal skins and negotiated a price per skin, as was the trade custom. Subsequently, the contract was mistakenly concluded at a price per pound which the plaintiffs accepted. They were prevented from enforcing the deal on the basis that they must have been aware of the defendants' mistake.

A unilateral mistake often arises out of a misrepresentation. Misrepresentation, however, renders a contract voidable not void, thus it may be impossible to recover any goods transferred under the contract. Under the voidable contract, the dishonest party obtains title to the goods and, if he sells them on before the contract is avoided, the party to whom he sold them acquires good title. Thus the party who was misled bears the loss. If, on the other hand, the contract is void for mistake, the dishonest party never acquires good title to the goods and the party who is misled may be able to recover the goods. Therefore, the decision as to whether a contract is voidable for misrepresentation or void for unilateral mistake may determine which of two innocent parties bears the loss. For further information on misrepresentation see A2.56 below.

For the contract to be void at common law for unilateral mistake, the mistake must be fundamental to the nature of the contract and it must induce the innocent party to enter into the contract.

What counts as a fundamental mistake?

Case Example: *Cundy v Lindsay (1877-78) 3 AC 459*

A fraudster called Blenkarn wrote to Cundy ordering goods, giving his address as 37 Wood Street and signing his name so that it appeared to be Blenkiron & Co, a respectable business with whom Cundy had traded on previous occasions and whose offices were at 123 Wood Street. Cundy sent the goods to 'Blenkiron' at 37 Wood Street and Blenkarn then sold them on to Lindsay. Cundy sued Lindsay to recover the value of the goods, claiming the contract was void for mistake. The court held that the contract was void for mistake. Cundy intended only to contract with Blenkiron and no title passed to Blenkarn.

If, however, the parties deal face-to-face rather than by letter or telephone, it is more likely that the contract will be voidable for fraudulent misrepresentation.

Case Example: *Lewis v Avery [1971] 3 All ER 907.*

The claimant advertised his car for sale. A dishonest person who claimed to be the actor Richard Green (who was famous at the time) came to buy it. A deal was agreed and the 'actor' signed a cheque, showing, as proof of identity, a pass for Pinewood Studios which had his name and photograph. Lewis accepted the cheque, which was dishonoured when presented at the bank. Meanwhile, the fraudster sold the car to Avery, who bought it in good faith with no knowledge of the fraud.

If the contract between Lewis and the fake Green was void for mistake, then Green never had title to the car and therefore neither did Avery. Lewis would get his car back and Avery would bear the loss. If, on the other hand, the contract between Lewis and Green was voidable for fraudulent misrepresentation, then Green did have good title to the car which he had passed on to Avery before Lewis avoided the contract. In that case, Lewis would bear the loss. The Court of Appeal found that the contract was not void for mistake because the evidence showed that Lewis intended to sell the car to the person who turned up at his house.

Case Example: *Hudson v Shogun Finance Ltd (Court of Appeal; 2001 WL 676716).*

A fraudster visited a motor dealer. He wanted to buy a car on hire purchase and showed a driving licence as proof of identity. That licence was not his. The dealer contacted the claimant finance company, which ran credit checks against the person named in the licence, and these revealed a good record. The deal went ahead. The fraudster then sold the car to an innocent third party. Under the *Hire Purchase Act 1964 (HPA 1964)*, an innocent party who takes a car subject to a hire purchase contract can obtain a good title. The question for the court was whether, in these circumstances, there was a hire purchase contract in the first place.

By a majority, the Court of Appeal, upholding the county court, ruled that the alleged contract was void for mistake. It was accepted that where a contract was negotiated face-to-face, then the principle was that the other party was intending to deal with the fraudster, and that a voidable contract would result, unless the evidence was such as to displace the application of that presumption. The Court of Appeal differed, however, as to whether this was a face-to-face contract, when negotiations were through the dealer. It was held that it was not a face-to-face contract.

It was also held, however, that even if the face-to-face principle did apply, this would be a case where the presumption that a voidable contract had resulted would be displaced by the facts of the case. The evidence led by the claimant was very much to the point that the identity of the person seeking finance was crucial. It laid stress in particular on the fact that, to comply with the requirements of the *Consumer Credit Act 1974*, in particular when it came to the issue of default notices, the correct identity of the debtor was essential.

The decision to dismiss the appeal was also reached by another route. In *Hector v Lyons (1988) P&CR 1567*, a father had sought to buy a house, but in his son's name. The Court of Appeal had ruled that the face-to-face principle does not apply to a case where there is a contract which is wholly in writing.

Accordingly, the appeal was dismissed on the short ground that the fraudster was not the party named in the hire purchase agreement. In the event, therefore, there was no hire purchase contract, and the provisions of *HPA 1964* did not apply.

Cases for Further Information:

Phillips v Brooks [1919] 2 KB 243; Ingram v Little [1961] 1 QB 31.

Misrepresentation   A2.56

In order for a misrepresentation to be actionable, it must be shown that the statement:

- was a statement of fact, not opinion;
- was untrue; and
- induced the innocent party to enter the contract.

Statement of fact

Case Example: *Bisset v Wilkinson [1927] AC 177.*

A landowner who sold his land to a sheep farmer, expressing the view that providing it was worked properly it could support 2,000 sheep, was not liable for misrepresentation when this turned out to be false. It was held that this was an honest statement of opinion as to the capacity of the farm, not a representation as to its actual capacity.

Case Example: *Esso Petroleum Co Ltd v Mardon [1976] 2 All ER 5.*

Esso represented to a prospective purchaser of a petrol station that it was likely that petrol sales for that station could reach 200,000 gallons a year. The defendant, relying on that estimate, bought the station with the help of a loan from Esso. The garage in fact only sold 78,000 gallons. The defendant could not keep up the payments and Esso sought to repossess the station. The defendant counter-claimed for misrepresentation. The Court of Appeal found Esso's statement of sales to be one of fact, not opinion, because they had experience and skill in the form of market research analysis.

Case Example: *BG plc v Nelson Group Services (Maintenance) Ltd [2002] EWCA 547.*

BG had contracted out the installation of gas appliances sold in its showrooms. In 1995, Nelson was awarded four regional contracts for installation work. The relationship between the parties terminated in 1997 and Nelson began proceedings claiming to have sustained losses of £1.7m from entering into the contracts which it was induced to do by BG's misrepresentations consisting of original forecasts which were negligently prepared, false, inaccurate and misleading. Nelson argued that BG had, by implication, represented that it knew all the facts which justified the forecasts and/or that they were based on substantial and reasonable grounds.

The court said that, on occasions, an expression of opinion might carry with it no implication other than that the opinion was genuinely held, but, on other occasions, as in the present case, the circumstances might be such that they give rise to an implied representation that the representor knew of facts which justified the opinion. When an opinion was expressed, the person who expressed it either did or did not know facts which justified the opinion. The existence of those facts, and the representor's state of mind, were themselves capable of being misrepresented by implication by virtue of the expression of opinion.

Cases for Further Information

Cremdean Properties Ltd v Nash (1977) 244 EG 547; Sumitomo Bank Ltd v BBL [1997] 1 Lloyd's Rep 487.

The effect of 'patter'   A2.57

Vague general claims about a product will be seen as 'sales talk', e.g. 'the car is a great little runner'; 'the washing powder will make your clothes brighter'; 'the land is improvable'. More precise wording, however, is more likely to be treated as a misrepresentation of fact if untrue.

Case Example: *Smith v Land and House Property Corp [1884] 28 Ch D 7.*

It was misrepresentation when a vendor claimed his property was let to a 'most desirable tenant' when that tenant was seriously in arrears with his rent.

Future intentions   A2.58

A statement which declares an intention to do something in the future may be actionable as a misrepresentation if it is not carried out.

Case Example: *Edgington v Fitzmaurice (1885) LR 29 Ch D 459.*

The directors of a company issued a prospectus in which they stated that the money raised by the sale of debentures would be used to complete alterations to the company's premises and develop the business. In fact, it was used to pay off pressing debts. They were held liable for misrepresentation.

An actual statement   A2.59

As a general rule there must be an untrue statement either written or spoken. Silence does not amount to a misrepresentation. For example, when buying goods it is for the buyer to ask questions, there is no duty on the seller to disclose what he knows about the product.

There are exceptions to this rule, however, in the following circumstances.

- Where the contract requires utmost good faith (*uberrimae fidei*) there is a duty to declare all relevant matters. Non-disclosure can result in the contract being voidable for misrepresentation, thus allowing the innocent party to rescind. A contract for insurance is such an example – failure to disclose for example a speeding conviction may mean that a claim against the insurance company, in the event of a motor accident, would not be paid. Contracts where there is a fiduciary relationship between the parties are also considered to be *uberrimae fidei*. Such relationships exist, for example, between solicitors or accountants and their clients, between partners in a firm, or between an agent and his principal. If such a relationship is claimed, then the burden of proof is on the party claiming its existence.

- There is a duty to correct a statement which, although true when first made, subsequently becomes untrue before the contract is concluded.

- If, by revealing only part of the truth, a representor misleads the other party, he may be liable for misrepresentation.

Case Example: *With v O'Flanagan [1936] Ch 575.*

A doctor told a prospective buyer that his practice was worth £200 per annum, which was true. The doctor then fell ill, so that the income fell substantially, but the buyer was not informed. It was held that the buyer could rescind the contract on the grounds of misrepresentation.

Case Example: *Dimmock v Hallett (1886) LR 2 Ch App 21.*

A seller of land declared to the buyer that all the farms on the land were let. The seller was under a duty to reveal that in fact the tenants were about to leave.

Statement must induce contract   **A2.60**

Even if the statement made is untrue, any claim for misrepresentation will fail if the innocent party did not rely on it. If they knew it was untrue, or they would have agreed to the deal without the inducement, there can be no remedy. In addition, the person to whom a representation is made has no obligation to verify its authenticity, even if given the opportunity to do so.

Case Example: *Redgrave v Hurd [1887] 20 Ch D 1.*

A solicitor was induced into buying a practice because he was told its income was £300 per year. The buyer was given the accounts but he did not take the opportunity to examine them. The buyer was allowed to rescind the contract. He had relied on the statement and was under no duty to investigate its accuracy.

Case Example: *Attwood v Small (1838) 6 Cl & Fin 232.*

The owners of a mine made claims regarding the mine's reserves. The prospective buyers' surveyors wrongly verified these claims and the sale was concluded. A claim by the buyers to have the contract rescinded for misrepresentation failed, since they relied on their own surveyors not the sellers' statements. If they had believed the vendors, they would not have checked.

Types of misrepresentation   **A2.61**

Misrepresentations may be fraudulent, negligent or innocent. The classification is important for determining the remedy available.

Fraudulent misrepresentation

An untrue statement will be a fraudulent misrepresentation if it is made in the knowledge that it is false, or with reckless disregard for whether it is true or false. In other words, there must be an element of dishonesty on the part of the person making the statement.

Case Example: *Derry v Peek [1889] 14 AC 337*

Company directors stated in a share prospectus that the company had the authority to run trams. In fact, the Board of Trade did not give it permission to do so. As a consequence, the directors were sued in the tort of deceit by those who bought shares on the strength of the prospectus. The House of Lords held that since the directors genuinely believed that Board of Trade consent was merely a formality, the directors were not dishonest. There was an untrue statement of fact which induced a contract, but it was not made fraudulently.

Any party misled by a fraudulent misrepresentation may rescind the contract and also, or instead, recover damages for losses by suing for deceit in tort.

Negligent misrepresentation

Negligent misrepresentation is a statement made in the belief that it is true, but with no reasonable grounds for that belief. There are two paths open to a party misled by a negligent statement to gain compensation.

Firstly, since the decision in *Hedley Byrne and Co Ltd v Heller and Partners Ltd [1964] AC 465*, it is possible to take action in tort for negligent misstatement, and provided the plaintiff can prove a special relationship with the defendants and therefore reliance on the skill of the defendants, compensatory damages will be payable.

Secondly, the innocent party may rescind the contract and claim damages under *MA 1967*. Under the Act it is the defendant who must prove that they had reasonable grounds for making the statement, whereas in tort it is the claimant who must prove that the defendants were negligent.

Case Example: *Howard Marine and Dredging Co Ltd v A Ogden & Sons (Excavations) Ltd [1978] QB 574.*

The claimants hired two barges from the defendants. The carrying capacity of the barges was crucial and the defendants misrepresented the sizes. They had based their information on facts from *Lloyds Register* which turned out to be wrong, but they could have checked with the

---

barge owners. The court was not sure whether there was a duty of care in the tort of negligence, but under *MA 1967* the defendants failed to prove that they had not been negligent.

Innocent misrepresentation

A statement made in the belief that it is true, and with reasonable grounds for that belief, is an innocent misrepresentation. The remedy for innocent misrepresentation is rescission of the contract, but under *MA 1967, s 2(2)* the court may, instead, award damages.

Loss of the right to rescind means that there is no right to damages under *s 2(2)*. That section operates only if the right to rescission still exists (*Zanzibar v British Aerospace (Lancaster House) Ltd [2001] 1 WLR 2333*).

Excluding liability for misrepresentation   A2.62

MA 1967, s 3, provides that any contract term excluding or restricting any liability for misrepresentation, or excluding or restricting a remedy otherwise available because of misrepresentation, is valid only if it satisfies the test of reasonableness laid down in the *Unfair Contract Terms Act 1977*.

When a clause has not been reasonable

Case Example: *Howard Marine and Dredging Co Ltd v A Ogden & Sons (Excavations) Ltd [1978] QB 574.*

A term provided that:

> '... charterer's acceptance of handing over the vessel shall be conclusive that [she is] ... in all respects fit for the intended and contemplated use by charterers and in every other way satisfactory to them'.

The Divisional Court found that it was not fair and reasonable to rely on this clause, a view which the majority of the Court of Appeal were not prepared to disturb though no specific view was expressed. Lord Denning, however, pointing out that the parties were commercial concerns of equal bargaining strength, and that the term was not foisted by one party on another, but contained in a contract the drafts of which had been passed between the parties, and also noting that the dispute which had arisen was just what such a clause sought to avoid, ruled that it was fair and reasonable to rely on this clause.

Case Example: *Walker v Boyle [1982] 1 WLR 495.*

A clause in the then edition of the *National Conditions of Sale* provided that there was no right of rescission for errors, misstatements or omissions in the preliminary answers, or in the sale plan or special conditions, 'nor (save where the error, misstatement or omission is in a written answer and relates to a matter materially affecting the description or value of the property) shall any damages be payable or compensation allowed by either party in respect thereof'.

Without specifying his reasons, the judge ruled that this clause had not been shown to be reasonable. He appears to have been influenced by the fact that the condition excluded compensation for any oral misstatement, however grave, even to the extent of being fraudulent.

Case Example: *Josef Marton v Southwestern General Property (Unreported, 6 May 1982).*

Land had been bought at auction in reliance upon a misrepresentation. The relevant clause stated:

> 'The property is believed to be and shall be taken to be correctly described and any incorrect statement, error or omission found in the particulars or conditions of sale shall not annul the sale or entitle the purchaser to be discharged from his purchase.'

The purchaser was also denied the right to take any point under town and country planning legislation, requiring him to 'take the properties as they are under the said Acts, rules and regulations'.

A further clause, 'quite obviously designed to avoid the effects' of the *Misrepresentation Act 1967* provided:

> 'All statements contained in the foregoing particulars are made without responsibility on the part of the auctioneers or the vendor and are statements of opinion and are not to be taken as or implying a statement or representation of fact and any intending purchaser must satisfy himself by inspection or otherwise as to the correctness of each statement contained in the particulars. The vendor does not give or make any representation or warranty in relation to the property nor has the auctioneer or any person in the employment of the auctioneer any authority to do so on his behalf.'

The vendors argued that the circumstances of auction sales necessitated such clauses, while the purchaser said that the misrepresentation was derived from matters solely within the knowledge of the vendors. The vendors further argued that the particulars did stress the need for purchasers to make their own enquiries, and that they were catering not just for private buyers, such as the present party, but also for other categories including speculators.

The judge, however, ruled that parties might well come to an auction, as did this particular buyer, when time no longer allowed for enquiries to be made. He stressed that he was to judge this particular contract and the particular circumstances of the case, also noting that the facts on which the misrepresentation was based were central to the purchase and peculiarly within the vendors' knowledge.

He held that they had not shown that the exclusion was reasonable; if it were otherwise, the vendors could have avoided liability 'for a failure to tell more than only a part of the facts which were among the most material to the whole contract of sale'.

Where a clause has been reasonable

Case Example: *McCullagh v Lane Fox and Partners Ltd [1996] PNLR 205*.

This case involved the purchase of property which had a smaller acreage than stated in the particulars. An exclusion clause was upheld, not least because the purchaser 'had ample opportunity to regulate his conduct having regard to the disclaimer. He could have obtained, had he so chosen, an independent check on the acreage. Indeed, he appears to have accepted in evidence that, even within the tight timetable which he was following, he did have the opportunity had he wished to avail himself of it.'

Case Example: *EA Grimstead & Son Ltd v McGarrigan (Unreported, QBENF 97/1641/C)*.

An agreement for the purchase of shares contained clauses by which the purchaser confirmed that he had not relied on any warranty or representation not expressly contained in the agreement.

The evidence showed that the draft accounts had been available and the purchaser had had the chance to make a full investigation of the books and records. When the agreement was made, both sides had the benefit of advice from solicitors and accountants. It was also the case that the party making the allegedly false statements was only prepared to enter the contract on the basis that the purchasers relied on his own investigations and judgement. The court said that:

'In such a case, it seems . . . wholly fair and reasonable that the purchaser should seek his remedies . . . within the four corners of the agreement and should not be permitted to rely on pre-contractual representations which are, deliberately, not reflected in contractual warranties.'

Unfair terms   A2.63

In the context of a consumer contract, a term excluding or restricting liability for misrepresentation would be subject to the fairness test laid down in the *Unfair Terms in Consumer Contracts Regulations 1999 (SI 1999/2083)*.

Frustration   A2.64

A contract is frustrated when 'a contractual obligation has become incapable of being performed because the circumstances in which performance is called for would render a thing radically different from that which was undertaken by the contract' (*Davis Contractors Ltd v Fareham Urban District Council [1956] AC 696 729*). The effect of frustration is to discharge the parties from any further obligation under the contract. The application of the doctrine of frustration depends on the actual terms of the contract:

- to define the nature and basis of the performance, so that it can be determined whether the circumstances that have occurred have made performance radically different; and

- secondly, to determine whether the parties provided in the contract for the very event which occurred.

Other limits are that impossibility of contemplated performance must not have been foreseen by the parties, and must not be brought about by the fault or the choice of either party.

Frustration under the Sale of Goods Act 1979   A2.65

Section 7 of the *Sale of Goods Act 1979* provides that where there is an agreement to sell specific goods, and the goods perish before risk has passed, the agreement is at an end.

Meaning of 'perish'

Case Example: *Horn v Minister of Food [1948] 2 All ER 1036.*

The contract was for the sale of potatoes, which rotted and became useless. The court held that they could still be described as potatoes, for all that they had rotted, so *SGA 1979* did not apply.

When a contract is rendered void by the above provisions, the buyer can recover the price if already paid. There can be no adjustment for benefits conferred or expenses incurred before the time when the goods perished.

Case Example: *Turnbull v Rendell (1908) 27 NZLR 1067.*

The contract was for the sale of 'table potatoes' from a specific crop. At the time of the contract, some of the potatoes were so badly affected with secondary growth that they could no longer be described as 'table potatoes'. It was held that the potatoes had perished.

It would appear that goods can be said to have perished if they have been stolen (*Barrow, Lane & Ballard Ltd v Phillip Phillips & Co Ltd [1929] 1 KB 574*; or destroyed by fire (*Oldfield Asphalts v Grovedale Coolstores (1994) Ltd [1998] 3 NZLR 479*).

Contracting out of Section 7   A2.66

Unlike many other provisions of the *SGA 1979*, such as those relating to property and risk, the Act says nothing about the parties making their own provision as to the effect of perishing. Even so, it is arguably within the spirit of the Act to allow parties to allocate risk as they wish, so the following clause could be considered by a supplier:

> 'In those cases where the goods have perished before delivery to the buyer, the contract will be at an end, but the buyer will be liable for any costs and expenses incurred by the supplier in preparing for performance of the contract, and the buyer will be further liable to pay a reasonable sum for any benefits received. In no circumstances, however, will the buyer be liable for more than the contract price'.

Cases for Further Information

Duthie v Hilton (1868) LR 4 CP 138; *Asfar v Blundell [1895] 1 QB 126.*

Frustration outside the Sale of Goods Act 1979   A2.67

Where *SGA 1979, s 7* does not apply, a contract can be frustrated by any reason which makes performance radically different from that which was undertaken in the contract.

Instances of frustrating events

Case Examples:

- Illegality due to the outbreak of war (*Re Badische Co Ltd [1921] 2 Ch 331*).

- Requisitioning of goods (*Shipton Anderson & Co v Harrison Brothers & Co [1915] 3 KB 676*).

- Government restrictions on the purchase of contractual goods (*Societe Co-operative Suisse des Cereales et Matieres Fourrageres v La Plata Cereal Company SA (1947) 80 LlLR 530*).

- Inability to obtain export licences (*AV Pound & Co Ltd v MW Hardy & Co Inc [1956] AC 588*).

- Where goods were to be loaded on a particular vessel which was so damaged that it could not be loaded within the contractual period (*Nickoll & Knight v Ashton, Eldridge & Co [1901] 2 KB 126*).

Contracting out of the rules on frustration   A2.68

It will be difficult to draft a clause which excludes the possibility of frustration altogether. This is because it will be for the court to decide if it covers the events which have happened and even the widest of clauses might still not cover a very unusual or catastrophic event.

Case Example: *Metropolitan Water Board v Dick Kerr & Co [1918] AC 119.*

A contract for the construction of a reservoir provided for an extension of time in the event of delay 'whatsoever and howsoever occasioned'. This was held not to cover cessation of work due to government order, since the delay was such that it 'vitally and fundamentally changes the condition of the contract, and could not possibly have been in the contemplation of the parties when it was made'.

Consequences of frustration outside the Sale of Goods Act 1979   A2.69

The position in such cases is regulated by the *Law Reform (Frustrated Contracts) Act 1943 (LR(FC)A 1943)*. Any sums paid or payable can be recovered or will cease to be payable. The other side can, however, retain or recover payment to cover their costs. This would mean that, in a contract for the sale of goods where *SGA 1979, s 7* did not apply, any expenses involved in manufacturing the goods, or in customising manufacturing equipment, or in packing or transporting the goods is potentially recoverable.

LR(FC)A 1943 also provides that if before the frustrating event one party has conferred a valuable benefit on the other, the court may order the payment to the first party of such sum as it considers just, taking into account the valuable benefit.

LR(FC)A 1943 specifically allows the parties to make their own provisions in the contract for the effect of frustration, and thus to avoid the foregoing provisions.

Third party rights   A2.70

Privity of contract   A2.71

Under the 'privity of contract' doctrine, parties who are not actually parties to the contract cannot enforce it, even if the contract was specifically entered into for their benefit.

Case Example: *Tweddle v Atkinson (1861) 1 B & S 393.*

In consideration of an intended marriage between the claimant and the daughter of G, an agreement was made by the claimant's father whereby each promised to pay the claimant a sum of money. G did not do so and an action was brought by the claimant. The court ruled that the action must fail since 'no stranger to the consideration can take advantage of a contract, although made for his benefit'.

Case Example: *Beswick v Beswick [1968] Ac 58.*

A widow was refused enforcement in her own right of a contract made between her late husband and her nephew which required the latter to pay her £5 a week in return for the transfer to him of her husband's business.

Cases for Further Information

Gandy v Gandy (1885) 30 Ch D 57; The Pioneer Container [1994] 2 AC 324; Darlington BC v Wiltshier Northern Ltd [1995] 1 WLR 68; White v Jones [1995] 2 AC 207.

Contracts (Rights of Third Parties) Act 1999   A2.72

The position stated above remains the basic position, but significant inroads have been made into it by the *Contracts (Rights of Third Parties) Act 1999 (C(RTP)A 1999)*. *Section 1* of the Act provides that a person who is not actually a party to a contract may still enforce a term of the contract, if:

- the contract expressly provides that he may; or

- the term purports to confer a benefit on that party.

This, however, will not apply if, on a proper construction of the contract, it appears that the actual parties to the contract did not intend the term to be enforceable by the non–party.

C(RTP)A 1999 also requires that the non–party must be expressly identified in the contract by name, as a member of a class, or as answering a particular description, but need not be in existence when the contract is made. This would allow references in the contract to companies which have yet to be formed.

Sample Clause:

Draftsmen of commercial contracts would be well advised to consider, as a standard part of the drafting process, whether each provision which benefits a third party, who is also expressly designated in the contract, is capable of being directly enforced by that third party. If so, the draftsman will avoid all uncertainty if a right of enforceability is expressly conferred on the third party. If not, a provision should be included expressly excluding the third party rights of enforcement. For example, the draftsman might wish to provide that:

> 'except as otherwise expressly provided by this agreement, none of the terms and conditions of this agreement shall be enforceable by any person who is not a party to it',

so as to avoid any accidental conferring of enforceable rights on a third party.

Exclusion clauses and third parties   A2.73

C(RTP)A 1999 states that, where the exclusion clause is one seeking to exclude or restrict liability for negligence (other than relating to death or personal injury), the controls on such clauses imposed by the *Unfair Contract Terms Act 1977* shall not apply where the breach was in relation to the third party. In such cases, common law rules as to interpretation will apply. The absence of any reference to other provisions of the *UCTA*

1977, or to the *Unfair Terms in Consumer Contracts Regulations 1999 (SI 1999/2083),* will mean that they will apply in relation to third party actions on the contract.

Arbitration clauses   A2.74

C(RTP)A 1999 states that where a third party right of enforcement is given subject to a term of the contract which requires the submission of disputes to arbitration, the third party should be required to submit to arbitration to enforce his rights, and should be treated as a party to the arbitration agreement for that purpose.

Intellectual property rights   A2.75

There will be many contracts, such as licensing or technology agreements, or when the supplier of goods first develops and manufactures them with guidance from the buyer, where it will be necessary for intellectual property rights to be settled in the contract itself.

Sample Clauses:

The contract term should first define just what is meant by 'intellectual property rights'. Thus:

> '**"Intellectual Property"** means all rights in patents, registered and unregistered designs, copyright, trade marks, know-how and all other forms of intellectual property wherever in the world enforceable'.

It then becomes necessary to establish where ownership of such intellectual property is to lie, as follows.

> 'All intellectual property rights sued in or produced from or arising as a result of the performance of this contract shall, so far as not already so vested, become the absolute property of ourselves, and you will do all that is reasonably necessary to ensure that such rights vest in us (as, without prejudice to the generality of the foregoing) by the execution of appropriate instruments, or the making of agreements with third parties).'

If it is considered appropriate, the clause could go on to grant the other side a licence to use the intellectual property, as follows.

> 'At our discretion, we shall grant you a licence to use such intellectual property on such terms as to time, extent and royalty, and other appropriate matters, as we think appropriate.'

Confidentiality and non-disclosure A2.76

As with intellectual property, it is first necessary to define what is meant by 'confidential information'.

Sample Clauses:

The definition can be dealt with using the following clause.

> '"**Confidential information**" shall mean all information disclosed by us to you in any form or manner, provided that each such item of information would appear to a reasonable person to be confidential or is specifically stated by us to be confidential.'

This would then be followed by the following further clause.

> 'You will take all proper steps to keep confidential all confidential information disclosed to, or obtained by, you under or as a result of this agreement, and will not divulge such information to any third party. Without prejudice to the foregoing, such information may be divulged where this is necessary for the proper performance of this agreement and providing you ensure that the recipient of such information is under a like obligation to that spelled out in this clause. In addition, no liability will attach in relation to confidential information which, through no fault on your part, enters the public domain. It is further agreed that, on termination of this agreement, for whatever reason, you will return to us all equipment, articles, items, products and data, in whatever form recorded, and without retaining any copies, provided for the purposes of this agreement. Notwithstanding the termination of this contract, for whatever reason, the obligations and restrictions imposed by this clause shall be valid for a period of [x] years from the date of such termination.'

Service of notices A2.77

Proper provision for the service of notices is a necessary part of most agreements. Any such clause has to provide for the place or places at which notice is to be served, the method of service, and when any such notice will be deemed to have been delivered. Although oral notice is possible and permissible, the need for evidence of delivery effectively precludes such form of notice.

Sample Clause:

'All notices and communications given under this agreement shall be in writing or other durable form and shall be deemed to have been given:

- when delivered, if delivered personally or by messenger during normal business hours (or on the commencement of the first working day thereafter);

- when sent, if transmitted by telex, facsimile or electronic mail during normal business hours or on the commencement of the first working day thereafter); or

- on the second business day following mailing by certified or registered mail.

In all the above cases, the communication will be deemed to have been sent or delivered to the correct address or number if sent to the last address or number of which we have been advised by you.'

Signature   A2.78

A signature is only required in those cases where a contract must be in writing, such as contracts relating to real property, insurance and certain agreements relating to consumer credit. If, of course, a document is signed, that makes it that much easier to show that the contents were acknowledged and that a binding contract has resulted.

Binding nature of signature

Case Example: *L'Estrange v Graucob [1934] 2 KB 394.*

The buyer of a cigarette vending machine was bound by a clause which appeared in 'regrettably small print' in the seller's order form, and which the buyer signed.

Although probably not a major issue in commercial dealings, it should be noted that a person will only be allowed to deny the validity of his signature if he can show that the document signed was of an altogether different nature from what he thought he was signing (*Foster v McKinnon (1869) LR 4 CP 704; Saunders v Anglia Building Society [1971] AC 1004*). Under the provisions of the *Electronic Communications Act 2000*, provision is made for the use of electronic signatures, but no relevant Orders have yet been made under the Act.

Either party can stipulate that a contract will take effect only when signed by or on behalf of both parties.

Proper law clauses   A2.79

If goods are supplied to a party outside the jurisdiction, it is always advisable to include what is called a 'proper law' clause specifying whose law is to apply.

Sample Clause:

A typical clause would run: 'This agreement shall be governed by and construed in accordance with English law'. This is often bracketed with further wording giving English courts the exclusive right to determine any issues which may arise: 'Each party also agrees to submit to the exclusive jurisdiction of the English courts'.

Avoiding restrictions on exclusion clauses   A2.80

Although the parties have considerable flexibility in choosing the proper law, there are some restraints. Under the *Unfair Contract Terms Act 1977*, the Act will still apply if the parties choose a proper law outside the United Kingdom, if this was done to evade the operation of the Act; or if one of the parties was a consumer who was habitually resident in the United Kingdom, and the 'essential steps necessary' for making the contract were taken in the United Kingdom. Conversely, the Act also provides that where United Kingdom law applies only by virtue of a proper law clause, the provisions of the Act will not apply.

Competition issues   A2.81

Article 81 of the *Treaty of Rome* (also known as the *EC Treaty*) prohibits all agreements between undertakings, decisions by associations of undertakings and concerted practices which may affect trade between European Union Member States and which have as their object or effect the prevention, restriction or distortion of competition within the common market. The Treaty prohibits restrictions which:

- directly or indirectly fix purchase or selling prices or any other trading conditions;

- limit or control production, markets, technical development or investment;

- limit share markets or sources of supply;

- apply dissimilar conditions to equivalent transactions with other trading parties, thereby placing them at a competitive disadvantage; and

- make the conclusion of contracts subject to acceptance by the other parties of supplementary obligations which, by their nature or according to commercial usage, have no connection with the subject of such contracts. Such restrictions should therefore be left out when a contract is being drafted.

There are, however, a number of exemptions from these provisions, as follows.

- *Technology Transfer Agreements Regulation (96/240/EC)*
- *Motor Vehicle Distribution and Servicing Regulation (95/1475/EC)*
- *Specialisation Agreement Regulation (85/417/EEC)*
- *Research and Development Agreement Regulation (85/418/EEC)*
- *Vertical Agreements Regulation (99/2790/EC)*

Under the *Treaty of Rome*, an agreement which is anti-competitive can also be beneficial, and, if this is felt to be the case, an application can be made to the European Commission for an individual exemption.

Equivalent domestic provisions   A2.82

The Treaty broadly applies to agreements affecting trade within the European Union. Much the same provisions are, however, applied to transactions having only a domestic effect by the *Competition Act 1998 (CA 1998)*. The so-called *Chapter I* prohibition applies to agreements, decisions and concerted practices between undertakings or associations of undertakings which are implemented in the United Kingdom, and the purpose or effect of which is the prevention, restriction or distortion of competition in the UK. Exemptions can be granted by the Director General of Fair Trading. The Secretary of State may issue block exemptions. The Director General may impose fines of up to 10% of turnover.

Case Example:

Penalties were imposed on two bus companies, Arriva and FirstGroup. Staff from the companies had met and agreed that Arriva would withdraw from two routes, leaving FirstGroup with no competition on these routes. In turn, FirstGroup would withdraw from routes which Arriva would take on. Arriva was fined £318,175 and FirstGroup £529,852. These penalties were then reduced under the OFT's leniency programme under which businesses that inform the OFT about cartel activity and co-operate fully can be granted leniency.

FirstGroup asked for leniency at an early stage and was granted 100% leniency, thus eliminating the fine. Arriva asked for leniency second and co-operated, and its fine was reduced to £203,632.

Abuse of dominant position   **A2.83**

Article 82 of the Treaty, in provisions which are also matched in the *CA 1998*, prohibits the abuse of a dominant position.

Equivalent domestic provisions

The so-called *Chapter II* prohibition contained in the *CA 1998* is in comparable terms to that of the Treaty of Rome. Any conduct by an undertaking which amounts to an abuse of a dominant position will offend the prohibition. The Director General of Fair Trading may impose fines of up to 10% of turnover.

Case Example:

NAPP Pharmaceutical was fined £2.2m for supplying drugs used by cancer patients at excessively high prices to patients in the community while supplying hospitals at discount levels which blocked competition. Community prices were typically more than ten times Napp's hospital prices and up to six times higher than export prices. At least one competitor withdrew from the market.

Checklist   **A2.84**

- Have the goods to be supplied been clearly and closely defined?

- Are you, as a supplier, fully aware of your duties as to the supply of goods which are reasonably fit for their purpose and are of satisfactory quality?

- Have you, as a buyer, made known to the supplier just why you want the goods and what intentions, such as resale, you have in relation to the goods?

- Have you, as a supplier, made best use of the ways to avoid liability for the quality of the product?

- Do you think that any exclusion or limitation clauses you have drafted could be unreasonable or unfair?

- Are you sure that no exclusion or limitation clause you have used is going to give rise to a criminal offence?

- What provisions have been made as to the passing of property and the passing of risk?

- If the contract was meant to be by reference to a sample, has this been made clear?

- Do you understand the implications of the fact that duties can be imposed not just in relation to the actual contract goods, but also to all goods supplied under the contract?

- What measures have you, as supplier, taken to ensure that you have a proper retention of title clause in your contract. Have you considered the possibility that your goods might be used in the manufacture or construction of others?

- If you have drafted such a clause, have you considered that it might need registering to ensure that it is valid?

- What measures have you taken to exclude or limit your possible liability? Have you taken fully on board that there are statutory controls over the use of such clauses?

- When drafting such clauses, have you considered the possibility of making the clause a two stage one, so that there will be a limitation of liability as an alternative to a total exclusion of liability?

- If the contract you have made is with a consumer, have you ensured that the terms are drafted in plain and intelligible language?

- Have you considered making special provision in the contract for frustration, or for the impact on the contract of some supervening event?

- Have you considered if a non-party is to acquire benefits under your contract, and have you taken the appropriate steps to ensure that such person can enforce those rights?

- Have you ensured that you have secured all your intellectual property rights and also made provision for the non-disclosure of confidential information?

- What provision has been made to ensure that notices are served on the right people at the right address?

- Have you ensured that all necessary signatures have been provided?

- If the contract is made with a party outside the jurisdiction, have you checked the contract to make sure that express provision is made for the governing law?

- Are you certain that nothing in the agreement, or in your conduct, infringes competition law?

Chapter A3
Export Contracts – Special Issues

At a glance

- There are many statutory provisions controlling export sales.
- Proper export documentation must be obtained.
- There are various categories of invoice to be supplied.
- Sale of goods rules will apply when the export contract is subject to English law.
- There are a number of well established categories of contract used in export sales, of which FOB and CIF contracts are the best known.
- The seller under a CIF contract takes on more obligations than under an FOB contract.
- A model set of terms and conditions has been prepared by the International Chamber of Commerce. This is called 'Incoterms'.
- Incoterms are, however, generally restricted to matters relating to delivery.
- There are rules operating among EEA countries for determining which country's law shall apply. Special provision is made as to the applicability of UK law on exclusion clauses and unfair terms.
- A person dealing as consumer is given special protection as to which country's law will apply.
- There are also provisions determining the separate issue of which country's courts within the EEA have jurisdiction. A distinction is drawn between consumer and business contracts.
- There are restrictions on opting out of the rules on jurisdiction.
- Whether Internet advertising is directed at a particular country will depend on the circumstances of the case.
- Provision is made for the mutual recognition and enforcement of judgments within the EEA.
- Provision is also made for bringing actions against parties outside the EEA.

Legislative framework   A3.2

Military goods are covered under the *Export of Goods (Control) Order 1994 (SI 1994/1191)*, while industrial or so-called dual-use goods are covered under the *Dual-Use and Related Goods (Export Control) Regulations 1996 (SI 1996/2721)*.

The *Dual Use Regulation (94/3381/EC)* was implemented in July 1995, which is directly applicable to all EU Member States and establishes a basis for harmonised export control procedures in all EU countries.

There are a number of particular compliance issues which the EU regulation imposes on exporters of controlled goods, including registering with the Department of Trade and Industry Compliance Unit (see http://www.dti.gov.uk/export.control/).

The key requirements imposed on industry under the EC *Dual Use Regulation* are as follows.

- Classification of goods under the *Annex 1* control list (see A3.3 below).

- Checking whether goods are on *Annex 4* (see A3.3 below).

- Register with the DTI if shipping *Annex 1* controlled goods.

- Seek licences for *Annex 1* controlled goods for extra EU exports.

- Seek licences for all *Annex 4* controlled shipments, even intra-EU.

- Include destination control statements on invoices and shipping documents.

- Keep records of all shipments.

- Implement a procedure for compliance with the *Article 4* catch-all control.

The UK was one of the first countries to introduce an end use or 'catch-all control' in 1990. *Articles 4.1* and *4.2* of the EC *Dual Use Goods Regulation* and *Regulation 4.2(b)* of the *EC Dual Use Goods Regulation* together represent the control, sometimes called the catch-all, which applied to all goods and technology not otherwise controlled. Any attempt to export goods without an export licence is an offence.

The control list   A3.3

The EC *Dual Use Regulation* has lists of controlled goods comprised as follows:

- *Annex 1*, which is the agreed list of dual use goods (including atomic and nuclear goods) that are subject to control.

- *Annex 4*, which is the agreed list of goods which require a licence even for export to other EU Member States.

- *Schedule 2* is a list of dual use goods additional to *Annex 1*, the export of which the UK also controls.

- *Schedule 3* contains a few goods in *Annex 1* which do not appear in *Annex 4* but for which the UK requires individual licences even when being shipped to other EU Member States.

The main types of goods which require licence under the *Dual Use Regulation* are as follows.

(1) Goods capable of but not specially designed for military use, e.g. computers, electronic and instrumentation equipment, or machine tools.

(2) Nuclear-related goods including nuclear materials, nuclear reactors and nuclear processing plants.

(3) Chemical weapons precursors and related equipment and technology.

(4) Certain micro-organisms, biological equipment and technology.

(5) Goods used in weapons of mass destruction programmes.

Components, spare parts and technology for controlled goods may also require an export license.

List of goods in EC Regulation Annex I

The list of goods in *Annex I* to the *Dual Use Regulation* is arranged in the following way.

- Nuclear materials, facilities and equipment, including:
  - equipment, assemblies and components;
  - test, inspection and production equipment;
  - materials;
  - software; and
  - technology.

- Materials, chemicals, micro-organisms and toxins, including:
  - equipment, assemblies and components;
  - test, inspection and production equipment;
  - materials;
  - software; and
  - technology.

- Materials processing:
  - ○ equipment, assemblies and components;
  - ○ test, inspection and production equipment;
  - ○ materials;
  - ○ software;
  - ○ technology;
  - ○ electronics:
    - □ equipment, assemblies and components;
    - □ test, inspection and production equipment;
    - □ Materials;
    - □ software; and
    - □ technology.
- Computer:
  - ○ equipment, assemblies and components;
  - ○ test, inspection and production equipment;
  - ○ materials;
  - ○ software; and
  - ○ technology.
- Telecommunications and information security, including:
  - ○ telecommunications:
    - □ equipment, assemblies and components;
    - □ test, inspection and production equipment;
    - □ materials;
    - □ software; and
    - □ technology; or
  - ○ information security:
    - □ equipment, assemblies and components;
    - □ test, inspection and production equipment;
    - □ materials;
    - □ software; and
    - □ technology.
- Sensors and lasers, including:
  - ○ equipment, assemblies and components;
  - ○ test, inspection and production equipment;

- ○ materials;
- ○ software; and
- ○ technology.
- Navigation and avionics, including:
  - ○ equipment, assemblies and components;
  - ○ test, inspection and production equipment;
  - ○ materials;
  - ○ software; and
  - ○ technology.
- Marine:
  - ○ equipment, assemblies and components;
  - ○ test, inspection and production equipment;
  - ○ materials;
  - ○ software; and
  - ○ technology.
- Propulsion systems, space vehicles and related equipment, including:
  - ○ equipment, assemblies and components;
  - ○ inspection and production equipment;
  - ○ materials;
  - ○ software; and
  - ○ technology.

Non-technology goods   A3.4

In order to export live animals, cattle, goats, sheep and swine from Great Britain to all destinations licences are required from the appropriate agricultural department (Department for Environment, Food and Rural Affairs (www.defra.gov.uk), Department of Agriculture & Rural Development Northern Ireland (www.dardni.gov.uk), Scottish Executive Rural Affairs Department (www.scotland.gov.uk/who/dept_rural.asp) or the National Assembly for Wales (www.wales.gov.uk/subiagriculture/index.htm)).

Goods more than 50 years old   A3.5

The export without a licence of any goods manufactured or produced more than 50 years before the date of exportation is prohibited with the exceptions of:

- postage stamps and other articles of a philatelic nature;

- birth, marriage or death certificates, or other documents relating to the personal affairs of the exporter or the spouse of the exporter;

- letters or other writings written by or to the exporter or the spouse of the exporter; and

- other goods exported by and being the personal property of the manufacturer or producer thereof, or the spouse, widow or widower of that person.

Antiques   **A3.6**

An Open General Export Licence (The OGEL (Antiques)) permits the export to most destinations of certain classes of antiques providing the value is less than the figure specified in the OGEL for the relevant class. The Department for Culture, Media and Sport (www.culture.gov.uk) imposes controls on exports from the UK and the Isle of Man on works of art, antiques and collectors' items.

The Department of Trade and Industry (www.dti.gov.uk) remains responsible for granting licences for certain antiques produced between 50 and 100 years before the date of exportation and goods manufactured or produced more than 50 years before the date of exportation relating to industrial equipment capable of being used for chemical, biological or nuclear weapon purposes.

Types of licences   **A3.7**

There are three types of export licences issued by the DTI, which are the:

- Open General Export Licence (OGEL);

- Open Individual Export Licence (OIEL); and

- Individual Export Licence (IEL).

The OGEL does not have to be applied for but it may be used by any exporter provided the terms and conditions are met.

The OIEL has to be applied for and allows an individual exporter to ship a range of goods to a range of destinations.

The IEL is granted to an individual exporter and covers export of a specific quantity of named goods to a named customer.

The vast majority of export trade is legally made, without any requirement to use an OGEL or to apply for an individual licence.

The vast majority of goods appearing on the control list set out in the *Dual Use Regulation* may be traded freely within the EU without an export licence (see A3.8 below).

Provided the goods are not subject to export licence the exporter may export them without any reference to export licensing on the shipping documents or customs entry. If, however, United Nations or EC/EU full trade sanctions are imposed on a particular destination, then no exports may be made.

Intra-EU trade   A3.8

The vast majority of dual use goods may be shipped free of any export licence control throughout the EU. Only a minimal percentage of intra-EU trade is now subject to export licence. Goods which would require a licence if exported outside the EU are required to comply with a number of conditions.

Trade in military, military related or defence goods which remain subject to UK export control still require export licences to all destinations.

Exports to non-EU countries   A3.9

If goods are covered under either the *Export of Goods (Control) Order 1994 (SI 1994/1191) (EG(C)O 1994)* or the *Dual Use Regulation*, an export licence is required for shipments to all destinations outside the EU.

The export licence could be an IEL, an OIEL or an OGEL. All three types of licence are possible regardless of whether the goods are military items controlled by *EG(C)O 1994* or the EC *Dual Use Regulation*'s control dual use items.

The catch-all control must be considered when making shipments to any destination outside the European Union.

Export licensing – a summary

The following considerations should be made when reviewing an export contract.

- Whether the product is of a military nature and subject to the *Export of Goods (Control) Order 1994 (SI 1994/1191)*.

- Whether the product is subject to the *Dual Use and Related Goods (Export Control) Regulations 1996 (SI 1996/2721)*.

- Whether the product requires an export licence under either of these sets of Regulations.

- Whether the product could be utilised in the manufacture of weaponry.

- Is an OGEL, OIEL or IEL licence required? Is the product approved for export under licence conditions?

- Is the destination country sanctioned, embargoed, sensitive or somehow restricted? Does the selected licence apply for the country?

- Does the destination country have a history of weapons proliferation? Has compliance been assured with the licence conditions?

- Whether end use of product is defined as dual use for military purposes.

- What is the extent of knowledge of the customer's business? Is this an existing customer or a new user? Are there any suspicious aspects to the transaction? What is the potential for division or re-export of the goods?

- Is all necessary documentation, including licence, export control statement on shipping paperwork, shipping/transport instructions in order? Have copies been retained of all relevant documentation as required? For further information on documentation see A3.10 below

Export documentation   A3.10

There are a number of documents which have to be prepared by exporters, which must be completed carefully and checked before they are despatched.

Many of the forms are completed by freight forwarders, hauliers, airlines and shipping lines, as well as banks and other financial intermediaries.

Invoice   A3.11

An invoice must be raised for every shipment even if the goods are being supplied free of charge. The invoice is the basic document used in export and every other document draws upon the information that appears on it.

There are several different types of invoice.

Commercial invoice

The main features of an invoice are:

- name and address of consignor and consignee;
- description of the goods;
- value and terms of delivery (Incoterms, see A3.36 below);
- an outline summary of the packing and total weights;
- statement of the origin of the goods;
- signature of exporter;
- the tariff (HF) number; and
- the terms of payment.

Proforma invoice

Proforma invoices are generally used for quotations, to draw up a letter of credit or to apply for the foreign exchange to pay for the goods. The invoice is generally sent in advance of the goods, but does not differ from a standard commercial invoice.

Commercial invoice with declaration

Some countries require a specific declaration to be included on the invoice. This declaration can enable the buyer to take advantage of a lower rate of duty, as in the case of 'EUR forms', or to take account of import regulations in the country of destination.

Certified invoice

Certified invoices are generally certified by a Chamber of Commerce before goods are despatched. The exporter lodges authorised signatures with local chambers who verify the signature before stamping the documents.

Legalised invoice

Legalised invoices may be required by some Middle Eastern countries which require invoices to be presented to their embassy who then attach their stamp to the document. This is usually arranged through the Arab–British Chamber of Commerce (www.abcc.org.uk).

Consular invoice

Consular invoices are particularly common in South America where the details of the invoice are transferred on to a standard form, prepared in Spanish. A consular invoice is usually needed in addition to a normal commercial invoice.

Invoice with Combined Certificate of Value and Origin (CCVO)

CCVOs are still required by some, predominately African, countries. The invoice section of the document is enhanced by a certificate confirming the value and origin of the goods described therein. These documents often have to be signed and witnessed. The relevant forms are available from commercial stationers dealing in export documents and from some chambers of commerce.

Originally signed invoice

The customs authorities of some countries require originally signed invoices, as such an original signature should be added to each photo-copied, or computer generated, copy. Unless specifically required by the country of importation, or by a letter of credit, there is no legal obligation for export invoices to be signed.

Export contracts   A3.12

Assuming that a particular contract is subject to English law, the provisions of the *Sale of Goods Act 1979* will apply. In addition, the contract will generally be what is called CIF (cost, insurance, freight, see A3.28 below) or FOB (free on board, see A3.13 below) the terms of which have been developed by common law. Many export contracts are, however, made subject to Incoterms (see A3.36 below), and where the parties have adopted these, the duties of the parties are clearly spelled out. Where the parties have not made use of Incoterms, the rules of the common law set out below will apply. The parties are also free to incorporate terms and conditions developed by trade associations such as the Federation of Oils, Seeds and Fats Associations, and the Grain and Feed Trade Association.

FOB contracts   A3.13

The duties of a seller under an FOB, or 'free on board' contract, ultimately depend on the terms of the contract. While it is always open to the seller to assume additional duties, the seller's general duty is to place the goods free on board a ship to be named by the buyer during the contractual shipment period. The seller's obligations extend to all charges incurred before shipment, including loading charges, but not freight or insurance. It is the duty of the buyer to select both the port and date of shipment, as well as to make arrangements for shipment. Adequate notice must be given to the seller of the ship nominated. Compliance with the obligation to ship at the nominated port is a condition of the contract, meaning that breach entitles the buyer to claim damages and rescind the contract (*Petrograde Inc v Stinnes Handel GmbH (The Times, 27 July 1994)*).

Failure of carrier to load   A3.14

A seller who fails to deliver the goods on board the vessel or fails to load the goods is not necessarily in breach of contract. It will usually be the buyer who is in breach for failure to nominate an effective ship or provide effective shipping instructions.

Seller only obliged to deliver on board   A3.15

While the seller is bound to put the goods on board the vessel in accordance with the terms of the contract, he is not generally obliged to deliver the goods in any other way (*Maine Spinning Co v Sutcliffe & Co (1917) LJKB 288*).

Delivery at port of shipment   A3.16

The terms of the contract should indicate the port of shipment, though this can be left to the option of either party. Where there is an option as to the port of shipment, the choice will be that of the buyer unless the circumstances show that the choice was to be that of the seller.

Cases for Further Information

David T Boyd & Co Ltd v Louis Louca [1973] 1 Lloyd's Rep 209; Gill & Duffus v Soc pour L'Exportation des Sucres [1985] 1 Lloyd's Rep 621.

Stipulations as to time   A3.17

Not least because of the costs involved in shipping, time is an important factor in the performance of FOB contracts. The contract will generally create a timetable for performance and it is essential for the timetable to be met in order to keep costs down. *Section 10* of the *Sale of Goods Act 1979* says that whether a stipulation as to time is of the essence is a question of the circumstances of the case. In FOB contracts, it is normally the case that time is of the essence.

Case Example: *Bunge Corporation New York v Tradax Export SA Panama [1981] 1 WLR 711.*

The contract provided that the 'buyers shall give at least 15 consecutive days' notice of probable readiness of vessel(s)'. The last day of the delivery period for the June shipment was 30 June, so the last day for notice was 12 June, though notice was not given until 17 June.

The House of Lords ruled that this was a major term, and hence condition, of the contract. It rejected the argument that a condition must be such that breach must deprive the victim of the substantial benefit of the contract. It was also the case that the law had generally treated stipulations as to time in commercial contracts as of the essence. Certainty was important in commercial contracts and that favoured classification of the term as a condition.

Account also had to be taken of the buyer's duty to notify the seller, and of the latter's duty to nominate the port of shipment. The court further stressed that the experience of businessmen was thought to support the conclusion that time stipulations were conditions. It was also the case that damages for breach of the term would be difficult to assess, and this pointed to the clause being a condition, breach of which allowed termination.

Completion of loading   A3.18

The seller must ship the goods at the latest by the end of the shipment period specified in the contract. The obligation so to do is a condition of the contract, so that any failure gives the buyer the right to terminate the contract (*Yelo v SM Machado & Co Ltd [1952] 1 Lloyd's Rep 183*).

Arrival at destination   A3.19

In an FOB contract, the seller is not generally under any obligation in relation to the arrival of the goods. The seller's obligation is to place the goods on board the vessel. It is, therefore, the time of shipment which matters, not the time at which the buyer takes delivery.

Case Example: *Frebold and Sturznicke (Trading as Panda OHG) v Circle Products Ltd [1970] 1 Lloyd's Rep 499.*

It was a term of the contract for the sale of toys that 'delivery of the consignment would be effected in good time for [the defendants] to catch the Christmas trade'. The goods were put on board on 2 November and reached their destination on 13 November. The buyers were not notified of the arrival and, on 27 December, cancelled the order. The seller's claim for damages succeeded. The vital factor was that the contract between the parties was FOB so that delivery was complete when the goods were put on board on 2 November. This being the case, the sellers were not responsible for what happened subsequently.

Cost of putting goods on board   **A3.20**

While the seller in an FOB contract is to bear the cost of putting the goods on board, he is not required to bear any subsequent carriage costs unless the terms of the contract so require. The parties can always agree that the seller will bear the cost of stowing the goods on board the vessel and other incidental costs incurred after the goods have been placed on board, hence the use of the terms 'FOB stowed' and 'FOB stored and trimmed'.

Seller's duty as to contract of carriage   **A3.21**

In what is sometimes called the 'classic' FOB contract, the contract for the carriage of the goods is between the seller and the shipowner. This means that the seller must, unless the contract is to the contrary, comply with *s 32(2)* of the *SGA 1979* and 'make such contract with the carrier on behalf of the buyer as may be reasonable having regard to the nature of the goods and the other circumstances of the case and if the seller omits to do so, and the goods are lost or damaged in the course of transit, the buyer may decline to treat the delivery to the carrier as delivery to himself, or may hold the seller responsible in damages'.

Case Example: *Thomas Young & Sons Ltd v Hobson & Partners (1949) 65 TLR 365.*

Goods were damaged in transit because they were insecurely fixed. Had the sellers made a reasonable contract with the carriers (that is, had they sent the goods at the company's risk as per the usual practice for goods of that kind instead of at owner's risk) the loss would not have occurred. The Court of Appeal held the buyers were entitled to reject the goods.

Insurance   **A3.22**

While the terms of the contract may require the seller to insure the goods while they are in transit, the general rule is that an FOB seller is not responsible for insuring the goods while they are in transit (*Wimble Sons & Co v Rosenberg [1913] 3 KB 743*).

Incoterms guidelines

Incoterms 2000 A3 expressly state that the seller is under no obligation in relation to the contract of insurance. The FOB seller is, however, required by *s 32(3)* of the *Sale of Goods Act 1979* to give notice to the buyer to enable him to insure the goods during sea transit. Incoterms 2000 A10 states that:

> 'The seller must provide the buyer, upon request, with the necessary information for procuring insurance'.

Accordingly, Incoterms place the onus on the buyer to request such information.

Passing of risk and property   **A3.23**

The almost universal rule is that risk passes as soon as the goods are over the ship's rail. This is because the duty of the seller is to deliver the goods free on board. Once they are on board, the seller has delivered them to the buyer, thus making it natural that they should thereafter be at the seller's risk (see *Frebold and Sturznicke (Trading as Panda OHG) v Circle Products Ltd [1970] 1 Lloyd's Rep 499* at A3.19 above).

The loading of the goods is probably an unconditional appropriation of the goods, which passes the property in the goods to the buyer under *s 18, Rule 5* of the *SGA 1979*. In modern times, any general presumption that property passes with risk on shipment in an FOB contract has probably largely disappeared. Although this may sometimes be the case if the contract contains no contrary provision, the practice of treating the shipping documents as security for payment is now so well-established in international sales that contractual terms requiring payment in exchange for the shipping documents is the norm in FOB contracts. Where payment is to be made only against the documents, the seller will normally have himself named as the consignee in the bill of lading (that is the goods will be deliverable to or to the order of the seller), so the provisions of *s 19* of the *Sale of Goods Act 1979* become relevant. A bill of lading is a document acknowledging the shipment of a consignor's goods for carriage by sea, often used when the ship is carrying goods belonging to a number of consignores.

Section 19(1) provides that a seller may reserve the right of disposal of the goods until certain conditions are fulfilled, with the result that, notwithstanding delivery of the goods to the buyer, carrier or other bailee for transmission to the buyer, property does not pass until the particular conditions are fulfilled. *Section 19(2)* provides that, where goods are shipped, and the bill of lading states that the goods are deliverable to the order of the seller, the seller is *prima facie* to be taken as having reserved the right of disposal. The result is that shipment is treated as amounting only to a conditional appropriation, the condition being that the seller must be paid before property passes.

Obtaining a licence A3.24

For the various licences which are required in export contracts, see A3.7 above.

The obligation of the seller is simply to pay the cost of putting the goods on board the vessel at the port of shipment unless he assumed some further obligation under the terms of the contract. It follows that he is, therefore, not responsible for the cost of obtaining the licence which might be required for export.

Incoterms guidelines

Incoterms 2000 draw a clear line between import and export licences. The obligation of a seller is to 'obtain at his own risk and expense any import licence or other official authorisation and carry out, where applicable, all customs formalities necessary for the export of the goods' (A2). The buyer is stated to be obliged to 'obtain at his own risk and expense any import licence or other official authorisation and carry out, where applicable, all customs formalities for the import of the goods and, where necessary, for their transit through any country' (B2).

In the absence of any express term in the contract governing the matter, there will be occasions where there will be an implied duty on the buyer to obtain the export licence.

Case Example: *HO Brandt & Co v HN Morris & Co Ltd [1917] 2 KB 784.*

The parties entered into a contract for the sale of aniline oil FOB Manchester. The contract was for monthly deliveries over a period of five months but, after the contract was made, the export of this product was banned by government order and the prohibition ran for the greater part of the five months, although licences were granted in certain cases. The buyers sued for non–delivery. It was held that it was the duty of the buyers to obtain the necessary export licences, therefore they could not maintain an action for damages when the failure of the seller to deliver was due to their own failure to obtain the requisite licences. The Court of Appeal indicated that it was generally the duty of the buyer under an FOB contract to obtain the necessary export licences.

> **Case Example**: *A V Pound & Co Ltd v MW Hardy & Co Inc [1956] AC 588.*
>
> This ruling somewhat limited the scope of the above case. The House of Lords said that the earlier case was authority 'only for the proposition that where a British buyer has bought goods for export from Britain, and a British prohibition on export except with a licence supervenes, then there is a duty on such buyer to apply for a licence, because not only is he entitled to apply to the relevant British authority but he alone knows the full facts regarding the destination of the goods'.
>
> In the *Pound* case itself, a US company agreed to buy from an English company Portuguese gum spirits of turpentine FAS (free alongside ship). The sellers knew at the time when they made the contract that the goods were for East Germany. Under Portuguese law, the goods could not be exported without a licence and that licence could be obtained only by the seller's suppliers, the name of whom had not been disclosed to the buyers. The sellers then bought the goods from their Portuguese suppliers on terms expressly subject to the grant of a licence. A licence was refused. The buyers' vessel arrived in Lisbon and was ready to load the goods on board, but loading did not take place because the buyers declined to provide another destination for the goods and a licence for export to East Germany had been refused. The sellers failed in their action against the buyers because it was their duty to obtain a licence. The factors which persuaded the House of Lords to decide that it was the sellers' duty to obtain the licence were that the sellers knew that the buyers wished to export the goods to East Germany and that only their suppliers, whose identity had been deliberately withheld, could apply for the necessary licence.

It would seem to follow from this ruling that, where the parties are in different countries, the duty to obtain the export licence will be that of the seller, since he is in the better position to do so.

Whoever bears the duty of obtaining a licence, the further question remains whether that duty is absolute, or whether the relevant party is required only to use his best endeavours. If this is not covered by the contract itself, the *prima facie* approach of the courts is to require only that the relevant party uses his best endeavours or reasonable diligence (*Re Anglo-Russian Merchant Traders and John Batt & Co (London) Ltd [1917] 2KB 679*).

Documentary obligations   **A3.25**

It is essentially a question of the terms to determine if the seller has any documentary obligations. The terms of any letter of credit may be particularly relevant in this context. The terms of the contract may impose other documentary obligations on the seller, such as a duty to supply a certificate of quality in relation to the goods.

Force majeure or prohibition of export clauses   **A3.26**

The implication referred to in A3.24 above that the duty to obtain a licence is a duty to use best endeavours is not inevitable, since the courts on occasions have found that a more onerous obligation has been assumed. An important factor in determining this issue can be the presence in the contract of a *force majeure* or prohibition of export clause. *Force majeure* is the term generally used to indicate some supervening event, outside the control of the parties, which makes performance of the contract impossible or impractical.

> **Case Example**: *C Czarnikow Ltd v Centrala Handlu Zagranicznego 'Rolimpex' [1979] AC 351.*
>
> Where there is such a clause, and the clause states that the failure to obtain a licence is not a *force majeure* event, the court may be prepared to accept that the parties intended that the obligation to obtain a licence was stricter than an obligation merely to use best endeavours.
>
> **Case Example**: *Colonie Import-Export v Loumidis Sons [1978] 2 Lloyd's Rep 560.*
>
> Conversely, where the *force majeure* clause makes no reference to the failure of one party to obtain a licence, the court may be more willing to infer that the duty is only to use best endeavours.

Other obligations   **A3.27**

The terms of the contract may impose other obligations on the seller than those set out above.

> **Incoterms guidelines**
>
> Incoterms 2000 A10 states that:
>
> > 'The seller must render the buyer at the latter's request, risk and expense, every assistance in obtaining any documents or equivalent electronic messages (other than those mentioned in A8) issued or transmitted in the country of shipment and/or of origin which the buyer may require for the import of the goods and, where necessary, for their transit through any country'.

Other duties which may be imposed on the seller by the terms of the contract include the obligation to give a performance guarantee.

Sample Clause:

> 'We undertake to furnish you with a 10% guarantee that we will deliver the goods to your forwarding agents in Antwerp as soon as we receive confirmation from your bankers that the necessary letter of credit, valid not less than six weeks, will be established in our favour in free transferable US dollars'

(Heisler v Anglo-Dal Ltd [1954] 1 WLR 1273.)

CIF Contracts   A3.28

A seller under a CIF contract (cost, insurance, freight) assumes more obligations than the seller under an FOB contract. The seller under a CIF contract agrees to sell the goods at an inclusive price which covers the cost of the goods, and also their insurance and freight.

Shipment   A3.29

Unless the terms of the contract stipulate to the contrary, the CIF seller is not obliged physically to load the goods on board a particular vessel. Instead, he can purchase goods already on board and allocate them to the particular contract. The terms of the contract will dictate the obligations of the seller in this regard.

The terms of the contract dealing with time and place of shipment are generally regarded as conditions, breach of which entitles the buyer to rescind the contract and to claim damages.

Case Example: *Bowes v Shand (1877) 2 App Cas 455.*

Shipment was to be 'during the months of March and/or April 1874'. In fact, the vast majority of the goods were shipped in February and, of four bills of lading, three were issued in late February. It was held that shipment could be rejected.

Time of notification of appropriation   A3.30

When the seller is required by the contract to give the buyer notice of appropriation, the time limits specified for giving notice must be complied with, so that a failure to comply will generally entitle the buyer to reject the documents and the goods: (*Societe Italo-Belge pour le Commerce et l'Industries SA v Palm and Vegetable Oils (Malaysian) Sdn Bhd (The Post Chaser) [1982] 1 All ER 19*).

The terms of the contract may specify in some detail the form and content of the notice, and the seller must comply with those requirements; a failure to do so will allow the buyer to rescind the contract and claim damages.

The entitlement of the seller to withdraw a notice once given may be regulated by the terms of the contract. It is not uncommon for a contract to contain a provision to the effect that 'a valid notice of appropriation when once given shall not be withdrawn' (*Ross T Smyth & Co Ltd v TD Bailey, Son & Co [1940] 3 All ER 60*).

Such a clause applies only to attempts by the seller to withdraw a notice, not to correct or amend it. The right of a seller to amend or correct a notice may be limited by the terms of the contract. In particular, where the contract contains a term which entitles the seller to amend or correct a notice of appropriation within certain narrow limits, this contractual entitlement to correct or amend may be held to be the sum total of the seller's right to do so, with the result that a seller who fails to comply with the term of the contract entitling him to correct will have no further power to do so.

Sample Clause:

An instance of a term entitling the seller to amend or correct a notice of appropriation is:

> 'Every such notice of appropriation shall be open to correction of any errors occurring in transmission, provided that the sender is not responsible for such errors, and for any previous error in transmission which has been repeated in good faith'

(*Kleinjan and Holst NV Rotterdam v Bremer Handelgesselschaft mbH Hamburg [1972] 2 Lloyd's Rep 11.*)

Route of shipment – deviation provisions **A3.31**

The contract of sale may provide for a particular route of shipment. Where this is the case, the seller must tender a bill of lading for shipment via the route specified in the contract. So-called deviation clauses are now a common feature of bills of lading, however, and it may be that such a clause may no longer entitle the buyer to reject such a bill. A buyer who wishes to ensure that the goods are carried straight to the agreed destination should ensure that the contract contains a clause which states that the ship shall sail direct from the port of loading to the destination for unloading of cargo.

Insurance **A3.32**

The seller must tender to the buyer insurance documentation which covers the goods for the duration of their sea transit. The documents must relate to an enforceable contract. The main cause of uncertainty in this area is not the existence of the seller's obligation to tender insurance documents, but the nature of the documentary obligation which has been assumed by the seller or, possibly, imposed on him. The question which arises is whether the seller is to tender the insurance policy itself, or whether it is enough for the seller to tender a certificate of insurance entitling the buyer to call for the policy itself.

Incoterms guidelines

There is no clear authority on this point at the moment, so this is a matter which must be covered in the contract. As a result, Incoterms 2000 A3 state that:

> 'The seller must obtain at his own expense cargo insurance as agreed in the contract, such that the buyer, or any other person having an insurable interest in the goods, shall be entitled to claim directly from the insurer and provide the buyer with the insurance policy or other evidence of insurance cover.
>
> The insurance shall be contracted with underwriters or an insurance company of good repute and, failing express agreement to the contrary, be in accordance with minimum cover of the Institute Cargo Clauses (Institute of London Underwriters) or any similar set of clauses. The duration of insurance cover shall be in accordance with B5 and B4.
>
> When required by the buyer, the seller shall provide at the buyer's expense war, strikes, riots and civil commotion risk insurance if procurable. The minimum insurance shall cover the price provided in the contract plus ten per cent (i.e. 110%) and shall be provided in the currency of the contract'.

Clause B5 states that:

> 'The buyer must bear all risks of loss of or damage to the goods from the time they have passed the ship's rail at the

---

> port of shipment. The buyer must, should he fail to give notice in accordance with B7, bear all risks of loss or damage to the goods from the agreed date or the expiry date of the period fixed for shipment provided, however, that the goods have been duly appropriated to the contract, that is to say, clearly set aside or otherwise identified as the contract goods'.
>
> B4 states that the 'buyer must accept delivery of the goods when they have been delivered in accordance with A4 and receive them from the carrier at the named port of destination'.

In the absence of such a provision as Incoterms A3, it would be necessary to look at the common law, although the relevant cases are somewhat old and do not reflect modern commercial practice.

Invoice   **A3.33**

The seller must tender to the buyer an invoice for the goods. The form and content of the invoice may be regulated by the terms of the contract itself. Buyers who wish to obtain an invoice in a particular form, or with a particular content, should stipulate for this in the contract of sale.

Other documents   **A3.34**

The seller may be required by the terms of the contract to tender other documents to the buyer. For instance, the seller may be required to tender a certificate of origin, quality or inspection.

Incoterms guidelines

It will generally be the responsibility of the seller to obtain an export licence for the goods (Incoterms 2000 A2 and *Congimex Compahania Geral SARL v Tradax Export SA [1983] 1 Lloyd's Rep 250*). Import licences are more likely to be a matter for the buyer (Incoterms 2000 B 2 and *Mitchell Cotts & Co v Hairco Ltd [1943] 2 All ER 552*).

Tender of shipping documents   **A3.35**

The contract will generally make provision for the time at which the documents are to be tendered to the buyer. Where the contract requires the buyer to pay against the documents, a provision which fixes the date on which the buyer is to make payment may also fix the date on which the seller must tender the documents (*Alfred C Toepfer v Lenersan-Poortman NV [1980] 1 Lloyd's Rep 143*).

As for the place of tender, there is no clear authority. In practice, therefore, this is an issue usually dealt with in the terms and conditions. For example, if the contract provides for payment to be made by letter of credit, the place of tender is likely to be the offices of the collecting bank.

The time at which the goods arrive at the port of destination is normally of no concern to the seller. That said, it may be particularly important for the buyer to know when that delivery will take place. In such a case, the buyer must insert into the contract an express term imposing on the seller an obligation to ensure that delivery takes place within a particular period of time, or an obligation to give the buyer appropriate notice of the arrival of the vessel. The clause should be drafted in such a way as to impose on the seller an obligation to ensure that the goods actually arrive at the port of destination within the stipulated period of time and not in such a way as to impose nothing more than an obligation to load the goods at such a time as will enable the ship to arrive at the port at the relevant time.

Incoterms   A3.36

When quoting and pricing for export it must be quite clear to buyer and seller which party is responsible for the various costs, tasks and responsibilities in the export supply chain. To facilitate this, the International Chamber of Commerce publishes a set of terms which, when used to qualify a price, establishes:

- which costs are included in the price, for example:
  - documentation;
  - export packing;
  - inland freight;
  - terminal charges at port/airport of export;
  - overseas freight;
  - cargo insurance;
  - terminal charges at port/airport of arrival;
  - import customs clearance;
  - payment of import duties and taxes; and
  - inland freight to buyer's premises;
- the point at which risk passes from seller to buyer;
- the delivery and transport responsibilities of the parties;

- the division of functions between seller and buyer; and
- the overall division of responsibilities.

Incorporating Incoterms

Incoterms 2000 should be included in all international trade contracts and, additionally, all export invoices should include the clause 'Subject to Incoterms 2000 (or such later version if Incoterms has been replaced or amended)'.

Incoterms designation – the codes   **A3.37**

Each Incoterm is designated by a three letter code. The code must precede a named place, for example: 'EXW Liverpool'.

The individual codes and their meanings are set out below.

EXW	ex works
FCA	free carrier
FAS	free alongside ship
FOB	free on board
CFR	cost and freight
CIF	cost, insurance, and freight
CPT	carriage paid to
CIP	carriage and insurance paid to
DAF	delivered at frontier
DES	delivered ex ship
DEQ	delivered ex quay
DDU	delivered duty unpaid
DDP	delivered duty paid

Matters not covered by Incoterms

Incoterms do not deal with:

- the transfer of property rights in goods;

- relief from obligations and exemptions from liability in the case of unexpected or unforeseeable events; or

- the consequences of various breaches of contract except those relating to the passing of risk, and costs when the buyer is in breach of his obligations to accept the goods or to nominate the carrier under an F-term (this is a reference to the FCS, FAS and FOB terms referred to above).

Incoterms are only rules for the interpretation of terms of delivery and not other terms relating to a contract of sale. They deal only with obligations in connection with terms as to delivery, such as the obligations to give notice, provide documents, procure insurance, pack the goods properly and clear them for export and import. In areas outside the scope of Incoterms, the contracting parties should be careful to set out the relevant contract terms as to sale and purchase.

Jurisdiction and choice of law   A3.38

The presence in any contract of what might be called a 'foreign element' necessitates a discussion of issues as to which country's law will apply; and which country has jurisdiction to hear disputes arising under the contract.

Applicable law   A3.39

The Rome Convention applies to litigation within the EEA between sellers and buyers wherever situated. The EEA consists of the 15 EU countries, Norway, Iceland and Liechtenstein. It is given effect in the United Kingdom by the *Contracts (Applicable Law) Act 1990*.

The choice of the parties

The general rule is that a contract is in the first place to be governed by the law chosen by the parties.

In the absence of such a choice, the contract will be governed by the law of the country with which it is most closely connected. It is presumed that the contract is most closely connected with the country where the party who is to effect the performance which characterises the contract has – at the time of the contract – his habitual residence (or, in the case of a body corporate or unincorporate, its central administration).

The parties are at any time entitled to agree to subject the contract to a law other than that which previously governed the contract.

Unfair terms

In certain circumstances, a party may wish to rely on the *Unfair Contract Terms Act 1977 (UCTA 1977)*, even though the contract is not to be governed by English law. The position is that, under *s 27(2)* of *UCTA 1977*, the provisions of the Act will apply regardless of any contract term which seeks to apply the law of a country outside the United Kingdom where that term was imposed wholly or mainly to enable the relevant party to evade the Act, or if the other party was a consumer habitually resident in the United Kingdom and the essential steps necessary for making the contract were taken in the United Kingdom.

Similarly, *Reg 9* of the *Unfair Terms in Consumer Contracts Regulations 1999* (*SI 1999/2083*) has a mandatory effect, in that the Regulations will apply notwithstanding any term seeking to apply the law of a country outside the EEA if the contract has a close connection with the territory of a Member State.

Consumer contracts

The Convention contains special rules for determining the law applicable to certain consumer contracts, the aim of which is to provide a degree of protection to the party perceived to be in the weaker bargaining position which, in the case of a contract for the sale of goods, is the buyer.

The choice of the parties

In summary, the parties are free to choose the applicable law, but any such choice shall be ineffective to deprive the consumer of the protection afforded him by the mandatory rules of law of the country in which he has his habitual residence. In the absence of choice, the consumer will be governed by the law of the country of his habitual residence. *UCTA 1977* and the 1999 Regulations are examples of mandatory provisions, and it may be that other measures of consumer protection, such as the *Consumer Credit Act 1974* may be so treated by the courts.

Uniform law on international sales   A3.40

The Uniform Law on the International Sale of Goods 1964 was implemented in the United Kingdom by the *Uniform Laws on International Sales Act 1967*. Under the Act, the Convention applies only if chosen by the parties. The Convention deals with the obligations of the parties, the availability of remedies and the passing of risk, but not the passing of property. The Convention is very rarely used.

Jurisdiction   A3.41

Separate from the question of whose law is to apply is the further question of which courts have the jurisdiction to apply the relevant law. Between the Member States of the EEA, this is now governed by Council Regulation (EC) No 44/2001 of 22 December 2000 on jurisdiction and the recognition and enforcement of judgments in civil and commercial matters. This Regulation is now in force.

Business contracts – the rules

- In the case of persons (which will include both natural and legal persons) domiciled in a Member State, whatever their nationality, they are to be sued in the courts of that Member State.

- Persons who are not nationals of the Member State in which they are domiciled shall be governed by the rules of jurisdiction applicable to nationals of that State.

- Persons domiciled in a Member State may be sued in the courts of another Member State only by virtue of the rules set out in the Regulation.

- If the defendant is not domiciled in a Member State, the jurisdiction of the courts of each Member State shall be determined by the law of that Member State.

- As against such a defendant, any person domiciled in a Member State may, whatever his nationality, avail himself in that State of the rules of jurisdiction there in force.

- A person domiciled in a Member State may, in another Member State, be sued in matters relating to a contract, in the courts for the place of performance of the obligation in question. For the purpose of this provision and unless otherwise agreed, the place of performance of the obligation in question shall be:

  ○ in the case of the sale of goods, the place in a Member State where, under the contract, the goods were delivered or should have been delivered;

  ○ in the case of the provision of services, the place in a Member State where, under the contract, the services were provided or should have been provided; or

  ○ as regards a dispute arising out of the operations of a branch, agency or other establishment, in the courts for the place in which the branch, agency or other establishment is situated.

- A person domiciled in a Member State may also be sued:

  ○ where he is one of a number of defendants, in the courts for the place where any one of them is domiciled, provided the claims are so closely connected that it is expedient to hear and determine them together to avoid the risk of irreconcilable judgments resulting from separate proceedings;

  ○ as a third party in an action on a warranty or guarantee or in any other third party proceedings, in the court seised of the original proceedings, unless these were instituted solely with the object of removing him from the jurisdiction of the court which would be competent in his case; or

> ○ on a counter-claim arising from the same contract or facts on which the original claim was based, in the court in which the original claim is pending.

Place of domicile A3.42

A company or other legal person or association of natural or legal persons is domiciled at the place where it has its:

- registered office or, where there is no such office anywhere, the place of incorporation or, where there is no such place anywhere, the place under the law of which the formation took place;

- central administration, or

- principal place of business.

Contracting out of the Regulation A3.43

If the parties, one or more of whom is domiciled in a Member State, have agreed that a court or the courts of a Member State are to have jurisdiction to settle any disputes which have arisen or which may arise in connection with a particular legal relationship, that court or those courts shall have jurisdiction. Such jurisdiction shall be exclusive unless the parties have agreed otherwise.

Agreements conferring jurisdiction – the rules

Such agreements must be:

- in writing or evidenced in writing;

- in a form which accords with practices which the parties have established between themselves; or

- in international trade or commerce, in a form which accords with a usage of which the parties are or ought to have been aware and which in such trade or commerce is widely known to, and regularly observed by, parties to contracts of the type involved in the particular trade or commerce concerned.

Any communication by electronic means which provides a durable record of the agreement shall be equivalent to 'writing'.

Where such an agreement is concluded by parties, none of whom is domiciled in a Member State, the courts of other Member States shall

111

have no jurisdiction over their disputes unless the court or courts chosen have declined jurisdiction

Consumer contracts – the rules   **A3.44**

The Regulation provides that the 'weaker party should be protected by rules on jurisdiction more favourable to his interests than the general rules provide for'. In accordance with this principle, the Regulation provides that jurisdiction is to be determined by the following rules, where the contract is:

- for the sale of goods on instalment credit terms;
- for a loan repayable by instalments;
- for any other form of credit, made to finance the sale of goods; or
- in all other cases, the contract has been concluded with a person who pursues commercial or professional activities in the Member State of the consumer's domicile, or, by any means, directs such activities to that Member State, or several Member States including that Member State, and the contract falls within the scope of such activities.

Where a consumer enters into a contract with a party not domiciled in the Member State, but has a branch, agency or other establishment in one of the Member States, that party shall, in disputes arising out of the operations of the branch, agency or establishment, be deemed to be domiciled in that State.

Proceedings may only be brought against consumers in the courts of the Member State where the consumer is domiciled.

Contracting-out   **A3.45**

Careful control is exercised over this in the context of consumer contracts.

> **Departing from the Regulation – the rules**
>
> The Regulations may be departed from only by an agreement:
>
> - which is entered into after the dispute has arisen;
> - which allows the consumer to bring proceedings in courts other than those indicated above; or
> - which is entered into by the consumer and the other party to the contract, both of whom are at the time of conclusion of the con-

> tract domiciled or habitually resident in the same Member State, and which confers jurisdiction on the courts of that Member State, provided that such an agreement is not contrary to the law of that Member State.

Internet advertising   **A3.46**

A key phrase above referred to business who 'direct' their activities to a particular Member State. It would be necessary to look at the nature of any given website to see if it was directed to consumers in a particular jurisdiction. If the website gave information in different Community languages and currencies, and offered to deliver to EU countries, then it would fairly clearly be directed at consumers in the EU. If, however, it was specifically stated that the offer applied only to a designated country, or countries, then it would be directed only to consumers in the designated territory.

Recognition and enforcement   **A3.47**

The Regulation provides that a judgment given in a Member State shall be recognised in the other Member States without any special procedure being required.

Non-recognition of a judgment – the rules

In certain circumstances a judgment will not be recognised where:

- such recognition is manifestly contrary to public policy in the Member State in which recognition is sought; or where it was given in default of appearance, if the defendant was not served with the document which instituted the proceedings or with an equivalent document in sufficient time and in such a way as to enable him to arrange for his defence, unless the defendant failed to commence proceedings to challenge the judgment when it was possible for him to do so;

- if it is irreconcilable with a judgment given in a dispute between the same parties in the Member State in which recognition is sought; or

- if it is irreconcilable with an earlier judgment given in another Member State or in a third State involving the same cause of action and between the same parties, provided that the earlier judgment fulfils the conditions necessary for its recognition in the Member State addressed.

A judgment given in a Member State and enforceable in that State shall be enforced in another Member State when, on the application of any interested party, it has been declared enforceable there.

In the United Kingdom, such a judgment shall be enforced in England and Wales, in Scotland, or in Northern Ireland when, on the application of any interested party, it has been registered for enforcement in that part of the United Kingdom. The application shall be submitted to the court or competent authority indicated in the Regulation (which, for England and Wales, is the High Court). The declaration of enforceability shall be served on the party against whom enforcement is sought, accompanied by the judgment, if not already served on that party.

Seller outside the EEA   A3.48

For an English buyer to sue a seller outside the EEA, leave to serve the claim outside the jurisdiction must be obtained under the Civil Procedure Rules.

Bringing claims outside the EEA – the rules

Broadly, claims in contract may be brought with leave of the court if the contract:

- was made within the jurisdiction;

- was made by or through an agent trading or residing within the jurisdiction on behalf of a principal trading or residing out of the jurisdiction;

- is by its terms, or implication, governed by English law; or

- contains a term to the effect that the High Court shall have jurisdiction to hear and determine any claim in respect of the contract.

Case Example: *Brinkibon v Stalig Stahl under Stahlwarenhandelgessellschaft MBH [1983] 2 AC 34.*

The issue was whether the contract had been made within the jurisdiction. An English company sought leave to appeal to serve an Austrian company for breach of contract (Austria not at that time being an EU member). The contract had been made by telex with the buyer in London accepting a counter-offer made by the seller situated in Vienna. It was held that the contract had been made in Vienna where the acceptance had been received.

Checklist   **A3.49**

- Have you made sure that all necessary export licences have been obtained?

- Are you sure that your documentation, particularly with regard to invoices, is in order?

- Have you decided on what kind of contract you are going to use: in particular, has consideration been given to whether the contract will be FOB or CIF?

- Has proper attention been given to the terms of the particular contract, not least with regard to such matters as delivery, loading and payment?

- Does the contract make special provision for the passing of property and risk and for obtaining necessary export licences?

- Has thought been given to using trade association terms or those drafted by the ICC?

- Has the contract made provision as to which country's law is to apply?

- If the contract is with a consumer, has note been taken of the restrictions imposed on determining the applicable law?

- Have you given thought to using the Uniform Law on International Sales?

- Are you fully aware of the provisions as to jurisdiction and enforcement?

- Have you determined the precise place of domicile of the other party?

- To what extent have you contracted out of the rules on jurisdiction and to what extent, when so doing, have you distinguished between business and consumer contracts?

- Are you aware of what must be done to sue a seller based outside the EEA?

Chapter A4
Software Contracts – Special Issues

At a glance   A4.1

- A software contract can involve both goods (the disk) and services (the actual software).

- Issues as to whether the contract is for goods and/or services can be settled by an appropriate contract term.

- There is automatic copyright protection in a computer program, but this can be reinforced by a specific contract term.

- Failure to provide clear instructions for use can produce a breach of contract.

- Licensees should take care to ensure that the functional specifications of the software are drafted to meet their special needs. These specifications should be accompanied by appropriate systems specifications.

- The licence should clearly indicate what rights there are as to user manuals.

- Warranties are often linked to exclusion or limitation clauses. The latter are subject to statutory control, and their use can give rise to a criminal offence.

- The buyer receives automatic statutory protection to the effect that his use of the software will not of itself violate the intellectual property rights of a third party. As above, these rights can be excluded or limited subject to strict statutory control.

- Software writing contracts can make provision for who will own copyright.

- The terms and conditions contained within a shrink-wrap purchase, insofar as they relate to the manufacturer and not the actual supplier, probably have no legal validity because of the absence of consideration.

- Customer registration cards often found in shrink-wrap purchases could, if returned to the manufacturer, provide consideration to make the terms and conditions binding.

- A licence clause will set out the rights of the purchaser in relation to his use of the software.

- The contract can provide for acceptance tests to be imposed as a pre-condition to the licensee accepting the software.

- The licence can set out specific restrictions on the use of the software.

- The contract should contain specific provisions as to confidentiality and disclosure, if only to affirm provisions implied by law.

- Provision can and should be made for the source code to be lodged with a third party.

- The contract should spell out details of any training provided in the use of the software.

- An indemnity can be offered against the use of the software by the licensee infringing the rights of a third party.

- There are a number of points which should be considered in the case of a contract for bespoke software.

Whether software is 'goods'   A4.2

It is clear from the observations in *St Albans City and District Council v International Computers Ltd [1996] 4 All ER 481*, that a computer disk falls within the definition of 'goods'. Accordingly, the terms implied by the *Sale of Goods Act 1979* as to description, quality and fitness for purpose will apply. Similarly, the sale of an entire computer system, including hardware and software, will be a sale of 'goods'.

This, however, is clear only in respect of the disk itself. What is less clear is the status of the software contained within the disk.

Case Example: *Advent Systems Ltd v Unisys Corporation 925F.2d 670 (1991).*

In this American case, it was indicated that software does 'constitute' goods for the purposes of sale of goods legislation.

Case Example: *St Albans City and District Council v International Computers Ltd [1996] 4 All ER 481.*

In this case, in contrast, it was stated that the computer program itself is not goods, but the sale of the disk 'onto which a program designed and intended to instruct or enable a computer to achieve particular functions has been encoded' can constitute a sale of goods.

Case Example: *Beta Computers (Europe) Ltd v Adobe Systems (Europe) Ltd 1996 SLT 604.*

A Scottish court said that an order for a standard package to upgrade an existing system was a discrete category of agreement which contained elements of a contract of sale and a contract of licence. It was said to be an essential feature of such a contract that the supplier undertook both to supply the medium on which the program was recorded, and the right to access and use the software.

Ultimately, the point may be more academic than practical. If the agreement is one for the supply of goods, then the implied terms referred to above will apply. If the contract falls within the remit of the *Supply of Goods and Services Act 1982*, then identical provisions apply. If, for whatever reason, no particular Act applies, then the common law will certainly apply much the same terms in any event.

Case Example: *Horace Holman Group Ltd v Sherwood International Group Ltd (Technology and Construction Court; 12 April 2000).*

The Court felt it 'probable' that a contract for the supply of software was not a contract for the supply of goods, in which case a term as to reasonable fitness (and one may assume merchantable quality) would be implied at common law.

The purchaser would be well advised to avoid any problems as to which Act applies by specifically incorporating into the contract appropriate terms.

Sample Clause:

'It is agreed that the subject matter of this contract, including both hardware and software, in whatever form, in all respects corresponds with any description made, and are, in all respects, of satisfactory quality and reasonably fit for the purpose for which they are supplied. These undertakings are in addition to, and not in derogation of, any other applicable provisions implied by law'.

Intellectual property   A4.3

A computer program is stated to be a literary work under the provisions of *s 3(1)* of the *Copyright, Designs and Patents Act 1988 (CDPA 1988)*. This applies if the program is 'written'. *Section 178* states that 'writing' includes (so the definition is illustrative rather than exhaustive) 'any form of notation or code, whether by hand or otherwise and regardless of the method by which, or medium in or on which, it is recorded'. It is difficult to envisage any form of software which would not be in writing.

Given that a computer program does have copyright protection, this means that it cannot be copied in whole or in substantial part without the consent of the copyright owner. The copyright in computer-generated works lasts for 50 years from the end of the year in which the work was made (*s 12(7), CDPA 1988*). Whether or not a software program is computer-generated will depend on an analysis of the facts leading to its creation. It is thought likely that the individual skill of the program-writer will mean that in many, perhaps most cases, the software will not be computer-generated. In such a case, copyright protection will last for 70 years from the end of the year in which the program-writer died; or 70 years from the year in which the program was first made available if the author is unknown (*s 12(1), CDPA 1988*. This particular period of protection will, however, not apply if the country of origin of the work is outside the European Economic Area and the author is not an EEA national, in which case the duration of copyright is that of the country of origin so long as that does not exceed the 70 year period (*s 12(6), CDPA 1988*). The EEA consists of the Member States of the European Union, Norway, Liechtenstein and Iceland.

Although it is strictly unnecessary for the supplier to spell out his copyright protection, it may be useful to do so, perhaps with a limited permission to make copies.

Sample Clause:

'No part of any software may be copied or stored in any medium without the supplier's prior written consent, except that no more than [X] copies may be made for backup or archive purposes'.

Instructions for use   A4.4

It is an unfortunate fact that many of the instructions accompanying computer material are sometimes misleading, and more often than not confusing, and thus making the subject matter of the contract difficult or even impossible to use.

Case Example: *Wormell v RHM Agriculture (East) Ltd [1987] 1 WLR 1091.*

It was accepted that misleading instructions would mean that the goods would not be reasonably fit for their purpose, and, one would imagine, not of satisfactory quality.

Where goods are ordered from a non-English speaking country by a party in the United Kingdom, the buyer presumably takes the risk that the instructions might not be in English.

Documentation   A4.5

The nature and quality of the documentation provided with the software will be of particular importance. The most important documentation will be as set out in A4.6 to A4.8 below.

Functional specification   A4.6

This will set out, in ordinary language, and some detail, the functions to be performed by the software. In the case of packaged software, this may be the supplier's document stating what the software does, rather than stating the customer's requirements. From the licensee's point of view, it is far better that the specifications should have been drawn up by the licensee, setting out his requirements for the software. In this case, the supplier will be concerned to ensure either that he can meet the specifications, or that he states the respects in which he will not.

System specification   A4.7

This will consist of the detailed, technical specification of the software, detailing how the functional requirements will be realised.

User manual   A4.8

This will describe how the software is to be used.

The right of the user to obtain copies of the above documents, the number to which he is entitled, when they are to be delivered, his right to copy, and the ownership in them, should all be clearly addressed in the licence.

Warranties and limitation of liability   A4.9

It is not uncommon to find in a contract a provision which both offers a limited warranty on the product, but which also takes away from the buyer such other rights as he might have at law.

Sample Clause:

> 'We make no warranties with respect to the items supplied under this contract other than to guarantee the original items against faulty materials or workmanship for 90 days from the date the items were supplied'.

This may then be followed by such a clause as:

> 'The foregoing warranty is in lieu of all other warranties, express or implied, including but not limited to the implied warranties as to description, quality and fitness for purpose. In no event will we be liable for consequential damages even if we have been advised in advance of the possibility of such damages'.

The 90 day warranty is lawful, but there may be a problem with the exclusion of liability if this occurs in a contract made between businesses. On the safe assumption that the clause is part of a contract on written standard terms, then, under the provisions of the *Unfair Contract Terms Act 1977 (UCTA 1977)*, it will be valid only if the party seeking to rely on it can show that it is reasonable.

If the purchaser of the system was a private consumer, then the position is more stringent. *UCTA 1977* provides that the exclusion clause is automatically void. Furthermore, under the provisions of the *Consumer Transactions (Restrictions on Statements) Order 1976 (SI 1976/1813)*, the use of the exclusion clause will constitute a criminal offence (this does not apply if the clause is used in a business-to-business contract).

UCTA 1977 makes the use of the exclusion clause automatically void in a contract with a consumer. It is likely, though not inevitable, that the same result would be reached by the *Unfair Terms in Consumer Contracts Regulations 1999 (SI 1999/2083)*. This renders void those terms which are unfair. There is nothing which automatically makes any term void in the way this is done under *UCTA 1977*.

Purchaser's safeguard against intellectual property infringements   A4.10

It will be implicit in any contract involving the supply of software that the buyer can lawfully use that software; that is to say, that his doing so will not infringe the intellectual property rights, such as copyright or patent rights, of a third party. Insofar as any such clause as above seeks by implication (or it might expressly spell it out) such a duty, then it will fall to be governed by *UCTA 1977* and the *Unfair Terms in Consumer Contract*

Regulations 1999 (SI 1999/2083), with the result differing, depending on whether the contract is between businesses or made with a consumer. *UCTA 1977* does not apply to contracts so far as the contract relates to the creation or transfer of any right or interest in intellectual property. A contract for the supply of items, even though they may be subject to copyrights or patents, is not such a contract. In any event, if the contract was with a consumer, the 1999 Regulations apply, and these contain no exclusion of terms relating to intellectual property rights.

The scope of the exclusion from *UCTA 1977* of terms relating to the creation of transfer of intellectual property rights has been subject to a restrictive interpretation.

Case Example: *The Salvage Association v CAP Financial Services Ltd [1995] FSR 654.*

The contract in dispute related to the installation of computer software. It was argued that, since all the issues in the case related to the creation or transfer of interests in intellectual property, then the matter fell within the exclusion. This argument was rejected. The court ruled that the exclusion applied only to those provisions of a contract actually dealing with the creation or transfer of a right or interest in the relevant intellectual property:

> 'It does not extend generally to all the terms of a contract simply because the contract is concerned overall with the provision of a service, performance of which will result in a product to which the law affords the protection of one or more of the specified intellectual property rights.'

The court agreed that the exclusion from *UCTA 1977* would apply to any term concerned with the creation or transfer of a right or interest in intellectual property; but if a term was one concerned with other aspects of the contract, then the exclusion would not apply. Where a term does fall within the exclusion from *UCTA 1977*, then it will be judged on common law principles, which effectively means that the court will construe it to determine its precise scope and applicability.

It should again be pointed out that the *Unfair Terms in Consumer Contract Regulations 1999 (SI 1999/2083)* apply as much to contract terms relating to intellectual property rights as to any other, and that a clause will be held void if the consumer can show it unfair.

Use and licence of software   A4.11

A contract for the supply of a specially written computer program can provide for the writer to retain copyright or for copyright to pass to the client, though the former is more usual.

Shrink-wrap licences   **A4.12**

Many software packages sold in shops are wrapped in cellophane, or some other wrapper, on which there appears a notice indicating that, by opening the package, the buyer agrees to be bound by various terms supplied alongside the notice or inside the package. Typically, the 'shrink-wrap' terms will include an undertaking by the purchaser not to claim against the manufacturer for consequential loss arising out of defective software, as well as restrictions on the use of the software itself. In return, the manufacturer might agree to replace defective disks.

It has yet to be decided in the courts if the purchaser is bound by the licence, but it is unlikely that he would be. His contract would only be with the supplier of the goods, and not with the manufacturer. Even if the purchaser expects to be aware that there will be terms and conditions contained in the package (perhaps from previous purchases), he has supplied no consideration to the manufacturer and hence still cannot be bound by them.

Customer registration   **A4.13**

It is frequently the case that a shrink-wrap licence will contain a term asking the purchaser to complete and return to the manufacturer a registration card. This could entitle him to updates and the use of a telephone helpline and other assistance. It is arguable that, by returning the card, the purchaser is accepting the terms and conditions contained in the licence, and providing the consideration to support a contract containing those terms, though this point still remains to be settled.

Licence clause   **A4.14**

The main purpose of a licence is to grant a permission to do something which the licensee would otherwise have no right to do. For instance, unless the licence expressly gives the right to make back-up or archive copies, there is no right to do so. The licence would also have to consider an 'internal purposes' clause. The reason for such wording would be to prevent the software being used for the provision of a bureau service to businesses or persons who would otherwise themselves have to obtain a licence from the supplier. It will also have the effect of restricting use to the purposes of the particular company which obtained the licence. Where the company is a member of a group, and it is envisaged that other members of the group may wish to use the software, the licence should specifically cover such use.

Acceptance tests   **A4.15**

The idea of acceptance tests is important in relation to software. The purpose of such tests is to determine whether the software performs required functions, so that the licensee can decide whether to accept the software and proceed with the contract, or terminate the contract, return the software and obtain a return of any money paid.

The nature of the acceptance tests can vary widely. At one extreme will be a detailed set of tests, comprehensively stated in a document negotiated as part of the contract. At the other extreme, acceptance may be a simple provision by which the licensee will be taken to have accepted the software if he uses it for a fixed period without rejection. The key to such provisions is that they should be clear and definitive; they should not involve an agreement to agree unless there is a procedure established for the determination of issues in the event of a disagreement.

Restrictions on use **A4.16**

The basic restrictions on the use of the software will be contained in the licence clause (see A4.14 above) since, by saying what can be done, this will preclude any other use. Software licences do, however, often lay down further restrictions, the most common of which are set out below.

No modifications

The licensee will, in practice, be unable to create any modifications without the software source code. Legally, however, in the absence of an express prohibition, there would seem to be no reason why he should not modify the software except to the extent that by doing so he does something impermissible such as infringe the copyright in the software.

Use with other hardware or software

The terms of the licence will often limit the hardware with which the software can be used. In addition, the licensee may be restricted from using the software with other software. For example, the licensee may decide to write some software of his own to perform additional functions, or alter the way in which the licensed software operates. A restriction as to the hardware to be used with the software will normally be reasonable provided that it permits use with replacement or standby hardware. The licensee should resist limits on the source of such hardware; the test should be compatibility with the software, not the source.

Use by skilled operator in accordance with manual

The supplier may impose some such restriction because of a concern for problems which may reflect unfairly on him. Such a restriction is, though, difficult to police.

Confidentiality   A4.17

Software is generally protected by the law of copyright and the law of confidence. The latter does not require the existence of any specific provision in the contract, but enforcement becomes more straightforward if the licensee explicitly agrees to maintain confidentiality. Accordingly, in most software licences, the supplier will impose an obligation on the licensee to keep the software and all associated documentation, confidential.

Such a clause is reasonable so long as the items to be protected are confined to those belonging to the licensor. If they are, for example, extended to include data or specifications belonging to the licensee, this will impinge on the latter's business. The licensee should also ensure that the clause permits him to disclose the software to his employees, or at least those who need to know, and others with a legitimate right to know (such as auditors, consultants, lawyers or other advisers), and that the obligation of confidence ceases when the information falls into the public domain. The clause should also not impinge on the scope of the licensee to use the software. If, for example, subsidiaries of the licensee are permitted to use the software, disclosure to them should be not be a breach of the undertaking as to confidentiality.

Source code escrow   A4.18

The default or disappearance of the licensor will almost certainly have serious consequences for the licensee. For example, the licensee may no longer be able to have errors corrected or modifications carried out. The licensee will generally have only the object code version of the software and, without the source code, will be unable to do any of these things for himself.

The solution to this is the 'source code escrow agreement'. A tripartite agreement is entered into between the licensor, the licensee and the escrow agent. The licensor agrees to deposit a copy of the software source code with the agent, and to update it as and when new releases of the software are supplied to the licensee. The licensor will agree with the licensee that, on the happening of a number of defined events (such as the insolvency of the licensor, or his failure to provide maintenance) the source code will be released to the licensee. The escrow agent agrees that he will release the source code when such events are notified to him.

Training   A4.19

Training may constitute an important part of the arrangements for both parties. Full details of any courses offered, their location, the payment of travel and accommodation expenses, the number of persons who can attend each course, and the like, should be included in the licence.

Patent/Copyright indemnity A4.20

Generally, licensors will be prepared to give a limited indemnity in relation to the infringement by the software of any intellectual property rights
owned by a third party. This would constitute a breach by the licensor of
the provisions of the *SGA 1979*, as to quiet possession and freedom from
encumbrances (*Niblett v Confectioners' Materials Co Ltd [1921] 3 KB 387*;
Microbeads AG v Vinhurst Road Markings Ltd [1975] 1 WLR 218).

Indemnities often contain a limitation to the effect that they will not
apply if the infringement arises from the combination of the licensor's
goods with those not so supplied. Patents can be granted for new combi-
nations of old inventions, and, as a result, infringements can occur when
two non-infringing items are combined.

Drafting tips:

Practical drafting points to bear in mind are that the person providing
the indemnity will:

- wish to have control, or the right to take control, of any action
  brought or negotiations for its settlement;

- require the other party to notify him immediately of any claim;
  and

- require him not to make any admission of liability.

Provision is often made to the effect that, in the event of a claim, the
indemnifying party may modify the equipment so that it ceases to
infringe, or obtain a licence from the third party who brought the
claim, or terminate the agreement.

Bespoke software A4.21

While a contract for the provision of bespoke software will have many
similarities to what might be called off-the-shelf software, there will be
differences arising from the fact that such software has been expressly
written for the purposes of the particular contract.

Functional specification A4.22

The question arises as to how to define the user's requirements. This
answer will lie in the functional (or requirements) specification which will
describe, in detail, the functions to be performed by the software. The
preparation of the functional specification should be undertaken with
great care, since it will become the benchmark for the project and will

determine whether or not the supplier fulfils or breaches its obligations, is entitled to be paid, and whether or not the software meets the user's requirements. The functional specification is best prepared by the user alone, possibly with the help of independent consultants, or by a combination of the user and the suppler, with the user maintaining the ultimate control over content. It should not be prepared by the supplier alone since the essence of the specification is that it sets out what the user wants, not what the supplier is willing or able to supply.

It is important that the copyright and other rights in the specification should vest in the user. If the intention is that the rights to the software itself should vest in the user, then any different agreement as to the specification could lead to legal difficulties. Furthermore, the user should be able to take the functional specification to any software supplier and have the software written by them; if the rights in the functional specification are vested in a third party, such as the software house concerned in the preparation, this would be prevented.

A system specification and user manual should also be produced as part of the contract (see A4.5 above).

Defining responsibilities   **A4.23**

The primary obligation will be on the supplier to write and deliver software complying with the user's requirements. At the same time, the supplier will be dependent on the user providing him with information about the latter's business, accepting the functional specification as complete, supplying trial data, providing employees of the required standard for training and so forth. The contract should spell these matters out, so that the division of responsibilities is clear. This should be done in the implementation plan, a document which sets out the detailed timing of the project. It will set dates for the exchange of information, the production of specifications, the availability of the site, the achievement of various planned stages, acceptance testing and the delivery of documentation.

Dealing with changes   **A4.24**

The contract should specify a procedure for specifying and agreeing on changes to the contract work. The procedure should allow the user to specify a change, with a period allowing the supplier to respond with a statement as to cost of implementing the change, the consequences for delivery and other dates, and any other consequences. It should be made clear who is to pay for the cost of such response.

It would also be sensible for the contract to provide for any changes which might be suggested by the supplier.

Price and payment **A4.25**

The price for bespoke software can either be a fixed price agreed in advance, or on a time and materials basis. The former suits the user, the latter, the supplier. Just which payment method is adopted will depend on the negotiations between the parties, and, in particular, their relative bargaining strengths. As a general rule, it would be unusual for bespoke software to be written entirely on a time and materials basis.

Performance stages **A4.26**

The contract should specify details as to the:

- delivery of functional specifications;
- delivery of system specifications; and
- acceptance of software.

Many other stages may be identified as suitable for consideration in the contract. Where the software consists of a number of discrete modules, the stages might be linked to the achievement of particular stages in relation to each module, with overall system acceptance being the final stage.

Acceptance testing **A4.27**

Acceptance testing will generally test each separate phase of the development as it is completed, and then the total installation. The acceptance tests should be specified in a contractual document and agreed at the outset. If the tests cannot be agreed on at the outset, a procedure should be laid down for determining the tests in the event of a failure to agree, such as determination by an independent third party.

Intellectual property **A4.28**

A major area of possible dispute concerns the ownership of the intellectual property in bespoke software, not least because there is no general presumption in English law that the person who commissions, and pays for, a piece of work owns the copyright in it. If the parties expressly agree on the matter, that will resolve any disputes. If not, the courts will have to decide what has been implied as to ownership. To do this, it will look at all the circumstances of the case, such as the amount paid, the extent to which the software was specifically written for the user, the extent to which it embodied the supplier's standard software, and whether it was intended to confer a commercial advantage on the user.

An indication in the agreement that will be of major significance will be a licensing clause. If the user is licensed to use the software, this will be almost conclusive evidence that the intellectual property belongs to the supplier. The absence of a licence may indicate that intellectual property vests in the user.

> **Case Example**: *Saphena Computing Ltd v Allied Collection Agencies Ltd (22 July 1986).*
>
> The Recorder rejected a customer's submission that the commissioning of a computer program of itself vested the copyright in that program in the customer. He also declined to find any basis on which to imply a term that the beneficial interest should pass to the customer.

The matter should normally be explicitly addressed in a bespoke contract, and will often constitute a major area of negotiation.

> **Matters to consider**:
>
> Ownership may be clearly allocated to one side or the other, but a range of intermediate solutions is possible taking account of such matters as the distinction between trade secrets and general skill and experience.
>
> The supplier can legitimately be expected not to claim ownership of anything which is a trade secret of the user, but could expect to make use of the general knowledge and experience acquired while performing the contract.

Distinction between specially written and standard codes   A4.29

The bespoke software may be written entirely for the user, or may consist of modifications to a standard package. It may be agreed that the whole of such specially written software should belong to the user. Even within the specially written software, however, there might be segments of code which are standard and owned by the supplier. It might, therefore, be agreed that the supplier should retain ownership of the standard code, so that only the copyright in the codes written specifically for the user should belong to him.

Joint ownership   A4.30

This is something which can arise in two ways. Firstly, the software may be created by programmers employed by both parties. In the absence of any specific agreement, such software will belong jointly to both parties.

Secondly, the parties may themselves agree on joint ownership. The respective rights of joint owners of copyright at law are unclear, but it would seem that each party would have the right to use the software and reproduce it for his own use, but could not sub-licence its use without the consent of the other.

Marketing rights   A4.31

Rather than ownership of the rights, the user's main concern may be to prevent the competition from obtaining the advantage of similar software too quickly or too early. The supplier, in contrast, will be concerned that if it relinquishes ownership of the software, it will be hampered in future work by concern that it is infringing the rights of the user. The solution could lie in an agreement as to the marketing of the software similar to that written for the first user. For example, the rights might vest in the supplier, but it might be prevented from marketing any similar systems for a defined period, or to defined types of customer. It may also agree on the payment of a royalty on sales to other customers as a *quid pro quo* for its ownership of the rights. The arrangement need not necessarily involve the supplier owning the rights; they could vest in the user, with an exclusive licence being granted to the supplier allowing it to market the software.

Sub-contractors   A4.32

It may well be that the supplier needs the assistance of third parties to fulfil the contract with the user. If there is nothing personal about the reason the user contracted with the particular supplier, the latter will be able to sub-contract all or part of the task. If, therefore, the user is particularly concerned that only employees of the supplier should work on the contract, this should be spelled out in the contract.

Matters to Consider:

- prohibitions on disclosure of information should cover sub-contractors;

- the sub-contractor should agree that, as between himself and the supplier, the copyright and other rights in the software will vest in the supplier. If the user is actually to own these rights, this will happen automatically under the main contract.

- the user should consider taking direct undertakings from the sub-contractor as to such matters as quality, performance, non-disclosure. Since there is no direct contract with the sub-contractor, these undertakings should be made under seal, or supported by a nominal consideration.

Non-competition clauses A4.33

The user may require the supplier to enter into an agreement not to market similar software to any competitor within a defined period. Any such clause, however, is subject to both the *Treaty of Rome* and the *Competition Act 1998*, to the effect that an agreement is void if it has the object or effect of preventing, restricting or distorting trade.

Solicitation of employees A4.34

Since there may well be close co-operation between one party and the employees of the other, even to the extent of employees working on the other's premises, it can be worthwhile stating in the agreement that neither party can entice or even employ another's employee for a period of, say, twelve months from the termination of the contract. Any such clause would have to be reasonable to avoid being an unfair restraint on trade, and possibly also anti-competitive as referred to immediately above.

Other terms A4.35

Reference should be made to the terms considered above in relation to software contracts generally.

Checklist A4.36

- Has the issue of whether software can cover the supply of goods and also the supply of services been properly addressed in the contract?

- Has thought been given to the protection of your intellectual property rights?

- Has care been taken to ensure that the instructions for use have been given in clear, intelligible language?

- Has proper thought been given to all the contents of the documentation?

- Has full use been made of exclusion and limitation clauses? Has care been taken to avoid the use of any such clauses which might be illegal?

- Are you sure that the use by the buyer/licensee of the software will not infringe third party intellectual property rights?

- As the manufacturer of software, are you are aware that the terms and conditions you seek to impose might not be binding against a party who buys from a retail supplier?

- Has use been made of a registration card as a possible way of a buyer providing consideration?

- Have the rights of the licensee been clearly spelled out? In particular, have all the relevant restrictions on use been clearly identified?

- As a purchaser, have you set out the acceptance tests which must be run before you are prepared to accept the software?

- What provision has been made in relation to confidentiality and non-disclosure?

- Does this agreement contain provision for the deposit of the source code with a third party?

- What provision has been made for training in the use of the software?

- Has an indemnity been offered against any possible infringement of a third party's intellectual property rights?

- Bespoke software raises special problems. Have all the relevant issues been considered in the contract?

Chapter A5
Consumer Contracts –
Special Issues

At a glance

- Generally, consumers have the same rights as businesses under *SGA 1979*.

- In some areas, notably in areas dealing with rights of rejection and the effect of exclusion clauses, the consumer has greater protection.

- Specific guidance is given as to when a person deals as a consumer.

- There is no requirement to provide a guarantee, but the provision of a guarantee does have legal consequences.

- Provision is made for indemnities required in consumer contracts.

- The manner in which the price is indicated is subject to legislative control.

- There are various requirements for contracts made at a distance.

- Inertia selling is not itself illegal, but is still subject to control.

- Provision has been made in law for facilitating electronic commerce, with regard to the need for documents to be in writing.

- EU law, yet to be implemented in the United Kingdom, considerably affects consumer rights and remedies.

Consumer rights   A5.2

The provisions of the *Sale of Goods Act 1979* (*SGA 1979*) apply as much to consumers as they do to those buying in the course of a business. Exactly the same is true with regard to the *Supply of Goods and Services Act 1982*. As a result, the consumer has rights against the seller as to title, fitness for purpose and as to the satisfactory quality of the goods.

Consumer remedies   A5.3

The provisions as to passing of property and risk, acceptance and rejection, and actions for damages also apply equally to those buying as consumer. In one sense, the rights of a consumer are greater than those of the business buyer. Acceptance, and hence the loss of the right to reject, takes place if, among other things, a buyer intimates acceptance or, following delivery of the goods, the buyer performs any act inconsistent with the seller's ownership. Where the buyer has not been able to examine the goods, there is no acceptance under these provisions until the buyer has had a reasonable chance to examine the goods.

Special position of consumer

SGA 1979 goes onto say that a buyer dealing as consumer does not lose his right to rely on this right to examine by virtue of any agreement, waiver or any other act. This means, for example, that a consumer who signs an acceptance note will not, because of that, be deemed to have accepted the goods and hence to have lost any right of rejection.

Exclusion clauses   A5.4

The consumer has, in this context too, more protection than someone who deals as a business.

The *Unfair Contract Terms Act 1977* (*UCTA 1977*) covers both businesses and consumers, but its scope and effect is broader for the latter.

For instance, *s 3* of *UCTA 1977* applies the reasonableness test to clauses which seek to:

- exclude or limit liability for breach;

- allow a substantially different performance from that which was reasonably expected; or

- allow no performance at all.

In the case of contracts with a business, these provisions are applicable only if the contract is on written standard terms. In the case of a consumer contract, they apply to contracts in whatever form.

UCTA 1977 also applies to clauses which seek to exclude or limit liability for the terms implied by *SGA 1979* (and corresponding Acts) as to description, quality and fitness for purpose. In the case of contracts with a business, the reasonableness test will apply to such contracts. In the case of contracts with a consumer, however, such clauses are automatically void and of no effect.

The difference is emphasised by the provisions of the *Consumer Transactions (Restrictions on Statements) Order 1976* (*SI 1976/1813*). This makes it a criminal offence to include in a consumer contract an exclusion or limitation clause rendered void by *UCTA 1977*.

Under the Act, a person deals as consumer when:

- the relevant party neither makes the contract in the course of a business nor holds himself out as so doing;
- the other party does deal in the course of a business; and
- the goods are of a type ordinarily supplied for private consumption.

Case Example: *R & B Customs Brokers [1988] 1 WLR 321.*

The claimant company purchased a car, with a term of the agreement excluding the implied terms as to quality and fitness. The car was the second or third acquired by the claimants on credit terms. They were in business as shipping brokers and freight forwarding agents. This particular car was bought for both personal and business use. The Court of Appeal ruled that the purchase was only incidental to the claimant's business activity and that a degree of regularity was required before the transaction could be said to be an integral part of the business and hence entered into for the purposes of business. The present case lacked any such regularity and the contract was therefore a consumer contract.

Case Example: *Brigden v American Express Bank Ltd [2000] IRLR 94.*

It was held that, where a person enters into a contract of employment as an employee, he neither makes the contract in the course of a business nor holds himself out as so doing, but the other party does, the result being that the employee deals as consumer.

Case for Further Information: *Rasbora v JCL Marine [1977] 1 Lloyd's Rep 645.*

What these cases show, given that the use of exclusion clauses can be a criminal offence as explained above, is that businesses whose contracts might be used by both business and consumer customers, should indicate that the exclusion clauses will not apply to those contracting as consumers. Crucially, *s 12(3)* of *UCTA 1977* states that a contract is deemed to be a consumer contract until the contrary is proved.

Choosing between the Act and the Regulations   **A5.5**

The *Unfair Terms in Consumer Contracts Regulations 1999 (SI 1999/2083)*, by definition, apply only to contracts with consumers. This is defined by *Reg 3(1)* as any 'natural person' who is acting for purposes outside his business or profession. There is no presumption as to whether a particular contract is one made with a consumer as thus defined, so it will be the task of the person bringing an action to show that he comes within the Regulations and hence was acting as consumer. This could mean in some circumstances that an action is better brought under *UCTA 1977*.

Greater scope of Regulations

The Regulations have a broader scope than *UCTA 1977* in that, while the Act in general applies to exclusion and limitation clauses, the Regulations apply to any contract term which has not been individually negotiated and which is unfair because, contrary to the requirements of good faith, it causes a significant imbalance in the parties' rights and obligations to the detriment of the consumer.

Guarantees   A5.6

It is manufacturers rather than retailers who provide guarantees (or warranties) covering the goods supplied. Usually, they will offer the consumer a level of protection and redress greater than would otherwise arise by operation of law, as under the *Sale of Goods Act 1979*. For instance, there is no requirement in law for the seller to offer to repair or replace defective goods, since the sole remedy otherwise available to the consumer is rescission of the contract and a claim for the purchase price if already paid (or to damages if he has accepted the goods). It is doubtful if a manufacturer's guarantee is legally enforceable, since no consideration passes between consumer and manufacturer. Assuming that a guarantee is, however, legally valid (as it certainly would be when actually given by a retailer), *UCTA 1977* provides that nothing in any guarantee can exclude or limit liability for damage resulting from negligence by the manufacturer or distributor where the goods proved defective while in consumer use. A retailer could not, therefore, disclaim his liability under the *SGA 1979* by a provision in the guarantee to the effect that no liability is accepted for any defects in the goods arising from, for example, negligence in the course of production or on the part of any carrier.

Mandatory wording to accompany guarantees   A5.7

This position is supported by the *Consumer Transactions (Restrictions on Statements) Order 1976 (SI 1976/1813)*, which requires guarantees, where they assume obligations in the event of the goods being defective, not of satisfactory quality, or not being reasonably fit for their purpose (and whether such obligations are legally enforceable or not) to be accompanied by an indication that the guarantee does not affect the consumer's statutory rights. Although no wording is prescribed by the Order, the almost invariable form of words is: 'Your statutory rights are not affected'.

> **Sample Statement**:
>
> 'We guarantee that if the goods fail due to defective workmanship or materials within twelve months of purchase, and if the goods are returned to us in their original packaging together with proof of date of purchase, we will refund your postage costs and, in our absolute discretion, refund the purchase price, repair the goods and return them to you at our cost, or send you new goods as a replacement. This guarantee is in addition to and does not affect your statutory rights'.

The Order would not, however, apply to the following:

> 'We guarantee that if the goods fail to satisfy you in any way, and you return them by post with proof of date of purchase, within one month of purchase, to the address below, we will refund the purchase price and the cost of return'.

The Order only applies when the guarantee relates to the goods not conforming to their description, or not being of satisfactory quality or reasonably fit. This particular guarantee goes further, and would cover any reason for dissatisfaction with the goods.

Indemnity clauses – when given by consumer   A5.8

A contract term, particularly where the contract is for the provision of a service, might require the consumer to indemnify the service provider against any liability which the latter might incur to a third party. Thus, a car ferry service might require the car owner to indemnify the company against any liability it might incur to other owners if an employee of the company manoeuvres the consumer's car into another. Any such clause is rendered ineffective by *UCTA 1977* unless it can be shown to be reasonable. Such a clause could also be challenged under the *Unfair Terms in Consumer Contracts Regulations 1999 (SI 1999/2083)*.

Indemnity clauses – when given by business   A5.9

It can be a good selling point for the contract specifically to state that the consumer will not only be compensated for any loss which he incurs because of a defective product or service, but that any liability which he incurs to third parties will also be made good.

> **Sample Clause**:
>
> The following clause can be used in any contract, whether for goods or services:

> 'The supplier undertakes to indemnify the customer against all proceedings, costs, expenses, liabilities, injury, death, loss or damage arising out of the breach or negligent performance or failure in performance by the supplier of this agreement in any way whatsoever.'

The above clause is wide enough to cover third party claims which might be made against the consumer.

Sample Proviso:

If the supplier wants to guard against a possible open-ended liability, he can add the following:

'... provided that the customer:

* promptly notifies the supplier of any third party claims;

* allows the supplier if he so requests to conduct and control, at the supplier's sole cost, the defence of any such claim and related negotiations; and

* affords the supplier all reasonable assistance, at the supplier's sole cost, and makes no admission prejudicial to the defence of any such claim.'

Price indications   A5.10

There is no requirement for the price to be stated in the contract itself, though, as a practical matter, this is unavoidable, and it will be specifically stated in the contract, or in documents to which the contract refers.

Under the terms of the *Price Marking Order 1999 (SI 1999/3042)*:

* a business must indicate the price at which goods are sold to a consumer, and this must be placed in proximity to the goods to which it relates;

* any indication of charges for postage, packing or delivery must be unambiguous, easily identifiable and clearly legible. (The Order does not actually say that there must be an indication of these matters, though, if they are omitted and must be paid if the consumer is to obtain the goods, the price indication would be misleading and contrary to the provisions of the *Consumer Protection Act 1987*);

* the statement of the selling price must be inclusive of all taxes including VAT. There is no actual requirement for the price to state that it does include VAT, it is enough that it does; and

- the price indication must be in sterling, but a foreign currency can also be quoted, so long as it is accompanied by an indication as to any commission charges which might be payable. If, however, payment is made by payment card or Uniform Eurocheque, it must be stated that the foreign currency price does not apply to such forms of payment.

The requirements as to price indications are specifically stated not to extend to advertisements.

Distance selling   A5.11

The regulation of distance contracts is subject to the *Consumer Protection (Distance Selling) Regulations 2000 (SI 2000/2334)* (the 'Distance Selling Regulations').

The main requirements of the Regulations are:

- for the contract to be in written form;
- for the contract to contain certain terms and conditions;
- for there to be a right to cancel; and
- for the contract to be performed within a stated time.

The Regulations are enforced by injunctions to restrain further breach. In addition, speedy action to prevent infringements of the Regulations can be brought under the provisions of the *Stop Now Orders (ECDirective) Regulations 2001 (SI 2001/1422)*. Action can be brought under these Regulations in EEA courts.

Case Example:

A scheme involving unsolicited first aid kits was stopped in a cross-border case. The OFT, working closely with the Dutch Consumers Association (Consumentenbond), used its powers to take action against Royal Consulting, a Dutch company which had been sending unsolicited first aid kits to UK residents accompanied by demands for payment.

Such activities are in breach of the *Distance Selling Regulations*. Consumers who receive unsolicited goods may keep them and demands for payment for such goods are unlawful. The OFT had received over a hundred complaints about the company and it subsequently obtained written assurances from Royal Consulting BV, and its parent company Royal Consulting AS, that they will not make demands for payment for unsolicited first aid kits. Any breach of the written assurances will lead to action in the Dutch courts.

Inertia selling   **A5.12**

Under the *Distance Selling Regulations*, unsolicited goods are treated as an unconditional gift to the recipient. A person who has no reasonable cause to suppose that he has a right to payment commits an offence if he demands payment. This applies only if the sender knew that the goods were unsolicited goods sent for the purposes of acquisition other than for business purposes. Similar provisions apply to unsolicited services.

The *Unsolicited Goods and Services Act 1971* and the *Unsolicited Goods and Services (Amendment) Act 1975* also make special provision for directory entries, requiring certain formalities to be completed before any person can be lawfully charged for such an entry. Following an order under the *Electronic Communications Act 2000* (see A5.13 below), the relevant signature to a request for a directory entry can be made electronically.

Electronic commerce   **A5.13**

The *Electronic Communications Act 2000* has the main aim of making it easier to use electronic commerce tools, such as the Internet, to enter into binding arrangements. At present many Acts, notably the *Consumer Credit Act 1974*, require certain agreements to be in writing and signed by the consumer. This currently precludes such agreements being entered into via the Internet. *ECA 2000* allows the Government by order to amend the relevant legislation to allow for electronic commerce.

Consumer guarantees – the EU Directive   **A5.14**

Directive 1999/44/EC on certain aspects of the sale of consumer goods and associated guarantees was due to be implemented in the United Kingdom by 1 January 2002. This deadline has been missed, therefore below the principles of the Directive which are to be incorporated eventually into the law of the United Kingdom are set out.

Scope

The Directive is limited to contracts made by a 'consumer' buyer with a professional 'seller'.

Conformity with Contract

The Directive provides that a seller must deliver goods to the consumer which are in conformity with the contract of sale. The corresponding obligations under *ss 13-15* of the *Sale of Goods Act 1979* are dealt with at A5.2 above.

Presumption of conformity

The Directive provides for a presumption of conformity if certain criteria are met.

Showing Conformity:

One factor giving rise to the presumption of conformity is that the goods 'comply with the description given by the seller'.

A second is if they are 'fit for the purposes for which goods of the same type are normally used'.

It is also provided that the goods must:

> 'show the quality and performance which are normal in goods of the same type and which the consumer can reasonably expect, given the nature of the goods and taking into account any public statements on the specific characteristics of the goods made about them by the seller, the producer or his representative, particularly in advertising or on labelling'.

Durability

The Directive states that any lack of conformity coming to light within six months of the delivery of goods shall be presumed to have existed at the time of delivery.

Minor breaches

The Directive states that the consumer will not be able to rescind the contract 'if the lack of conformity is minor'. *Section 15A* of the *Sale of Goods Act 1979* only imposes this restriction where the buyer is a business. The Directive does, however, allow EU Member Sates to retain measures of law offering a higher degree of consumer protection, so it may be that existing UK law, allowing rescission for minor breaches where the buyer is a consumer will be retained.

Remedies

The Directive gives the consumer four remedies, which are:

● repair;

● replacement;

- reduction in the price; or
- rescission of the contract.

Under the law as its stands at present, the only remedies available to a buyer (consumer or business) are those of rescission of the contract and damages; or damages alone.

Requirement of proportionality:

These remedies have to be possible and not disproportionate.

A remedy is deemed disproportionate if it imposes costs on the seller which, in comparison with the alternative remedies, are unreasonable, taking into account:

- the value of the goods:
- the significance of the lack of conformity; and
- whether any alternative remedy could be completed without significant inconvenience to the consumer.

Repair or remedy must be carried out in a reasonable time.

Duration of liability

The seller remains liable for two years for any lack of conformity which existed at the time of delivery.

Notification of defects

The seller must be informed of the lack of conformity within two months of its discovery by the consumer. Sellers who are liable under these provisions can pass their liability back up the distribution chain to the producer.

Guarantees

A guarantee is defined in the Directive as 'any undertaking by a seller or producer to the consumer, given without extra charge, to reimburse the price paid or to replace, repair or handle consumer goods in any way if they do not meet the specifications set out in the guarantee statement or in the relevant advertising'. This definition covers both sellers' and manufacturers' guarantees. Since it applies to guarantees given without extra charge, it will not cover maintenance contracts often taken out in relation to various consumer goods. Since, in effect, the definition applies only to defective items, it will not cover the 'money back if not completely satisfied' type of guarantee.

The Directive provides that: 'A guarantee shall be legally binding on the offeror under the conditions laid down in the guarantee statement and the associated advertising'.

Contents of guarantee

The Directive contains only minimal requirements as to what the guarantee must contain. It must:

- state that the consumer has legal rights under applicable national legislation governing the sale of consumer goods and make clear that those rights are not affected by the guarantee;
- set out in plain intelligible language the contents of the guarantee and the essential particulars for making claims under the guarantee, notably:
  - the duration and territorial scope of the guarantee; and
  - the name and address of the guarantor.

Guarantees can be oral as well as in writing, but, in the former case, the consumer has the right to require that the guarantee is made available in writing or other durable medium.

Despite these requirements, guarantees do remain voluntary.

Checklist   A5.15

- Do you fully understand that, in some areas, these rights and remedies can be greater than those afforded to businesses?
- With regard to exclusion clauses, have you remembered that the use of certain clauses in consumer contracts can give rise to a criminal offence?
- Are you also aware of just what it means, for the purposes of the law, if someone is 'dealing as consumer'?
- Do you understand that, while giving guarantees is not mandatory, there are legal consequences attached if a guarantee is given?
- Have you checked that any indemnity you might require a consumer to give is likely to satisfy the reasonableness test?
- Have you also made sure that any indication as to price is given in the way required by the law?

- What steps have been taken to ensure that a distance contract is in the correct form?

- The EU *Consumer Guarantees Directive* is not in force but will bring about major changes when it is. Are you sure that you are being kept informed as to its implementation in the United Kingdom?

Section B:
Business-to-business
Contracts

Chapter B1
Terms and Conditions for the Sale of Goods

At a glance

- A contract for the sale of goods means a contract where property in those goods passes from one party to another.

- Generally speaking, no formalities are required for a contract of sale.

- Statute implied obligations as to title into contracts for the sale of goods.

- Statute also implies a requirement that goods must conform to their contract description.

- The goods as supplied must conform very closely to their contract description.

- Statute further requires that goods supplied must be of a particular quality and capacity.

- The obligations as to description and quality are strict, meaning that blame or intention is irrelevant to the question of a breach.

- There are obligations incurred when the sale is a sale by sample.

- Exclusions are permitted from the obligations as to quality and capacity in certain well-defined circumstances.

- Apart from the above, statute places severe control on the use of exclusion or limitation clauses.

- Exclusion clauses can be subject to a reasonableness test.

- There are statutory provisions as to when property and risk is to pass.

- These statutory provisions are, however, subject to the terms of the contract.

- It is a general rule that a person who has no title cannot himself pass a valid title, but there are many exceptions to this rule.

- Prompt payment is not generally of the essence of the contract, although this is subject to the terms of the contract.

- Late payment can incur statutory interest.
- Duties are imposed on a seller as to delivery, and as to delivery of the right quantity.
- A buyer has right as to the examination of the goods, but these are subject to the terms of the contract.
- Acceptance of the contract goods carries with it the loss of the right to reject.
- Acceptance is defined by law.
- An unpaid seller has certain rights, such as a right to a lien and a right to stop the goods in transit.
- Such a seller also has rights of resale and to damages.
- Provision is also made for the seller to sue for the actual price.
- Statute also provides for the rights of the buyer, notably with regard to specific performance and damages.

General   B1.2

Many aspects of contract of sale, and of purchase, are determined by the *Sale of Goods Act 1979*. The major points of the Act are set out below.

Definition of 'sale'   B1.3

Section 2(1) of *SGA 1979* defines a 'sale' as a contract by which the seller 'transfers or agrees to transfer the property in goods to the buyer for a money consideration...' This definition excludes contracts of hire purchase, hire, for the supply of goods and services, and barter or exchange. It remains unclear whether the definition of 'sale' includes a contract whereby the buyer pays in cash and also tenders a trade-in. In many ways, the distinction between a contract of sale and other contracts is academic in that legislation such as the *Supply of Goods (Implied Terms) Act 1973* and the *Supply of Goods and Services Act 1982*, imply terms into the contract identical in most respects to those implied by the *Sale of Goods Act 1979*.

Formalities   B1.4

There are no formalities attached to a contract of sale, nor requirements as to copies. A contract can be made in any form (entirely oral, entirely written, or a combination). In commercial contracts, of course, a written agreement is, for practical purposes, essential.

Implied terms as to title   B1.5

The following sections set out implied terms as to title.

Conditions   B1.6

In a contract of sale, *section 12* of *SGA 1979* states that there is an implied condition that the seller has the right to sell the goods. A 'condition' is a major term of the contract which means that, on breach, the buyer can rescind the contract and claim damages (*Wallis, Son and Wells v Pratt and Haynes [1910] 2 KB 1003*).

Warranties   B1.7

SGA 1979 also implies warranties as to title. A 'warranty' can be regarded as a minor term of the contract, breach of which entitles the buyer to claim damages, but the contract remains valid and cannot be rescinded. The implied warranties are that:

- the goods are free from any charge or encumbrance not disclosed or known to the buyer when the contract is made; and

- the buyer will enjoy quiet possession of the goods except so far as it may be disturbed by the owner or other person entitled to the benefit of any charge or encumbrance so disclosed or known.

In many cases, the implied warranties will overlap with the implied condition.

> **Case Example**: *Mason v Burningham [1949] 2KB 545.*
>
> The purchaser of a stolen typewriter was entitled to cover the cost of repairs for breach of the warranty as to quiet possession, when he could equally have succeeded in an action for breach of the implied condition.

At the same time, it is possible for there to be breaches of the warranties in circumstances when there would be no breach of condition.

> **Case Example**: *Microbeads AG v Vinhurst Road Markings Ltd [1975] 1 All ER 529.*
>
> This involved the sale of a product over which a third party had a patent and who could, therefore, seek delivery of the patented product.

> **Case Example**: *Rubicon Computer Systems Ltd v United Paints Ltd (2000) 2 TCLR 453.*
>
> A computer was installed with a time-lock device, which rendered the computer unusable, this being held to infringe the warranty of quiet possession.

In each of these cases, there was no breach of the implied condition since the goods had always been the property of the seller who had, therefore, a complete right to pass title.

Limited title   B1.8

In those circumstances where it is to be inferred that the seller is transferring only such title as he or a third person may have, none of the foregoing implied conditions or warranties apply. Instead, there is an implied warranty that all charges and encumbrances known to the seller were disclosed to the buyer prior to the making of the contract, and an implied warranty that none of the following will disturb the buyer's quiet possession:

- the seller;
- the third party (in those cases where the seller is to transfer only such title as a third party might have); and
- anyone claiming through or under the seller or third party, except in relation to a charge of encumbrance disclosed or known to the buyer before the contract was made.

Implied term as to description   B1.9

Section 13 of the *SGA 1979* implies a condition into contracts of sale by description, meaning that the goods will correspond with the description given.

A contract is a sale by description when 'even though the buyer is buying something displayed before him on the counter a thing is sold by description, though it is specific, so long as it is sold not merely as a specific thing but as a thing corresponding to a description' (*Grant v Australian Knitting Mills [1936] AC 85100*).

A sale will, therefore, not be by description if the buyer makes it clear that he is buying a particular thing because of its own unique qualities and that no other will do. Nor will a sale be by description if it was not within the contemplation of the parties that the buyer will be relying on the description (*Harlingdon & Leinster Enterprises Ltd v Christopher Hull Fine Arts Ltd [1991] 1 QB 564*).

Close conformity to description required   B1.10

Any variation from the agreed description will cause an infringement.

> **Case Example**: *Arcos Ltd v Ronaasen and Son [1933] AC 470.*
>
> A contract was for the supply of a quantity of staves for use in making cement barrels, and it stated that the staves were to be half an inch thick. A breach of the implied term arose when only 5% conformed to the description, even though all the staves remained fit for their intended use:

Microscopic variations will, however, be disregarded on the *de minimis* principle. The *de minimis* principle requires the courts to disregard anything which can be fairly regarded as too small or insignificant to be worthy of notice.

> **Case Example**: *Moralice (London) Ltd v E, D & F Man [1954] 2 Lloyd's Rep 526.*
>
> It was said that, where the price is payable by means of a documentary credit against shipping documents, the *de minimis* principle had no application as between seller and bank. The shipping documents were to comply strictly with the requirements of the letter of credit.

Breadth of 'description'   B1.11

The description can include the way in which goods are packed.

> **Case Example**: *Re Moore & Co and Landauer & Co's Arbitration [1921] 2 KB 519.*
>
> It was held that packing tins in cases of 24, when the contract specified 30, infringed the implied condition even though the correct number of tins were packed.
>
> **Case Example**: *Albright & Wilson UK Ltd v Biachem [2001] 2 All ER (Comm) 537.*
>
> It was held that, where a buyer contracted with different sellers for the supply of different chemicals, but delivery was to be by the same firm, there was a breach of the implied term as to description where one supply of chemicals was accompanied by a delivery note referring to the other supply.

Strict liability   **B1.12**

There is a breach of *SGA 1979, s 13* regardless of any element of blame. An infringement arises if the goods do not conform to the contract description, whether or not the breach was innocent or inadvertent.

Satisfactory quality   **B1.13**

Section 14(2) of *SGA 1979* implies a condition that the goods supplied under the contract must be of satisfactory quality.

Meaning of 'satisfactory'

Section 14(2A) of *SGA 1979* provides that goods will meet this standard if a reasonable person would regard them as satisfactory, taking account of any description of the goods, the price (if relevant) and all the other relevant circumstances.

The 'quality' of the goods is said by *SGA 1979, s 14(2B)* to include their state and condition and the following are examples of the matters to be taken into account:

- fitness for all the purposes for which goods of the kind in question are commonly supplied;
- appearance and finish;
- freedom from minor defects;
- safety; and
- durability.

There is little by way of precedent as to what satisfactory quality means, but some cases under the old law, which required goods to be of merchantable quality may provide some guidance.

> **Case Example**: *Ashington Piggeries Ltd v Christopher Hill Ltd [1972] AC 441.*
>
> Animal feed was held unmerchantable when contaminated with poison.
>
> **Case Example**: *Bernstein v Pamson Motors (Golders Green) Ltd [1987] 2 All ER 220.*
>
> A car was unmerchantable when it had a safety defect which could have caused a serious accident.

Case Example: *Wormell v RHM Agriculture (East) Ltd [1987] 3 All ER 75.*

Goods are unmerchantable if, though in proper condition, the accompanying instructions are misleading.

Exceptions to obligation as to quality

Section 14(2C) of *SGA 1979* provides that the implied term as to satisfactory quality is inapplicable where:

- the defects were specifically drawn to the buyer's attention before the contract was made, or
- where the buyer examines the goods beforehand, in relation to defects which that examination ought to have revealed.

Reasonable fitness for purpose   **B1.14**

Section 14(3) of the *SGA 1979* provides that where the buyer expressly or by implication makes known any particular purpose for which the goods are being bought, there is an implied condition that the goods should be reasonably fit for that purpose. The requirement to make known any particular purpose is automatically fulfilled when the goods have only one ordinary purpose. If the goods have more than one purpose, the duty is on the seller to provide goods fit for such of the purposes as the seller indicated: see the *Australian Knitting Mills* case at B1.9 above. The seller will not, however, be in breach if the unsuitability of the goods arises from a special feature relating to the buyer not disclosed to the seller.

Case Example: *Slater v Finnings Ltd [1996] 3 All ER 398.*

A new camshaft fitted to a fishing vessel failed, as did two further replacement camshafts. This failure was not due to the camshafts themselves, but to the fact that the vessel had an abnormal tendency to produce excessive torsional resonance when fitted with the new type of camshaft which, in turn, caused excessive wear on the camshaft. The House of Lords held that there was no breach of the implied term where the failure of the goods to meet their intended purpose arose from an abnormal feature or idiosyncrasy, not made known to the seller, in the buyer or in the circumstances of the use of the goods by the buyer, regardless of whether or not the buyer himself was aware of such abnormality.

For a further example, see *Griffith v Peter Conway Ltd [1939] 1 All ER 685.*

Exceptions to obligation as to quality

The implied term is stated by *SGA 1979, s 14(3)* as inapplicable where the circumstances show that the buyer does not rely on the seller's skill or judgement, or that any reliance was unreasonable. It was said in the *Australian Knitting Mills* case (see B1.9 above) that this provision is generally interpreted in favour of the buyer.

Case Example: *Henry Kendall & Sons v William Lillico & Sons Ltd [1969] 2 AC 31.*

It was said that the fact that the buyer proposed to analyse or test the goods on delivery does not mean an absence of reliance.

Case Example: *Wren v Holt [1903] 1 KB 610.*

Where the buyer was aware that the seller could supply only one particular brand, there was evidence of an absence of reliance.

Case Example: *Phoenix Distributors Ltd v L B Clarke (London) Ltd [1967] 1 Lloyd's Rep 518.*

It was said that a buyer who is given a certificate as to the goods supplied by an independent third party can be said not to be relying on the seller in respect of matters covered by the certificate.

Case Example: *Cammell Laird & Co v Manganese Bronze and Brass Co Ltd [1934] AC 402.*

Partial reliance suffices if the breach is in the area of such reliance.

Liability does not depend on any blame on the part of the seller.

Case Example: *Frost v Aylesbury Dairy Co Ltd [1905] 1 KB 608.*

Milk was sold which was infected by typhoid. At the time, there was no test which could have disclosed this. The seller was still held liable for failing to supply goods which were reasonably fit for their purpose.

Sales by sample   B1.15

Section 15 of the *SGA 1979* provides that a contract is a sale by sample when there is an express or implied term to that effect. To satisfy this test, the parties must contract by reference to a sample on the understanding that the sample provided a description of the quality of the goods and that the bulk must conform to the sample (*Drummond v Van Ingen (1887) 12 App Cas 284*).

Section 15 further provides that, when a contract is a sale by sample, then certain conditions are implied, which are:

- that the bulk will correspond with the sample in quality; and

- that the goods are free from any defect, making their quality unsatisfactory.

If the sale is by description then there is an implied term that the goods must also correspond with the description.

Excluding the implied terms   **B1.16**

The *Unfair Contract Terms Act 1977* severely limits the effectiveness of clauses by which a seller seeks to exclude or limit his liability for breach of any of the above implied terms. In the case of the implied terms as to description, quality, fitness for purpose, and those implied when the contract is a sale by sample, an exclusion or limitation clause will be valid, but only if the seller can show that it is reasonable.

If a term seeks to exclude liability other than in relation the above implied terms (the seller might exclude liability for late delivery; or the buyer liability for non acceptance), the *UCTA 1977* also applies if the contract is on written standard terms.

What is meant by 'written standard terms'   **B1.17**

No definition is given of 'written standard terms', but it seems that a contract is made on written standard terms even if some of the terms have been individually negotiated (*McCrone v Boots Farm Sales Ltd 1981 SLT 103*; *Salvage Association v CAP Financial Services Ltd [1995] FSR 654* at pp 671-672; *St Albans City and District Council v International Computers Ltd [1996] 4 All ER 481* at p 491).

The reasonableness test   **B1.18**

Where *SGA 1979* does apply, it subjects any contractual clause to the test of reasonableness which:

- seeks to exclude or restrict liability for breach;

- seeks to allow the provision of a contractual performance which is a substantially different performance from that which was reasonably expected; or

- seeks to allow no performance at all.

No contract, whether on written standard terms or not, can exclude or limit liability for negligence resulting in death or personal injury. Subject to the test of reasonableness, however, a clause can exclude or limit liability for negligence having other consequences, such as damage to property, or which causes economic loss.

Cases where the reasonableness test has been applied

Flamar Interocean Ltd v Denmac Ltd [1990] 1 Lloyd's Rep 434; The Salvage Association v CAP Financial Services Ltd [1995] FSR 654; St Albans City and District Council v International Computers Ltd [1996] 4 All ER 481; Overland Shoes Ltd v Schenkers Ltd [1998] 1 Lloyd's Rep 498; British Fermentation Products v Compare Reavell Ltd [1999] 2 All ER (Comm) 389; Overseas Medical Supplies Ltd v Orient Transport Services Ltd [1999] 2 Lloyd's Rep 273; Britvic Soft Drinks Ltd and Others v Messer UK Ltd and Another (Court of Appeal; 30 April 2002).

Excluding liability for misrepresentation

In the case of any contract, a term seeking to exclude or limit liability for misrepresentation is only valid, by the *Misrepresentation Act 1967*, if it can be shown to be reasonable.

Cases where the reasonableness test has been applied

Josef Marton v Southwestern General Property (unreported, 6 May 1982); Walker v Boyle [1982] 1 WLR 495.

It should always be remembered that decisions on reasonableness have only limited value as precedent, since a clause can be reasonable in one case, but that same clause might be unreasonable in another given that the circumstances of the latter might differ from those of the former.

Passing of property and risk   B1.19

The parties are always free to make their own provision as to when the property (which may be equated with ownership) of the goods passes. The seller will want it to pass at the latest possible moment, usually on full payment; while the buyer will want it to pass no later than delivery.

If the contract says nothing on this point, then certain Rules laid down by *s 18* of *SGA 1979* will apply.

Specific and identified goods   **B1.20**

In the case of specific goods (particularly those agreed on and identified when the contract is made), property passes when the contract is made so long as the goods are in a deliverable state.

Where something remains to be done to put the goods in a deliverable state, property passes when this has been done and the buyer has been informed. Where the goods are in a deliverable state, but the price has yet to be ascertained, property passes when this is done and the buyer informed.

Where the goods are delivered to the buyer on approval, or subject to sale or return or similar terms, property passes when the buyer does any act adopting the transaction, for example:

- by signifying acceptance or approval;
- if the goods are retained without notice of rejection after the time fixed for their return; or
- if the goods are retained after the lapse of a reasonable time if no specific time was fixed.

Non-specific goods   **B1.21**

If the goods are not specific, that is to say they had not been specifically agreed on and identified at the time of the contract, property passes when goods of the relevant description are unconditionally appropriated to the contract by either party with the assent of the other, express or implied. Assent can be given before or after appropriation. There are also specific rules as to the passing of property of goods contained within a bulk.

Just as with the passing of property, the parties are left free by *SGA 1979* to provide for when risk is to pass. In this instance, the seller will want risk to pass as soon as possible, while the buyer will only want risk to pass when he has safely received the goods in good condition. If, however, nothing is said in the contract as to the passing of risk, the Act provides that it passes with property.

Transfer of title by non-owner   **B1.22**

Although property might not have passed to the buyer, it is always possible that he will seek to sell the goods on, innocently or fraudulently.

Section 21(1) of SGA 1979 provides the basic rule that any such disposition cannot pass title even to an innocent third party, but numerous exceptions to this rule are laid down, both in the Act and elsewhere.

The exceptions

The seller can be estopped by his conduct. This means that he can act in such a way that he gives the impression that a third party, not himself, is the owner of the goods, or that a third party has the authority to sell or dispose of the goods. The common law principles of principal and agent can also apply. If one person is the agent of another, the agent might appear to be authorised to sell the principal's goods, even if this is not the case.

In addition, *ss 24–25* of the *SGA 1979* apply exceptions in the case of the seller and buyer in possession. Thus, under *s 24*, a seller who remains in possession of goods after a sale can make a further sale of the same goods to a third party and pass a valid title to him.

Section 25 further provides that a person who has bought or agreed to buy goods, and who obtains possession of them with the seller's consent, can pass a good title to a third party. When the buyer is paying for the goods in instalments, and where title only passes on payment of the final instalment, he does not count as someone who has agreed to buy goods if the amount of credit advanced to him is not more than £25,000. This limit can be changed and a check should always be made on the current limit.

The *SGA 1979* specifically preserves the operation of the *Factors Act 1889*, in relation to mercantile agency. A mercantile agent is one who, in the normal course of his business, has the authority to sell goods, consign goods for the purposes of sale, to buy goods or to raise money on the security of goods. Any sale by a mercantile agent to a *bona fide* third party passes the latter a good title.

The *Hire Purchase Act 1964* must also be considered. This provides that the disposition by any party of a motor vehicle to a *bona fide* third party who is not a dealer passes good title to that party. This also applies to conditional sale agreements within the limit referred to above.

Duty as to payment   **B1.23**

The *SGA 1979* provides that, once the price has been agreed, it is the duty of the buyer to pay that price. The Act also says that unless a different intention appears from the contract, the time for payment is not of the essence. This means that late payment does not allow the seller to terminate the contract and claim damages, but he can claim damages alone. The seller who wishes to protect his position, therefore, should always write into the contract a term specifically stating that time of payment is of the essence. This will allow termination of the contract in the event of non–payment.

The seller's position in relation to late payment has also been much affected by the *Late Payment of Commercial Debts (Interest) Act, 1998*. This provides – whether or not it is specified in the contract itself – interest of 8% above base rate on all overdue payments. Payment is late where a supplier has agreed, either orally or in writing, a credit period with the purchaser, and payment is made after the last date of the credit period. If no credit period has been agreed, *LPCD(I)A 1998* sets a period of 30 days after which interest can run. The 30 day period starts from whichever is the later of:

- the delivery of the goods or the performance of the service by the supplier; or

- the day on which the purchaser has notice of the amount of the debt.

If a clause in a contract seeks to postpone the time at which interest would otherwise start to run, the *LPCD(I)A 1998* treats such a clause as subject to the reasonableness test under the *Unfair Contract Terms Act 1977*.

Under the *Late Payment of Commercial Debts Regulations 2002* (*SI 2002/1674*) once a party becomes entitled to statutory interest, he can also claim a fixed sum up to the following maxima.

- For a debt less than £1,000, the sum of £40.

- For a debt of £1,000 or more, but less than £10,000, the sum of £70.

- For a debt of £10,000 or more, the sum of £100.

The Regulations also provide that a representative body may bring proceedings in the High Court on behalf of small and medium-sized enterprises where standard terms put forward by a purchaser into contracts to which the *LPCD(I)A 1998* applies include a term purporting to oust or vary the right to statutory interest in relation to debts created by those contracts. The Court may grant an injunction restraining use of the term, where it finds that the term is void under the provisions of *ss 8* and *9* of the *LPCD(I)A 1998*, on such basis as it sees fit.

'Small and medium-sized enterprises' are defined in Annex 1 to Commission Regulation EC/70/2001 of 12 January 2001 on the applications of *Articles 87* and *88* of the *EC Treaty* to State aid to small and medium-sized enterprises. In summary, they are enterprises which have fewer than 250 employees and have either an annual turnover not exceeding €40 million, or an annual balance sheet not exceeding €27 million, and conform to the criterion of independence which in general limits the ownership of such enterprises by other enterprises, falling outside the definition of small and medium-sized enterprises, to 25% of the capital or voting rights.

'Representative body' is defined as an organisation established to represent the collective interests of small and medium-sized enterprises in general or in a particular sector or geographical area.

The provisions of the Regulations apply only to contracts made on or after 7 August 2002.

Duty as to delivery   B1.24

Section 27 of the *Sale of Goods Act 1979* states that it is the duty of the seller to deliver the goods, a duty which is stated to be concurrent with the buyer's duty to pay the price.

Meaning of 'delivery'.

Section 61 of *SGA 1979* defines 'delivery' to mean a 'voluntary transfer of possession'. *Section 29* says that whether it is for the buyer to take possession, or for the seller to send, depends on the express or implied terms of the contract. It is always better for the contract to be specific on this point, rather than leave it to what may be implied from the contract.

Delivery of the incorrect amount   B1.25

The *Sale of Goods Act 1979* provides for several situations where the wrong amount of goods is delivered.

Where less is delivered

Where less than the agreed amount is delivered, *SGA 1979* gives the buyer the right to reject what is delivered, or accept it, paying the contract rate.

Where too much is delivered

Similarly, *SGA 1979* provides that if more is delivered, the buyer can reject the surplus, reject the whole consignment, or accept the whole consignment paying for it at the contract rate.

Minimal variations

The Act also imposes a *de minimis* rule so that if the shortfall or excess is so small that rejection would be unreasonable, and the buyer is acting as a business, then rejection will not be allowed. It is for the seller to show that rejection would be unreasonable.

Delivery in instalments   B1.26

SGA 1979 provides that, unless otherwise agreed, the buyer is not obliged to accept delivery in instalments, nor demand such delivery.

Examination   B1.27

Subject to what the contract might say, *SGA 1979* gives the buyer the right on request to a reasonable opportunity to examine the goods before he accepts delivery and, in the case of a contract for sale by sample to compare the bulk with the sample (see B1.15 above).

Acceptance   B1.28

Whether or not a buyer has accepted the goods is crucial, since *SGA 1979* provides that, on acceptance, the buyer loses his right of rejection for any breach, although not his right to damages.

When the buyer has accepted the goods

Acceptance arises when the buyer intimates acceptance of the goods.

> **Case Example**: *Libau Wood Co v WH Smith & Sons Ltd (1930) 37 Ll L Rep 296.*
>
> The mere receipt of goods without more, however, is not an intimation of acceptance.

Acceptance also arises where the goods have been delivered to the buyer and the buyer performs an act which is inconsistent with the ownership of the seller. An example might be making use of the goods, particularly if this has the effect of consuming them.

Section 35(1) of *SGA 1979*, however, provides that although a buyer might have appeared to have accepted goods within either of the above examples, the buyer will not have done so if the goods were delivered to him and he had not previously examined them, until such time as he has had a reasonable chance to examine the goods for the purpose of:

- ascertaining whether they are in compliance with the contract; or
- comparing the bulk with the sample, where the sale is by sample.

Acceptance also arises where the buyer retains the goods for more than a reasonable time.

What constitutes a 'reasonable time'

SGA 1979 provides that a 'reasonable time' is a question of fact, to be determined in all the circumstances of the case; and that in considering if a reasonable time has elapsed a court is to consider whether the buyer had a reasonable opportunity to examine or compare the goods as above.

Actions not constituting acceptance   B1.29

SGA 1979 further provides that a buyer is not taken to have accepted goods under any of the above provisions if he has done no more than ask for, or agree to, the repair of the goods by or under an arrangement with the seller; or because the goods have been delivered to a third party under a sub-sale or other disposition.

Goods sold in units   B1.30

Special provision is made in *SGA 1979* for the sale of goods making up one or more commercial units (division of which would materially impair the value of the goods or the character of the unit). Acceptance of any of the goods in such a unit is taken to be acceptance of them all. For example, the buyer who purchases a fleet of cars is deemed to have accepted them all if he accepts just one.

Rejection   B1.31

Where a buyer validly rejects goods, *SGA 1979* provides that unless there is an agreement to the contrary, the buyer is not obliged to return the goods. It is enough that he indicates to the seller that he has rejected them. On receipt of such notice, the seller is entitled to have the goods placed at his disposal so as to allow for his resumption of possession (*Kwei Tek Chao v British Traders & Shippers Ltd [1954] 2 QB 459* at p 488). Until the seller does resume possession, the buyer is a bailee of the goods and must take reasonable care of them (*Galbraith and Grant Ltd v Block [1922] 2 KB 155*).

Rights of unpaid seller   B1.32

The unpaid seller has a number of rights against the goods, and as to damages, as follows.

Lien

Even if property has passed, *SGA 1979* gives an unpaid seller a right to a lien for the price while he is in possession of the goods. The Act goes on to say that if property has not passed, the seller has the right to withhold delivery similar to an co-extensive with the right to a lien.

Although these rights exist only when the seller is in possession, a clause in the contract which gives the seller the right to resume possession in the event of default revives the lien once possession has been resumed (*Bines v Sankey [1958] NZLR 886*).

Stoppage in transit

SGA 1979 provides that where the buyer has become insolvent, the unpaid seller who has parted with possession may resume possession of the goods if they are in transit and retain them until payment. The position is the same whether or not property has passed.

Meaning of 'insolvency'

This is defined by *s 61(4)* of *SGA 1979* thus:

> 'A person is deemed to be insolvent within the meaning of this Act if he has either ceased to pay his debts in the ordinary course of business, or he cannot pay his debts as they fall due, whether he has committed an act of bankruptcy or not . . .'

The mere fact of insolvency is not by itself a repudiation of the contract. The trustee in bankruptcy can always tender the amount due to the seller.

Resale

SGA 1979 provides that the exercise of the right to a lien or to stop the goods in transit does not automatically end the contract. If such a buyer re-sells, however, then the Act further provides that the replacement buyer obtains a valid title.

Perishable goods

SGA 1979 further provides that where the goods are perishable, or the seller has given notice of his intention to resell, and the buyer still does not pay within a reasonable time, the seller can then resell the goods and recover any loss occasioned by the breach, such as having to sell for a lower price. Where the seller invokes a contractual right of resale in the event of default, the Act provides that the resale of the goods terminates the contract, but without prejudice to the seller's claim for damages.

Damages

SGA 1979 also gives the seller a right to claim damages where the buyer wrongfully neglects or refuses to accept and pay for the goods. The measure of damages is the estimated loss which directly and naturally results in the ordinary course of events from the breach.

SGA 1979 says that the *prima facie* measure of loss is the difference between the contract price and the market price at the time when the goods should have been accepted, or at the time of refusal to accept if no time was fixed for acceptance.

Claiming special loss

SGA 1979 makes it clear that this is only the *prima facie* measure and that, in appropriate circumstances, the seller can claim loss based, for example, on his loss of profit. To do so, he will have to show that the buyer contemplated such loss, on the basis of facts known to him when the contract was made, as a probable result of any breach (*Hadley v Baxendale (1854) 9 Ex 341*).

Action for price

Where property has passed and the buyer fails to pay, the seller is entitled by *SGA 1979* to sue for the price. There are no specific provisions as to the position where property has passed and the buyer wrongfully refuses to accept the goods. In such a case, the seller presumably has the option to sue for the price or to claim damages.

If property has not passed

The seller cannot sue for the price if property has not passed, since he is still the owner of the goods, and this is so even if it was the buyer who prevented property from passing (*Colley v Overseas Exporters [1921] 3 KB 302*). *SGA 1979* does provide that if the price is payable on a 'day certain', an action for the price can be brought, regardless of whether or not property has passed.

Rights of buyer   B1.33

The buyer has a number of rights against the goods, and as to damages, as follows.

Specific performance

Where there is a breach of a contract for specific or ascertained goods (that is, goods identified and agreed on at the time the contract is made), the buyer may seek under *SGA 1979* an order from the court specifically enforcing the contract without the seller being given the option of retaining the goods on payment of damages.

Discretionary nature of remedy

Specific performance, however, is a discretionary remedy, and not an order to which a buyer is automatically entitled. Generally, the courts will refuse an action if damages are an adequate remedy.

> **Case Example**: *Sky Petroleum Ltd v VIP Petroleum Ltd [1974] 1 All ER 954.*
>
> The claimants obtained an interlocutory injunction to restrain the defendants from breaking a contract to supply the claimants with all their petroleum requirements for ten years. The court treated the injunction as in effect a decree of specific performance, saying that the general rule against the grant of such a decree was inapplicable where damages would clearly not be an adequate remedy. In this case, there was a real danger that the claimants would be forced out of business if the defendants broke their contract at a time of exceptional disturbance in the oil market.

Damages

Where the seller wrongfully neglects or refuses to deliver the goods, the *SGA 1979* provides the buyer with an action in damages for non-delivery.

Prima facie measure

The *prima facie* measure of damages laid down is the difference between the contract price and the market price at the time when the goods ought to have been delivered, or the time of refusal to deliver if no time was fixed.

Where the breach relates to quality, the *SGA 1979* provides that the *prima facie* measure of damages is the amount by which the goods have been diminished in value.

Claiming special loss

The buyer will be able to displace the *prima facie* measure of damages and claim special damages. This can be done if the buyer can show that the seller, on the basis of facts known to him at the time the contract was made, contemplated that the special loss would be a probable result of any breach by him (*Hadley v Baxendale (1854) 9 Ex 341*).

> **Case Example**: *Re R&H Hall Ltd and WH Pim (Junior) & Co's Arbitration [1928] All ER Rep 763.*
>
> The sellers sold a specific cargo of corn in a specific ship to the buyers at 51 shillings and ninepence per quarter. The buyers resold at 56 shillings and ninepence but, when the vessel arrived, the market price had fallen to 53 shillings and ninepence. The sellers failed to deliver and the question was whether the measure of damages was the difference between the contract price and the resale price, or the contract price and the market price. It was held that the former was correct. The two critical factors werethat the sale was of a specific cargo on a specific ship and it was this same specific cargo which had been resold, and secondly the contract of sale by its terms actually provided for resale by the buyer in the sense that various contractual provisions dealt with this eventuality.

Checklist   B1.34

- Are you sure that the contract is one for sale, i.e. that it is one where property in the goods is to pass?

- Have you considered if this is one of the rare cases where the contract does require certain formalities?

- Are you certain that, as a seller, you can comply with the obligations as to title which are imposed on you; or have you considered the possibility of providing only a limited title?

- Are you satisfied that you will have no problems in meeting the statutory duties as to description, quality and fitness for purpose?

- Have you considered if the buyer might lose his rights in relation to fitness and quality by, for example, prior examination of the goods, or absence of reliance on the seller?

- Have you considered the possible use and effectiveness of any exclusion or limitation clauses?

- Have you considered whether you should make special provision as to the passing of property and risk, or are you content to rely on the statutory provisions?

- Are you aware of the exceptions to the basic rule that a person who has no valid title cannot himself pass a valid title?

- What provision has been made in the contract as to prompt payment? Are you aware that statutory interest may become payable?
- Are you aware of the duties relating to delivery of the goods and the position arising on delivery of too much or too little?
- Is provision made in the contract for a specific right to examine the goods?
- Are you aware of what constitutes acceptance of goods and of the consequences, in terms of remedies, of acceptance?
- Are you aware of the rights and duties of the parties in the event of rejection?
- Are you fully aware of the rights and remedies available to either party in the event of breach?

Precedent – Terms and Conditions of Sale; Specimen Contract

B1.35

1. GENERAL

These terms and conditions apply in preference to and supersede any terms and conditions referred to, offered or relied on by the buyer whether in negotiation or at any stage in the dealings between the parties with reference to the goods with which this contract is concerned. Without prejudice to the generality of the foregoing, the seller will not be bound by any standard or printed terms tendered by the buyer, unless the buyer specifically states in writing, separately from such terms, that it wishes such terms to apply and this has been acknowledged by the seller in writing.

> **Comment:**
>
> The aim of this clause is to ensure that the contract is solely on the seller's terms and conditions. It can, however, only operate if the seller ensures that the contract is made on his terms and conditions in the first place. To do this, he must ensure that he is the winner in the so-called 'battle of the forms' (see A1.7).

2. VARIATION

Neither the seller nor the buyer shall be bound by any variation, addition to, or amendment of these terms unless such is agreed in writing by the parties and signed on their behalf by a duly authorised party.

> **Comment**:
>
> Parties are always free to vary their agreements in whatever way they wish, and in whatever form. To avoid the problems which purely verbal variations may cause, this clause stipulates that changes must be in writing and signed. Even so, this clause cannot be regarded as foolproof, since a verbal agreement to override it is binding, if perhaps difficult to prove.

3. DESCRIPTION

Any description given or applied to these goods has been given by way of identification only and the use of such description shall not constitute a sale by description. For the avoidance of doubt, the buyer hereby affirms that he did not in any way rely on any description when entering into the contract.

> **Comment**:
>
> The *Sale of Goods Act 1979* implies into contracts of sale a condition that the goods will conform to that description and, if there is a breach, the buyer can rescind the contract and claim damages (for further information see B1.9 above). The implied condition operates only if there is a sale by description and if the buyer relied on the description, hence the wording of this clause. It is, however, subject to the reasonableness test imposed by the *Unfair Contract Terms Act 1977* and hence the seller will have to show it is reasonable if the buyer challenges it. Its success cannot be guaranteed, but it should be used just in case the seller can succeed in showing that the clause is reasonable.

4. SAMPLE

Notwithstanding that a sample of the goods might have been shown to and inspected by the buyer, the parties hereto accept that such sample was so shown and inspected for the sole purpose of enabling the buyer to judge for himself the quality of the bulk, and not so as to constitute a sale by sample.

> **Comment**:
>
> The aim of this clause is to avoid the terms otherwise implied in the case of a sale by sample. Since the clause is judged under the terms of the *Unfair Contract Terms Act 1977*, the comments made in relation to clause 3 above apply.

5. LIABILITY

(a)   No liability of any nature shall be incurred or accepted by the seller in respect of any representation made by the seller, or on his behalf, to the buyer, or to any party acting on his behalf, prior to the making of this contract where such representations were made or given in relation to:

   (i)   the correspondence of the goods with any description; or

   (ii)   the quality of the goods; or

   (iii) the fitness of the goods for any purpose(s) whatsoever.

(b)   No liability of any nature shall be accepted by the seller to the buyer in respect of any express term of this contract where such term relates in any way to:

   (i)   the correspondence of the goods with any description; or

   (ii)   the quality of the goods; or

   (iii) the fitness of the goods for any purpose(s) whatsoever.

(c)   All implied terms, conditions or warranties, statutory or common law, as to:

   (i)   the correspondence of the goods to any description; or

   (ii)   the satisfactory quality of the goods; or

   (iii) the fitness of the goods for any purpose whatsoever (whether made known to the seller or not) are hereby excluded from the contract.

(d)   Each provision of this clause is to be construed as a separate limitation, applying and surviving even if for any reason one or other of the foregoing provisions is held inapplicable or unreasonable in any circumstances, and shall remain in force notwithstanding termination of this contract.

Comment:

Clause 5(a) above attempts to exclude liability for a misrepresentation made prior to the contract. Such clauses are regulated by the *Misrepresentation Act 1967*. The position is that this clause will have no effect unless it can be shown to be reasonable.

Clause 5(b) is one of the two clauses which deals with the terms of a contract. It confines itself to express terms. The seller is attempting to exclude liability for any express terms incorporated into the contract. This clause too is subject to the reasonableness test set out in the *Unfair Contract Terms Act 1977*.

Clause 5(*c*) is intended to exclude liability for breach of those terms which otherwise would be implied into the contract by the *Sale of Goods Act 1979* but is again subject to the reasonableness test.

UCTA 1977 states that a clause is reasonable if it is 'a fair and reasonable one to be included' having regard to the circumstances known to the parties when the contract was made. The Act also provides a number of guidelines. Strictly, these apply only to cases concerning those contracts which contain a clause such as clause 5(*c*) above, but the courts have said on many occasions that the guidelines represent the factors to be taken into account whenever the issue of reasonableness is raised. There are three important guidelines which are set out below.

- **Bargaining strength.**

  This was a factor stressed by Lord Wilberforce in *Photo Production Ltd v Securicor Transport Ltd [1980] 1 All ER 556* who stated: 'After the [1977] Act, when the parties are not of unequal bargaining power, and when the risks are normally borne by insurance...there is everything to be said...for leaving the parties free to apportion the risks as they think fit and for respecting their decision'. This is, of course, not a factor which can be dealt with in the conditions of sale as it depends on extrinsic circumstances.

- **Choice.**

  A court is also to consider whether the buyer could have entered into a contract with a different party, but without the exclusion clause. It points to an alternative method of drafting, which is to offer the buyer a 'two tier system'. This would be a choice of business terms, with the seller accepting full liability for a higher price, but offering the goods at a lower price on terms which exclude liability. If the buyer chooses the latter, to save money, the courts are likely, though not certain, to find the clause reasonable.

- **Knowledge.**

  This guideline asks if the buyer 'knew or ought reasonably to have known of the existence and extent of the term'. This factor can be taken into account in the drafting. For example, the seller's position is likely to be weaker if the wording of the clause is complex, or the print is small and hardly legible, or the exclusion clause is hidden away in later clauses which are unlikely to be read. Some degree of clarity and prominence is therefore required.

Clause 5(d) has the self-evident aim of ensuring, should any of the clauses be held unreasonable, that the other clauses will remain in being. By also providing that the clause survives termination, clause 5(d) allows the exclusion clauses to be invoked in relation to claims accrued at the date of termination.

6. LIMITATION OF LIABILITY

Where any court or arbitrator determines that any part of Clause 5 above is, for whatever reason, unenforceable, the seller will accept liability for all loss or damage suffered by the buyer but in an amount not exceeding the contract price.

> **Comment**:
>
> This takes note of the fact that the total exclusion imposed by the pre-ceding clause could well fail the reasonableness test, and hence pro-poses an alternative approach. Even this, however, cannot be guaranteed success, since it too is subject to the reasonableness test. *UCTA 1977* says that the reasonableness of a limitation clause should be judged by reference to the resources which the relevant party could expect to be available for the purposes of meeting any liability, and how far it was open to that party to obtain insurance cover.
>
> In *Overseas Medical Supplies Ltd v Orient Transport Services Ltd [1999] 1 All ER (Comm) 981*, a contract of carriage contained terms limiting lia-bility to approximately £600. The contract also said that, by special agreement in writing, the carrier would accept a greater degree of lia-bility 'upon the customer agreeing to pay the company's additional charges for accepting such increased liability. Details of the company's additional charges will be provided on request'. There was also a clause providing for insurance cover to be effected if written instructions were given by the customer, and, when taking out a policy, the carrier would act as the customer's agent using its best endeavours to arrange such insurance. Instructions were given, but these were ignored. The clause was held to be unenforceable. The limit of £600 was said to be 'derisory'. The court noted that the carriers were offering the service of carriage and insurance, yet were limiting liability in each case. While there might well be cases involving package deals where a broad brush approach to limitation of liability might be reasonable, it was 'unjust and inappropriate' in the present case.
>
> Each case must be judged on its facts, and this case does not mean that a fixed limit is always unreasonable. On the other hand, it does indi-cate that a more flexible limitation should perhaps be considered. Sellers could, therefore, try limiting damages to 50% of all loss suffered. They should also ensure that they have insurance cover.

7. SELLER'S WARRANTY

The seller undertakes that it will, at its option, either repair or replace defective goods where defects are found notwithstanding the proper use of the goods, within [. . .] months from the date of delivery, provided that:

(*a*)   notice in writing of the claimed defects is given to the seller immediately on their appearance;

(*b*)   such defects are found to the seller's satisfaction to have arisen solely from faulty design, workmanship or materials; and

(*c*)   the goods claimed to be defective are returned to the seller at the expense of the buyer if so requested by the seller.

Any repaired or replacement goods shall be redelivered by the seller free of charge to the original point of delivery, but otherwise in accordance with these conditions of sale.

As an alternative to the above, the seller shall be entitled in its absolute discretion to refund the price of the defective goods in the event that such price has already been paid.

The remedies contained in this clause are without prejudice to the other terms of this contract, including, but without limitation, clauses 5 and 6 above.

Comment:

The aim of this clause is to give the seller a better chance of showing that clauses 5 and 6 are reasonable. Support for the efficacy of such clauses was given in *British Fermenetation Products Ltd v Compair Reavell Ltd [1999] 2 All ER (Comm) 389*, where the clause, linked to an exclusion clause, was said to represent 'good business sense'. The clause itself provided:

> 'If within 12 months after delivery there shall appear in the goods any defect which shall arise under proper use from faulty materials, workmanship, or design (other than a design made, furnished or specified by the purchaser for which the vendor had disclaimed responsibility), and the purchaser shall give notice thereof in writing to the vendor, the vendor shall, provided that the defective goods have been returned to the vendor if he shall have so required, make good the defects either by repair or, at his option, by the supply of a replacement. The vendor shall refund the cost of carriage on the return of the defective goods or parts and shall deliver any repaired or replaced goods or parts as if [the contract terms as to delivery] applied'.

8. ACKNOWLEDGMENT OF EXAMINATION

The buyer hereby acknowledges and accepts that he has satisfied himself as to the condition of the goods and acknowledges that no condition or warranty whatsoever has been given or is given by the seller as to their quality or fitness for any purpose and that all conditions or warranties whether express or implied and whether by statute or otherwise are expressly excluded and delivery of the goods to the buyer shall be conclusive evidence that the buyer has examined them and found them to be in complete accordance with the contract description, in good order and condition, of satisfactory quality and fit for any purpose for which they may be required.

Comment:

In *BTE Auto Repairs v H&H Factors Ltd (unreported, 26 January 1990)*, the county court was 'not impressed' by this clause, particularly since the relevant defects were not apparent at the time, indicating, perhaps that the clause might pass the reasonableness test under the *Unfair Contract Terms Act 1977* only in relation to patent defects The case went to the Court of Appeal but no definitive finding was made. In *EA Grimstead & Sons Ltd v McGarrigan (1999) (QBENF 97/1641/C)*, an examination clause was upheld as being reasonable.

This last case is also illustrative of the uses of such a clause as giving rise to an estoppel; that is to say, the buyer, having entered a contract with such clause, cannot later deny its effect. In the case, the clause ran:

> 'The purchaser confirms that it has not relied on any warranty representation or undertaking of or on behalf of the vendors (or any of them) or of any other person in respect of the subject matter of this agreement save for any representation or warranty or undertaking expressly set out in the body of this agreement and for the avoidance of doubt no representation or warranty is given in respect of any of the matters contained in Schedule 2 save in respect of the facts and to the extent as expressly therein stated'.

This was coupled with a clause which stated that the agreement set out the entire agreement between the parties, and which also stated that the other party had not relied on any representations, warranties or undertakings not set out in the agreement.

The Court of Appeal said that these clauses could act as an estoppel against the other party, but that this could be so only if three conditions were met, namely:

- the statement in the disputed clauses were clear and unequivocal;

- the purchaser had intended the other party to act on the statements in the clause; and

- the other party must have believed the statements to be true and to have acted on them.

The Court of Appeal held that the seller had failed in relation to this last requirement. In the absence of specific evidence, it would not be safe to conclude that the seller had entered into the agreement on the basis that the buyer was not relying on the relevant representations. If the representations had been made as alleged, then that could only to have been to persuade the buyer to enter the contract. In such a case, it would be open to hold that the seller knew that the acknowledgement of non-reliance clauses did not reflect the true position. If that were the case, then the seller could not rely on the estoppel which might otherwise have arisen.

Although the above cases suggest that it will always be very difficult to make use of non-reliance or examination clauses, there still remains the outside chance of success and they should be used. The chance of success would be enhanced if latent defects were specifically excluded; and if prominence were given to the clause as, perhaps, by placing it in a box or underlining it. This would support the argument that the buyer had accepted the clause specifically and that the seller had relied on that acceptance.

9. PRICE

(a)   All quotations and estimates issued by the seller are, except where expressly stated otherwise, subject to variation on or after acceptance.

(b)   Without prejudice to the generality of the forgoing, any change in the applicable rate of VAT or of any other Government tax or levy shall be to the buyer's account.

Comment:

There are no statutory controls on such clauses. It does not seems sustainable to argue that either clause purports to provide a performance substantially different from that which was reasonably expected within the *Unfair Contract Terms Act 1977* since nothing in it affects the seller's performance.

10. PAYMENT

(*a*)   Payment for goods supplied is due 30 days after delivery.

(*b*)   If payment of the price or any part thereof is not made by the due date, the seller shall be entitled to:

  (i)   charge interest on the outstanding amount at the rate of 9% per annum above the Bank of England's base rate, accruing daily;

  (ii) require payment in advance of delivery in relation to any goods not previously delivered;

  (iii) refuse to make delivery of any undelivered goods whether ordered under the contract or not and without incurring any liability whatever to the buyer for non–delivery or any delay in delivery;

  (iv) terminate the contract.

Comment:

One aspect to this clause − (*b*)(iv) − is that it overcomes the presumption contained in *s 10* of the *Sale of Goods Act 1979* that time of payment is not of the essence. If this presumption were not corrected, the seller could not terminate a contract for late payment.

At the same time, the clause extends credit to the buyer, when this is not required, since the basic position is that payment is due on conclusion of the contract.

The provision in (*b*)(ii) can readily be dispensed with, since the *Late Payment of Commercial Debts (Interest) Act 1998*, provides for interest to be payable on overdue bills of 8% above base rate, but the contract can provide for its own rate of interest, certainly where this provides for a 'substantial remedy', as it is put in *s 8* of the Act. It is even possible for an interest rate set just below the statutory rate of interest to be substantial. The one query which must remain is that if the contract sets an interest rate higher than the statutory rate, this could well constitute a penalty clause.

---

11. DELIVERY

The seller will deliver the goods carriage paid within the United Kingdom by such method of carriage as the seller may choose.

Comment:

Under this provision, the price includes the cost of delivery. The seller is always free to provide that the price is 'ex works', such that carriage charges are paid by the buyer. *Section 29* of the *SGA 1979* says that it depends on the express or implied terms of the contract as to whether it is for the buyer to collect the goods or for the seller to send them.

12. RISK

The risk in the goods will pass to the buyer at the moment the goods are dispatched from the seller's premises. Where the buyer chooses to collect the goods himself, risk will pass when the goods are entrusted to him or set aside for his collection, whichever happens first.

Comment:

This takes advantage of the provision in the *SGA 1979* that the parties are free to determine for themselves when risk is to pass. Since the buyer will have an insurable risk in the goods, even if property has not passed (see the following clause) the clause could indicate that the seller will arrange insurance cover on written request and at the buyer's expense.

13. PROPERTY

The property in the goods will not pass to the buyer until payment of the price has been made in full.

Comment:

This is the simplest form of retention of title clause and takes advantage of the provisions of the *SGA 1979* that the parties are free to make their own contract as to when property is to pass.

The real value of such clauses is that they offer the seller protection in case of the buyer's insolvency, since the seller can recover the goods as he has priority over other creditors of the buyer.

When drafting such clauses, it is crucial to reserve the whole title (as the above clause does) since anything less will reserve only what is called an equitable interest while still passing legal title to the buyer. An equitable interest is valid only if registered under the *Companies Act 1985 (Re Bond Worth [1980] Ch 228*).

The clause drafted above is useful when the contract relates to goods which are easily identifiable as the seller's property, such as unique capital goods and equipment, which often have identifying serial numbers.

There are certain useful ancillary provisions which could be added, such as those permitting the seller access to the buyer's premises to recover the goods.

ALTERNATIVE CLAUSES TO THE ABOVE

The following more elaborate clause could be considered to cover these various matters.

'Title in the goods will not pass to the buyer but shall be retained pending payment in full of the contract price. Until such time as title passes to the buyer, the seller shall have absolute authority to retake, sell or otherwise deal with or dispose of all or any part of the goods in which title remains vested in him.

For the purposes specified above, the seller or any of his agents or authorised representatives shall be entitled at any reasonable time during normal working hours to enter without notice onto any premises where the goods or any part of the goods are installed, stored or kept or are reasonably believed to be.

The seller shall also be entitled to seek an injunction to prevent the customer from selling, transferring or otherwise disposing of the goods.'

Comment:

It should be noted that, where a receiver contests a retention clause, but offers an undertaking to return the goods or their proceeds, the court is unlikely to grant an injunction (*Lipe Ltd v Leyland DAF [1994] 1 BCLC 84*). There is, though, nothing to stop the seller attempting to enforce his rights by refusing to deal with the receiver, by way of supply of further goods, unless the receiver chooses to return the goods immediately or pay their price (*Leyland DAF Ltd v Automotive Products plc [1994] 1 BCLC 245*).

It should always be remembered that, notwithstanding the presence of a retention clause, a buyer can still pass a good title in some circumstances to a third party. To cater for this possibility, the seller could extend the retention clause so that it provides:

'Where the buyer sells or disposes of the goods prior to full payment being received by the seller, the buyer shall pay the proceeds of such sale or disposition into a separate bank account clearly denoted as an account containing monies deposited for the benefit of the seller by the buyer acting in a fiduciary capacity'.

Such a clause would impose a trust in relation to the proceeds by virtue of the fiduciary relationship, with the result that the seller would be able to recover the proceeds which are easily identifiable as being held by him on trust in the separate account.

14. FORCE MAJEURE

If delivery is delayed by strikes, lock-outs, fire, accidents, defective materials, delays in receipt of raw materials or bought-in goods or components or any other cause beyond the reasonable control of the seller a reasonable extension of time shall be granted and the buyer shall pay such reasonable extra charges as shall have been occasioned by the delay. If the delay persists for such time as the seller considers unreasonable, he may, without liability on his part, terminate the contract.

Comment:

Such a clause is necessary, because English law generally only excuses breach of contract where the contract has become literally impossible to perform. The clause above extends this right and, since it seeks to excuse what would otherwise be a beach of contract, it will be valid only if reasonable under the provisions of the *UCTA 1977*. While success cannot be guaranteed, its limitation to events beyond the reasonable control of the seller should go some way to ensuring its validity.

15. DELAYED DELIVERY

If a firm delivery date is specifically provided for, and the seller fails to deliver the goods by such time for reasons other than matters beyond its reasonable control, the buyer shall be entitled to claim a reduction in price by giving the seller notice in writing within a reasonable time, unless it can be reasonably concluded from the circumstances that no loss has been suffered. Such reduction shall in no circumstances exceed 5% of the price.

> **Comment**:
>
> Since this clause limits liability, it will have to survive the reasonableness test laid down in the *Unfair Contract Terms Act 1977*. Bearing this in mind, the seller in an individual case, with full knowledge of the contract goods and their intended use, should adjust the limit so that it has a better chance of being proved reasonable.

16. RELATIONSHIP OF PARTIES

Nothing in this agreement shall be construed as establishing or implying any partnership or joint venture between the parties, and nothing in this agreement shall be deemed to constitute either of the parties as the agent of the other or authorise either party:

(*a*)   to incur any expense on behalf of the other party;

(*b*)   to enter into any engagement or make any representation or warranty on behalf of the other party;

(*c*)   to pledge the credit of, or otherwise bind or oblige the other party;

(*d*)   to commit the other party in any way whatsoever, without in each case obtaining the other party's' prior written consent.

> **Comment**:
>
> In the absence of any express provision such as this, many types of commercial agreement can set up unwanted relationships of agency or partnership between the parties. The general effect of any such relationship would be that one party could bind the other towards third parties, or one party could become liable to third parties in respect of acts or omissions of the other.
>
> If an agency or partnership is not a real possibility in the circumstances of a particular contract, this provision can be omitted.

17. ASSIGNMENT AND SUB-CONTRACTING

This agreement shall not be assigned or transferred, nor the performance of any obligation sub-contracted, in either case by the buyer, without the prior written consent of the seller.

> **Comment**:
>
> The case law on topics such as sub–contracting and assignment is complicated and not entirely certain. In addition, sub–contracting is often permitted under general law since the original party to the contract remains liable for the performance of the sub–contractor. As a result, these are matters which should be expressly regulated under the contract, particularly if the identity of the party is important.

18. COSTS AND OTHER EXPENSES

Except as specifically agreed to the contrary, any costs in relation to this agreement and its subject–matter which are incurred by either of the parties shall be borne in full by that party.

> **Comment**:
>
> On general legal principles, the costs of performance remain with the party who incurred them. The general law also provides as to which party is liable to bear sales or transfer taxes, VAT and stamp duties payable in respect of a transaction. It is useful to have these matters set out expressly, if only to avoid subsequent disagreements.

19. SEVERABILITY

If any terms or provision in this agreement shall be held to be illegal or unenforceable, in whole or in part, under any enactment or rule of law, such term or provision or part shall to that extent be deemed not to form any part of this agreement, but the validity and enforceability of the remainder of this agreement shall not be affected.

> **Comment**:
>
> This provision recognises that the provisions of the contract might turn out to be illegal (perhaps because of a subsequent change in the law) or unenforceable (perhaps because a clause is successfully challenged under the *UCTA 1977*.

20. TIME TO BE OF THE ESSENCE

Time shall be of the essence of this agreement, both as regards the dates and periods mentioned and as regards any dates and periods which may be substituted for them in accordance with this agreement or by agreement in writing between the parties.

> **Comment**:
>
> Where time is stated in a contract to be of the essence, failure to perform an obligation on time entitles the other party to terminate the contract immediately. Generally, time is not of the essence unless the contract actually says so, or by the subsequent service of a notice. Under English law, in a contract for the sale of goods, neither the time for payment nor of delivery are of the essence, unless expressly stated so in the contract. The above clause may be considered too severe in many cases, so it can always be drafted so as to apply only to particular clauses.

21. WAIVER

The waiver or forbearance or failure by or of a party in insisting in any one or more instances on the performance of any provision of this agreement shall not be construed in any circumstances as a waiver or abandonment of that party's rights to future performance of such provision and the other party's obligation in respect of such future performance shall continue in full force and effect.

> **Comment**:
>
> Under general principles, the failure of a party to enforce rights under an agreement can, in some circumstances, be construed as a waiver of those rights. Since parties often either deliberately or inadvertently fail to enforce their rights under an agreement, it is advisable to provide for this situation under express clauses.

22. PROPER LAW

This agreement shall be governed by and construed in accordance with English law and each party agrees to submit to the exclusive jurisdiction of the English courts as regards any claim or matter arising under this agreement.

> **Comment**:
>
> Such a clause can be useful if the parties to the contract are in differing jurisdictions (and remember that Scotland is a different jurisdiction to England).

23. ARBITRATION

Any disputes which arise out of or in connection with this agreement of whatsoever nature shall, if practicable, be settled by negotiation between the parties. If such disputes are not resolved within 21 days of such negotiations commencing, then the matter shall be referred to arbitration, the ruling in such arbitration being binding on the parties. The parties shall agree on the identity of the arbitrator and, in the event of their failure to agree, the arbitrator shall be appointed by the President of the London Chamber of Commerce.

> **Comment**:
>
> The fairly obvious point of this clause is to seek to have disputes resolved speedily and without recourse of expensive litigation.

24. DISPUTE SETTLEMENT

If any dispute arises between the parties with respect to any matter within the expertise of a technical expert, then such dispute shall at the instance of either party be referred to a person agreed between the parties, and, in default of agreement within 21 days of notice from either party to the other calling upon the other so to agree, to a person chosen on the application of either party by [insert appropriate body, such as British Computer Society]. Such person shall be appointed to act as an expert and not as an arbitrator and the decision of such person shall be final and binding. The costs of the expert shall be borne equally by the parties unless the expert decides that one party has acted unreasonably, in which case he shall have discretion as to the award of costs.

> **Comment**:
>
> Where the parties try to resolve a problem of fact, such as compliance with a technical specification, whether a particular standard has been reached, or the value of an item, it is possible (indeed advisable) to use an expert and to provide for his decision to be binding.

25. SET OFF

Whenever under this contract any sum of money is recoverable from or payable by any party, the same may be deducted from any sum then due or which at any time thereafter may become due to that party under this or any other contract between the parties. Any exercise of the rights granted by this contract shall be without prejudice to such other rights or remedies as may be available to the party exercising such right.

Comment:

The inclusion of an express right of set-off makes the use of this remedy easier, since the general law might impose some restrictions. The clause above is a wide one, since set-off is permitted not just of sums owed under the particular contract, but also of sums owed under other contracts with the party concerned.

Although the inclusion of such clauses is common, equally common are clauses excluding those rights, such as the following:

> 'All amounts due under this agreement shall be paid in full, without any deduction or withholding other than such as may be required by law, and the party owing such amounts shall not be entitled to assert any credit, set-off or counter-claim against the other party in order to justify the with-holding of payment of any such amount in whole or part'.

Such a term is, however, within the remit of the *Unfair Contract Terms Act 1977* and is valid only if it can be shown to be reasonable (*Stewart Gill Ltd v Horatio Myer & Co Ltd [1992] QB 600* and *Esso Petroleum v Milton [1997] 1 WLR 938*).

---

26. PRESERVATION OF RIGHTS

The provisions of this agreement, and the rights and remedies of the parties under this agreement, are cumulative and without prejudice and in addition to any rights or remedies a party may have at law or in equity; no exercise by a party of any right or remedy under this agreement, or in law or in equity, shall (save to the extent, if any, provided expressly in this agreement or at law or in equity) operate so as to hinder or prevent the exercise by it of any other such right or remedy.

Comment:

There is sometimes a presumption that the parties have written down the whole of the rules governing the relationship between them and, in so doing, have displaced any additional remedies that might otherwise be available. This clause preserves rights under the general law in addition to any specifically granted by the contract.

Chapter B2
Terms and Conditions
of Purchase

Checklist

- Are you sure that the contract is one for sale, that is to say it is one where property in the goods is to pass?

- Have you considered if this is one of the rare cases where the contract does require certain formalities?

- Are you certain that, as buyer, you will benefit fully from the implied the obligations as to title; or, as a buyer, have you considered the possibility that you might be getting only a limited title?

- Are you, as buyer, satisfied that you will have the benefit of the statutory duties imposed on the seller as to description, quality and fitness for purpose?

- Are you, as buyer, sure that you have not lost your rights in relation to fitness and quality by, for example, your prior examination of the goods, or your absence of reliance on the seller?

- Have you considered the possible use and effectiveness of any exclusion or limitation clauses?

- Have you considered whether you should make special provision as to the passing of property and risk, or are you content to rely on the statutory provisions?

- Are you aware of the exceptions to the basic rule that a person who has no valid title cannot himself pass a valid title?

- What provision has been made in the contract as to prompt payment? Are you aware that statutory interest may become payable?

- Are you aware of the duties relating to delivery of the goods and the position arising on delivery of too much or too little?

- Is provision made in the contract for a specific right to examine the goods?

- Are you aware of what constitutes acceptance of goods and of the consequences, in terms of remedies, of acceptance?

- Are you aware of the rights and duties of the parties in the event of rejection?

- Are you fully aware of the rights and remedies available to you in the event of breach?

Precedent – Terms and Conditions of Purchase; Specimen Contract

B2.2

1. GENERAL

These terms and conditions apply in preference to and supersede any other terms and conditions referred to, offered or relied on by the supplier whether in negotiation, and howsoever presented, at any stage in the dealings prior to conclusion of this contract. Without prejudice to the generality of the foregoing, the buyer will not be bound by any standard or printed terms presented by the seller in any of its documents, unless the seller specifically states, in writing, separately from such terms that it intends such terms to apply and the buyer separately acknowledges such notification in writing.

Comment:

The clear aim of this clause is to ensure that it is the buyer's terms and conditions which will prevail. To do this, the buyer will have to take care that he is the winner in any 'battle of the forms'.

An alternative version could read as follows.

'This agreement hereby cancels all previous agreements (if any) between the parties relating to the subject matter of this agreement, and also cancels and nullifies all rights (if any) of either party arising against the other by virtue of all or any of the said prior agreements, or any of the provisions thereof, notwithstanding the existence of any provision in any such prior agreement that any such rights or provisions shall survive its termination.'

Comment:

It is important to refer to the survival provisions of the previous agreement or the cancellation may be incomplete.

---

2. VARIATION

Neither party to this contract shall be bound by any variation, waiver of, or addition to these conditions except where such is agreed to in writing by both parties and signed on behalf of each.

Comment:

There is always a level of concern that employees in the buyer's organisation may prejudice the position of the organisation by agreeing on some change to the contract. If the relevant employee is part of the purchasing department, he will often appear to have the relevant authority, and thus be able to commit the organisation. Although, in legal principle, such variations may well not be enforceable, since no consideration is supplied for the variation, incorporation of such a clause as the above should avoid such problems from the outset.

An alternative clause to the above is:

> 'The parties may expressly agree in writing on any variation in the terms of this contract, provided that, unless expressly so agreed, no such agreement shall constitute or be construed as a general waiver of any of the provisions of this contract by any of the parties and the rights and obligations of the parties shall remain in full force and effect notwithstanding any variation agreed between the parties on any particular occasion'.

---

3. QUALITY ETC. OF GOODS

The supplier warrants and guarantees that all goods supplied under this agreement will be free from any defects, patent or latent, in material and workmanship, conform to applicable specifications and drawings and, to the extent that detailed designs were not provided by the buyer, will be free from design defects and in every aspect suitable for the purposes intended by the buyer, as to which the supplier hereby acknowledges that he has had due notice. The approval by the buyer of any designs provided by the seller shall not relieve the seller of its obligations under any provision contained in this term.

Comment:

The above clause restates the provisions which would be implied into the contract by virtue of the *Sale of Goods Act 1979* as to description,

---

quality and fitness for purpose. It also removes any doubt as to the applicability of the term as to fitness for purpose by avoiding any argument from the supplier that there was no reliance on his skill or judgement, or that such reliance was unreasonable. It is always useful for the supplier's duties to be clearly spelled out in the contract, not least because businessmen cannot be assumed to know of the statutory provisions.

The above clause could usefully be supplemented with a statement of the buyer's remedies and the period of time for which they are applicable. The following also contains a 'revolving warranty' in that the relevant repaired or replaced item can itself be repaired or replaced until it lasts for the appropriate time. The suggested addition is:

'The seller's obligations under this clause shall extend to any defect or non-conformity arising or manifesting itself within [period] from delivery. The buyer, without thereby waiving any rights or remedies otherwise provided by law and/or elsewhere in this agreement, may require the supplier:

(*a*)   to make good or replace such items at the seller's risk and expense, or

(*b*)   to refund such portion of the price as is equitable under all the circumstances.

Items repaired or replaced shall be subject to the provisions of this agreement in the same manner as those originally delivered under the agreement. If the supplier refuses or fails promptly to repair or replace items when requested under this provision, the buyer may itself, or through an agent or sub-contractor, or otherwise, repair or replace any item himself and the seller agrees to reimburse the buyer for any costs or expenses incurred'.

4. GUARANTEE AS TO TITLE

The supplier:

(*a*)   holds full clear and unencumbered title to all of the goods;

(*b*)   will on the date of delivery hold such title in and to all the goods; and

(*c*)   will on the date of delivery have the full and unrestricted right, power and authority to sell, transfer and deliver all of the goods to the buyer at which point the latter will acquire a valid and unencumbered title to the goods.

Comment:

This clause restates the provisions of the *SGA 1979* as to title (implied terms as to title), and hence make the supplier fully aware of his obligations at the outset. It should be remembered that, even if there is a breach of this provision, the buyer will in some circumstances be able to act as though he did have full title in the goods (transfer of title by non-owner).

5. PRICE

The prices stated in the contract are inclusive of all taxes and cannot be varied without the express prior consent of the buyer given in writing and signed by a duly authorised party.

Comment:

Many buyers think that, unless the contract expressly states the price to be fixed, the supplier is entitled to increase the cost to cover any increase in overheads since the agreement was made. In fact, the true legal position is that the price is fixed unless the contract itself states to the contrary. The above clause clarifies the position.

6. PAYMENT OF THE PRICE

The buyer will pay for the goods at the end of the month following the month in which the goods are received or in which the invoice for such goods is received, whichever is the later. In the event of late payment by the buyer, he shall be liable to pay the seller interest at a rate which compensates him for such loss as has been directly caused by late payment so long as this does not exceed the rate of statutory interest provided for in the *Late Payment of Commercial Debts (Interest) Act 1998*. In no circumstances shall the time for payment be of the essence of the agreement.

Comment:

Under the *SGA 1979*, any time stated for payment is not of the essence unless the contract states otherwise. The final sentence to this clause ensures that time for payment is not of the essence. In the event of late payment, however, there will still be a breach, for which the seller is entitled to compensation. Under the *Late Payment of Commercial Debts (Interest) Act 1998*, statutory interest of 4% above base rate is automatically payable by the buyer. *Section 8 of the LPCD(I)A*

1998 however, allows for contracting out so long as the contract provides for a 'substantial remedy'. A remedy is 'substantial', by virtue of *LPCD(I)A 1998, s 9*, unless it is insufficient for the purpose of compensating the seller or deterring late payment; and if it would not be fair and reasonable to allow the remedy stated in the contract to stand.

The above clause seeks to avoid payment of statutory interest, but still to ensure that the seller is compensated for his loss. An alternative approach would be to specify that any interest payable by the buyer shall be no more than 2% above base rate. In most cases, this would be enough to meet the requirements for a substantial remedy.

7. DELIVERY

The goods are to be delivered, carriage paid, to such location as the buyer shall direct. Any time agreed between the parties for such delivery shall be of the essence of the contract.

Comment:

The *SGA 1979* provides that it is a question of fact whether any stipulations as to time are of the essence. By making delivery time of the essence, the buyer thus secures his right to terminate the contract and to seek damages where the date for delivery is not met.

The Act also provides that it is up to the parties to specify whether the buyer is to collect the goods or have them sent; and that the goods are to be delivered to the buyer's place of business unless the contract says otherwise. The above clause clarifies the position in the buyer's favour.

8. DELIVERY IN INSTALMENTS

Unless agreed by the parties in writing, and in a document signed on the buyer's behalf, delivery is not to be made in instalments. Where there is such an agreement (or where the buyer agrees in any case to accept delivery in instalments), breach in relation to any instalment, of whatsoever nature, shall entitle the buyer, without prejudice to such other remedies as he might have, to terminate the contract and to claim damages.

Comment:

The *SGA 1979* states that the buyer is not obliged to accept instalments unless the contract states otherwise. It also states that where a contract is for separate instalments, it depends on the terms of the contract and the circumstances of the case as to whether a breach in relation to any instalment results in a repudiation of the entire contract. Although the Act requires satisfaction of two conditions, it must inevitably be the case that a specific term of the contract as above would allow the buyer to repudiate the entire agreement in the event of a breach in relation to just one instalment.

9. PASSING OF PROPERTY

The property in the goods will pass to the buyer when the goods are unconditionally appropriated (by either party or by or with the consent of either party) to the contract, or on delivery to the buyer, whichever happens first.

Comment:

The *SGA 1979* sets out a number of rules as to when property is to pass. These, however, apply only if the contract is silent on this point. The above clause takes advantage of this and ensures that property, which can be regarded as full ownership of the goods, passes from the earliest possible moment.

10. PASSING OF RISK

The goods will be and shall remain at the seller's risk until such time as they are delivered to the buyer (or at his direction), and are found to be in accordance with the requirements of the contract. It shall be the duty of the seller at all times to maintain a contract of insurance over the goods and, on request from the buyer, to assign to the buyer the benefits of such insurance. Without prejudice to the generality of the foregoing, the seller accepts the risk of deterioration in the goods which is necessarily incident to the course of transit.

Comment:

The *SGA 1979* provides that risk passes with property unless otherwise agreed. The above clause takes advantage of this and, taken with the previous clause, gives the buyer property from the earliest possible moment, while delaying the passing of risk until the last.

The final part of the clause derives from a further provision in the Act which states that where the seller agrees to deliver at his own risk the

> buyer must still – unless the contract provides to the contrary – take any risk of deterioration which is necessarily incident to the course of transit. In *Bull v Robison (1854) 10 Ex 342*, steel was despatched by carrier and rusted in transit. This was held to be a normal incident of the journey. In *Mash & Murrell Ltd v Joseph I Emmanuel Ltd [1962] 1 WLR 862*, potatoes deteriorated during transit from Cyprus to England. This was said not to be a normal incident of the journey but happened because of a defect in the goods when the journey got under way.

11. ACCEPTANCE

The buyer shall not be deemed to have accepted the goods until such time as, in writing signed by him, he has notified the seller that he has accepted the goods as being in complete compliance with the requirement. Notwithstanding any such acceptance as aforesaid, the buyer will remain entitled to reject the goods and to claim damages if, within [period] of any such written notice, the goods are found not to be in complete compliance as aforesaid.

> **Comment**:
>
> Acceptance of goods eliminates the right of the buyer to reject the goods for breach of contract. Under the *SGA 1979*, acceptance can take place when acceptance is intimated; for example after the lapse of a reasonable time, or when the buyer does an act inconsistent with the seller's ownership. Although the provisions stated in the Act as to acceptance are not stated to apply unless the parties agree otherwise, it is assumed that they are nevertheless free to specify in the contract just when acceptance takes place.
>
> An alternative formulation of this clause is:
>
> > 'If any of the goods, or the packages containing the goods, do not comply with the order or with any term of this contract including those relating to quantity, quality or description, the buyer shall be entitled to reject those goods or any part at any time after delivery, regardless of whether the buyer is to be regarded under the *SGA 1979* or otherwise as having accepted them. Any acceptance of such goods by the buyer shall be without prejudice to any rights that buyer might have against the supplier. The buyer shall be entitled to return any rejected goods, carriage paid by the supplier, at the risk of the supplier'.

12. NON-DELIVERY

If the supplier does not deliver the goods or any part within the time specified in the contract, the buyer will be entitled to terminate the contract, purchase other goods of the same or similar description, and to recover from the seller the amount by which the cost of so purchasing exceeds the price which would have been payable to the supplier in respect of the goods replaced by such purchase, and all without prejudice to any other remedy for breach of contract (see clause 13 below).

Comment:

In one sense, this condition is superfluous, since it essentially restates the law as expressed in the *SGA 1979* and as it also exists at common law. Its presence is due to the fact that it alerts the supplier to his duties, and thus avoids any possible recourse to litigation. Linked with the provision in clause 7 above, making time of delivery of the essence, this clause allows the buyer to take action if the goods are only, say, one day late. It will always be an option for the buyer, of course, to accept delivery of the goods in such a case (see clause 20 below).

The general rules about damages, based on the ruling in *Hadley v Baxendale (1854) 9 Ex 341*, is found in *s 51* of the *SGA 1979* which provides that an action for damages for non-delivery is available 'where the seller wrongfully neglects or refuses to deliver the goods', going on to say that damages will normally be 'the difference between the contract price and the market or current price of the goods at the time or times when they ought to have been delivered'.

---

13. CONSEQUENTIAL LOSS

Without prejudice to clause 12 above, or to such other rights as the buyer might have under statute or at law, the supplier shall also be liable, in the event of any breach of contract, for all indirect or direct consequential loss following from the breach.

Comment:

The aim of this clause is in some ways to side-step the difficulties caused by *Hadley v Baxendale* and the *SGA 1979* which state that the type of loss covered here is available only if the supplier had specific knowledge of all the relevant circumstances (such as that the buyer was buying for the purposes of a profitable resale) which might produce such loss in the event of a breach.

The presence of this clause will overcome the problems inherent in decisions such as *Victoria Laundry (Windsor) Ltd v Newman Industries Ltd [1949] 2 KB 528*. Here the defendants contracted to supply the claimants with a boiler. They knew that it was to be put to immediate use in the claimants' laundry business. The boiler was delivered several months late, and the claimants sued for profits lost because of the delay. The Court of Appeal held that the defendants were liable for the loss of profit which naturally flowed from their breach, but that they were not liable for the loss of profit on some exceptionally lucrative Government contracts. The defendants had not known of the existence of these contracts at the time the contract had been made. Had the contract contained such a clause as the above, the further losses could also have been recovered.

14. INDEMNITY

The supplier shall indemnify the buyer against all those claims, costs and expenses which the buyer may incur and which arise, directly or indirectly, from the supplier's breach of any of its obligations under this contract.

Comment:

This again is essentially a clause which states what the legal position is anyway. It makes it plain to the supplier that should the buyer, for example, incur costs through defending an action in relation to the goods (they might be defective and cause damage to a third party, or infringe a third party's patent or trade mark), then the supplier will be liable for such costs as legal fees.

15. ASSIGNMENT AND SUB-CONTRACTING

The supplier shall not assign or transfer the whole or any part of this contract, or sub-contract the production or supply of any goods to be supplied under this contract, without the prior written consent of the buyer.

Comment:

Since buyers pay much attention to the quality of the goods produced by prospective suppliers, they will generally not want the supplier to hand over the contract to a third party. This will be despite the fact that the original supplier will remain liable on the contract and hence responsible for any failures on the part of the third party. The general rule is that a contract can be assigned or sub-contracted unless it is evident in all the circumstances that a supplier was chosen for his unique qualities. This clause changes the rules to prevent any assignment or sub-contracting without prior written consent.

There will, of course, be cases such as where the contract is for the supply of a computer, where the manufacturer could well obtain some components from a third party. In such cases, this clause can be removed, since the buyer will obtain adequate protection by drafting the contract specifications in as clear and tight a way as possible. Alternatively, the clause could be retained but have the following wording added to the end:

'. . . provided that such consent shall not be necessary where any assignment or sub-contracting is necessary for the due performance of the contract by the supplier'.

16. FORCE MAJEURE

The buyer shall not be liable for any failure to fulfil its obligations under the contract where such failure is caused by circumstances beyond its reasonable control.

Comment:

It can be the case that the events which prevent a buyer from carrying out the contract will cause the contract to be frustrated, so that no liability would arise anyway. On the other hand, frustration is narrowly defined as occurring 'whenever the law recognises that without default of either party a contractual obligation has become incapable of being performed because the circumstances in which performance is called for would render it a thing radically different from that which was undertaken by the contract' (*Davis Contractors Ltd v Fareham UDC [1956] AC 696*).

It is unlikely that, for example, industrial action, or the drying up of the sole source of supply of an essential ingredient, would count as frustration. In *The Super Servant Two [1990] 1 Lloyd's Rep 1*, the defendants agreed to carry the claimants' drilling rig in one of two barges owned by them. The defendants scheduled barge A for use in other contracts, and barge B for use in this contract. The latter was destroyed in an accident. The Court of Appeal said that the contract was not frustrated since it had been the defendants' choice to use barge B in performance of the contract. It is arguable that the above clause would have relieved the defendants in this case.

The above clause can be varied in two main ways.

- As well as using the broad phrase 'circumstances beyond its reasonable control', specific causes can be identified as potentially disrupting the contract, for example fire, flood, or industrial disputes. If such illustrations are added, they should be accompanied by the phrase 'without prejudice to the generality of this clause', so as to make it clear that these examples are illustrative only and that the clause is not limited to such examples.

- The clause might be drafted so as to provide for an extension of time. Since it can rarely be clear in advance how long a particular circumstance will prevail, the clause should do no more than provide for the suspension of the contract 'for a reasonable time, such to be in the sole discretion of the buyer'.

A further question is whether such clauses are valid under the provisions of the *UCTA 1977*. Since the clause seeks to excuse what would otherwise be a breach of contract by the buyer, it will be valid only if shown to be reasonable. Given that it applies to circumstances beyond the buyer's reasonable control, the clause should be regarded favourably.

17. PROPER LAW

This contract shall be governed by and construed in accordance with English law. Each party agrees to submit to the non-exclusive jurisdiction of the English courts as regards any claim or matter arising under this contract.

> **Comment**:
>
> The grant of exclusive jurisdiction to the English courts does not prevent the use of an arbitration clause (see the following clause).

18. ARBITRATION

All disputes and differences which arise out of or in connection with this contract or its construction, operation, termination or liquidation shall, if practicable, be settled by means of negotiation between the parties. If the parties cannot settle any such dispute or difference within 28 days after first conferring, then such dispute or difference shall be settled by arbitration. The place, date and the arbitrator shall be agreed between the parties or, where the parties cannot so agree within a further 28 days, by the London Chamber of Commerce.

Comment:

The value of this clause is that it can enable disputes to be settled promptly and without undue expense. Provision should always be made for an independent third person to appoint an arbitrator if the parties cannot themselves agree on an appointment.

19. SUPERVENING ILLEGALITY

If any term of this contract is held by any court of law or in arbitration to be illegal or unenforceable, in whole or in part, such term or part shall to that extent be deemed not to be part of this contract, and the validity of the remainder of the contract shall not be affected.

Comment:

It is always possible that a subsequent change in the law can render a contract term unenforceable or illegal, or that a clause is deemed unenforceable, if it is found to fail the reasonableness test imposed by the *Unfair Contract Terms Act 1977*. The above clause seeks to overcome any problems which this might cause. It may be, however, that the invalid clause was central to the contract, with the result that its disappearance could fundamentally alter the nature of the contract. To cover this, the following words can be added:

> 'Provided that, where the buyer is of the view that it would not have entered into the contract in the absence of the particular term, it may terminate the contract forthwith by notice in writing to the supplier and without liability on its part, but without prejudice to such rights on its part which had already accrued'.

20. WAIVER

Any waiver by the buyer of its rights under this contract shall not be construed as a waiver of its rights in any future case and the supplier's obligations in respect of future performance shall continue in full force and effect.

Comment:

It is always possible for a court to rule that a party's failure to enforce its rights has amounted to a permanent waiver of those rights. This clause avoids this by providing that an instance of forbearance does not amount to a waiver of the same obligation in the future. Since a forbearance can actually happen by inadvertence, a clause such as this is essential.

21. COSTS AND OTHER EXPENSES

Except as specifically agreed to the contrary, any costs in relation to this agreement and its subject–matter which are incurred by either of the parties shall be borne in full by that party.

Comment:

On general legal principles, the costs of performance remain with the party who incurred them. The general law also provides as to which party is liable to bear sales or transfer taxes, VAT and stamp duties payable in respect of a transaction. It is useful to have these matters set out expressly, if only to avoid subsequent disagreements.

22. FURTHER ASSURANCES

The supplier agrees to use its best endeavours to do, or cause to be done, all those things which are necessary, proper, or advisable to execute this contract including, without limitation, the performance of such further acts or the execution and delivery of any additional instruments or documents as may be necessary, and to obtain any permits, approvals or licences which may be required for the proper performance of this contract.

Comment:

It is always possible that the performance of a contract requires other documents to be produced or obtained, such as formal assignments of a contract, the transfer of intellectual property rights, or approvals from regulatory authorities. Although an obligation to do these things is probably implied by law, it is convenient for them to be spelled out in the contract.

23. NO PARTNERSHIP ETC

This contract shall not operate so as to create a partnership or joint venture of any kind, or make either party the agent of the other.

Comment:

In the absence of an express clause such as this, many types of commercial agreement could set up unwanted relationships between the parties. If, for example, an agency were constituted, one party could bind the other to third parties, or one party could become liable to third parties in respect of the acts or omissions of the other.

Other possible clauses   **B2.3**

Packaging   **B2.4**

If the buyer has detailed requirements, these may be specified in a separate condition Such requirements may arise because the goods have to be shipped by sea or air, handling facilities in the buyer's warehouse might need special containers or pallets, or detailed information is required on the outside of the package to ensure safe use by employees or purchasers.

Instruction manuals   **B2.5**

With complex items such as computers, instruction manuals will be crucial to proper use. The supplier can be placed under a contractual obligation to provide these facilities, perhaps also extending to instruction courses.

Spares and after sales service   **B2.6**

Some machines and equipment can be serviced only by the manufacturer and, unless spares continue to be available, the goods can become unusable. In *L Gent & Sons (a firm) v Eastman Machine Co Ltd [1986] BTLC 17*, it was held that where there is no trade custom to such effect, a buyer has no cause of action where the contract does not contain an express term to the effect that a supply of spare parts will be available. Furthermore, where there is no such custom, a failure by a supplier to have spare parts is not of itself grounds for alleging that the goods are not of satisfactory quality. Accordingly, the existence of spare parts should be a matter actively considered by buyers in appropriate cases.

Performance tests   **B2.7**

Where the seller is to design an item to meet certain standards and performance criteria, the buyer will generally require tests to be carried out to satisfy him that these standards and criteria have been reached. The contract will need to provide for the type of tests to be carried out, the time, place and allocation of costs of such tests, and for the effect of any failure.

Cancellation   **B2.8**

A somewhat stringent clause sometimes inserted by buyers gives them the right to cancel the contract regardless of any breach. Since such an arbitrary clause would be unreasonable under the *UCTA 1977*, it should at the very least state that the buyer will pay for goods which have been wholly or partly manufactured prior to cancellation, as well as for the cost of materials bought in and which now cannot be used.

Confidentiality   **B2.9**

Where, in the course of design and manufacture, confidential information, drawings, specifications and other materials come into the hands of the seller, the buyer may wish to provide expressly that the seller will keep such matters confidential, and will return all such drawings and documents on completion of the contract.

Insolvency   **B2.10**

The insolvency of the seller will not bring an end to the contract unless this is expressly provided for in the contract. If the seller does have financial difficulties, the buyer, particularly if the contract is a long term one, may wish to terminate the contract and seek a more secure source of supply.

Chapter B3
Licence of Computer Software

At a glance   B3.1

- Draft to favour the Buyer.
- Covers licence of software and provision of computer support services.
- Detailed contract.

Commentary   B3.2

- This standard contract should be used by companies wishing to take a licence of computer software from a software licensor for relatively major procurements where the Supplier's standard software licence is inadequate or too one-sided.

- The agreement also includes software support. If the Buyer will not be taking software support from the Supplier then this contract should not be used.

- These kinds of contract vary substantially in practice. Rarely will any example such as this be appropriate for every arrangement or Supplier/Buyer. Customisation, ideally after taking legal advice, is usually necessary.

- The contract lists the main 'variables' such as the parties' names on the front page. This could instead be on a schedule. It is simply a matter of personal preference.

- In clause 3.1(a) the contract allows for one named software package to be supplied or as an alternative for the contract to be set up for all future purchases of software from time to time ordered and documented by the parties.

- Clause 3.1 sets out the various supplies which the Supplier/licensor may undertake including software support and also training. This will vary from contract to contract.

- Clause 4 sets out strong warranties which protect the Buyer. A licensor would not want such stringent requirements. Strong Buyers are often however able to negotiate such provisions.

- Clause 5 contains the software licence clause. The Buyer needs to consider carefully the full extent of any licence which is required. Issues to consider include where the software may be used and by what legal entities, whether an outsourcing or facilities management company acting on behalf of the Buyer may use the software or not and whether there may be any special considerations such as a proposed future sale of assets which should be anticipated in the licence clause. Clause 5.2 sets out the different kinds of licence which a user may require. Often a Supplier will charge very different fees depending on which of these kinds of licence are envisaged.

- Clause 7 is a fairly stringent security clause. Buyers not so concerned about conduct of Supplier personnel at their premises may not require the entirety of these provisions.

- Clause 8 provides that the secret source code part of the software which is needed to repair faults and which rarely does the Supplier give to the Buyer will be lodged to protect the Buyer with a third party 'escrow agent'. NCC Global is suggested as an agent, although other software escrow agents exist. The agent should be one familiar with software and ideally with the expertise to undertake verification of what is lodged. Whether Supplier or Buyer pays the fees which are typically a few hundred pounds is a matter of negotiation in each case. If instead the contract provided that the Supplier would hand the source code to the licensee if the Supplier went out of business or failed to support the software then there is a risk that may not happen. In the situation of a liquidation the liquidator of the Supplier would have a right to set aside onerous contracts under insolvency legislation, hence the necessity for deposit with a third party. If a Buyer is able to negotiate possession of source code of course, which is rare, that is even better.

- Clause 9 provides for payment and is drafted in the Buyer favour.

- Clause 11 is an intellectual property indemnity clause which all licensees of software will require. Software is protected by copyright and it is hard for a licensee to check, as the right in the UK is unregistered, whether the licensor is the true owner of the rights; thus an indemnity which should protect the licensee in the event that the licensee is sued where the software infringes a third party right, is common. Even Suppliers in their own standard software licence agreements will include such a provision.

- Clause 15.1 excludes both parties' liability for consequential loss to the other. A very tough Buyer might not include such a provision but every Supplier will require it so it is better that it is in the standard contract of the Buyer.

- Appendix 1 is the maintenance schedule and is only relevant if software support is to be provided by the other party.

- Appendix 2 would set out a description of the software.

- Appendix 3 would contain any detail about training to be provided.

Precedent – Licence of Computer Software and Purchase of Support Services

B3.3

Contract Number: _____

Estimated Contract Value: _____

Contract relating to:

The supply of software and related services.

[date]

CONTRACT

Between

'Buyer': _____Ltd

Registered Office: _____

Company Number: _____; and

'Supplier': _____Ltd

Registered Office: _____

Company Number: _____

For the fees set out in this Agreement paid by the Buyer, the Supplier shall supply to the Buyer such software and services (as the case may be) as the Buyer may order from time to time within the Contract Period in accordance with this contract which comprises this front sheet and the following appended documents:

Number	Description
1	Conditions
2	Appendix 1 – Maintenance
3	Appendix 2 – Software, Licence Types and Pricing
4	Appendix 3 – Training

These, in the case of conflict, have precedence in the order listed.

Signed for and on behalf of the Supplier (name, position):

_____   _____

Signed for and on behalf of the Buyer (name, position):

_____   _____

CONDITIONS

1. DEFINITIONS

In the Contract, the following expressions shall have the meanings, if any, ascribed to them:

- 'Acceptance' – deemed acceptance of the Supplies by the Buyer in accordance with the Condition headed 'Faulty Supplies'. 'Accept' and 'Accepted' in the context of 'Acceptance' shall be construed accordingly.

- 'Buyer' – _____Ltd, its successors and assigns and, for the purposes of all obligations of the Supplier and of all rights and licences granted by the Supplier, all companies within the Buyer's group of companies.

- 'Buyer's Commercial Contact' – _____

- 'Commencement Date' – _____

- 'Contract' – this contract.

- 'Contract Price' – the total sum payable to the Supplier by the Buyer for Supplies.

- 'Contract Period' – ____ years from Commencement Date.

- 'Contract Personnel' – the Supplier's employees, sub-contractors and agents (and their employees, sub-contractors and agents) engaged in the performance of the Contract.

- 'Functional Specification' – the Supplier's functional specification for the Software as supplied to the Buyer or as published by the Supplier.

- 'Information' – information whether written or oral or any other form, including, but not limited to, documentation, specifications, reports, data, notes, drawings, models, patterns, samples, software, computer outputs, designs, circuit diagrams, inventions, whether patentable or not and know-how.

- 'Intellectual Property Right(s)' – any patent, petty patent, registered design, copyright, database right, design right, semiconductor topography right, know-how, or any similar right exercisable in any part of the world and shall include any applications for the registration of any patents or registered designs or similar registrable rights in any part of the world.

- 'Site' – premises specified by the Buyer, upon which the Supplier is to install and/or deliver Supplies.

- 'Software' – all the Supplier's proprietary computer programs that may be supplied to the Buyer under the Contract as currently listed in Appendix 2 (including all updates, enhancements, modifications, versions, and all replacement or amendment products from time to time offering the same or similar functionality) and all appropriate documentation necessary to enable their proper operation and functionality.

- 'Supplier's Commercial Contact' – _____

- 'Supplies' – all Software and related services to be supplied to the Buyer under the Contract.

- 'Support Period' – _____ years.

- 'Virus' – any code which is designed to disrupt, disable, harm, or otherwise impede in any manner, including aesthetic disruptions or distortions, the operation of the Software, or any other associated hardware, software, firmware, computer system or network, or would disable the Software or impair in any way its operation based on the elapsing of a period of time, exceeding an authorised number of copies, advancement to a particular date or other numeral, or that would permit the Supplier or any other person to access the Software to cause such disablement or impairment, or which contains any other similar harmful, malicious or hidden procedures, routines or mechanisms which would cause such programs to cease functioning or to damage or corrupt data, storage media, programs, equipment or communications, or otherwise interfere with operations. It includes, without limitation, computer programs commonly referred to as worms or Trojan horses.

2. DURATION

The Contract shall last for the Contract Period unless ended sooner in accordance with its terms.

3. SUPPLY

3.1   The Supplier shall:

(a)   supply, deliver and install [the Software] [such Software as is ordered by the Buyer from time to time during the Contract Period] at the respective Sites specified by the Buyer;

(b)   maintain the Software in accordance with Appendix 1 for a period of 12 months from its respective Acceptance at no additional charge to the Buyer;

(c)   if so requested by the Buyer in writing, maintain the Software in accordance with Appendix 1 within the Support Period (or any part of it as required by the Buyer) at the price stated in the Contract, or, if no such price is stated, at a fair an reasonable price;

(d)   provide training to the Buyer's personnel in accordance with Appendix 4; and

(e)   provide the Buyer's Commercial Contact with quarterly reports detailing the Buyer's quarterly and cumulative expenditure under the Contract.

4. QUALITY OF SUPPLIES

4.1   The Supplier warrants:

(a)   that:

  (i)   here applicable, the Supplies, the Supplier's internal equipment and systems, and the Supplier's links with the Buyer (including, without limitation, electronic data interchange links) are fully compatible (without modification, loss of performance, loss of use, or work or expense on the part of the Buyer) with changes to inputs, outputs, data or other Information in relation to dates arising in the year 2000 and beyond; and

  (ii)   agrees that, notwithstanding anything to the contrary in the Contract, the Buyer may freely disclose all Information concerning such compatibility to third parties;

(b)   that the Software is free from:

  (i)   all Viruses that could have been detected by using the latest (at the date of despatch) commercially available virus detection software; and

  (ii)   all forms of 'electronic repossession' and 'logic bombs' (which expressions shall have meanings as they are generally understood within the computing industry) and the Supplier indemnifies Buyer against all actions, claims, proceedings, damages, costs, and expenses arising from any breach of this warranty;

(c)   that, after Acceptance by the Buyer, the Software will perform in accordance with the Functional Specification;

(*d*) that it has and shall use and adopt only good quality materials, techniques and standards in performing the Contract with the standards of care, skill and diligence required of good computing practice;

(*e*) that it shall comply with:

(i) the requirements of any written requirement of the Buyer, all applicable legislation, regulations or by-laws of a Local or other Authority; and

(ii) any Buyer site regulations that may be notified to the Supplier; and

(*f*) that it has obtained all necessary licences, authorities, consents and permits for the unrestricted export of the Software to the Buyer, and export or re-export to such countries as the Buyer shall have notified to the Supplier at any time before delivery to the Buyer and the Supplier indemnifies the Buyer against all costs, claims, or demands resulting directly or indirectly from any breach of such warranty.

5. LICENCE

5.1 The Supplier grants to the Buyer an irrevocable, non-exclusive, non-transferable, perpetual licences from its respective date of delivery to the Buyer for the Buyer by itself or by third parties on its behalf to use, copy, install, maintain, modify, enhance and adapt the Software for all Buyer design and development purposes in accordance with the relevant Licence Type (as described in paragraph 2 of this Condition).

5.2 The relevant Licence Type shall be as stated in Appendix 2 or as may be ordered by the Buyer and shall be either:

(*a*) Processor Licence – limited to a specified processor(s) irrespective of the power of the processor, size or model group, whether physically or logically linked. No limitation on location or number of users;

(*b*) Site Licence – limited to a specified geographical location(s). No limitation on type or power of processors or number of users;

(*c*) Corporate Licence – No limitation on type or power of processor(s), location(s) or number of users;

(*d*) Enterprise Wide Licence – as Corporate Licence save that the expression 'Buyer' shall be deemed to include also any undertaking or entity in which the Buyer has a commercial interest from time to time anywhere in the world; or

(*e*) Other – Having limitations as may be agreed from time to time by the parties in writing.

5.3 Notwithstanding any limitations imposed by a relevant Licence Type, the Buyer shall have the right, without charge, to:

(*a*)   use any alternative processor for Software test and evaluation purposes or where Software cannot for any reason be used on any specified processor;

(*b*)   copy, install and use Software on any processor for back-up, archive or disaster recovery purposes;

(*c*)   transfer any Processor Licence to an alternative processor (whether or not at the same location); and

(*d*)   require the Supplier to promptly deliver and install (and the Supplier shall so deliver and install), where the Buyer elects to change an operating system, a new version of the Software compatible with such new operating system.

5.4   Notwithstanding any other Condition, the Supplier grants to the Buyer non-exclusive, royalty free, world-wide rights, by or on behalf of the Buyer, to copy and use Information supplied under the Contract or derived by the Buyer from the Supplies as necessary for the purpose of interfacing with other equipment as may form part of the Buyer Network or any other telecommunications network. For such purpose, the Supplier shall promptly provide such additional Information as the Buyer may request. The Buyer shall pay the costs of the collation, reproduction and despatch of the Information. In this Condition 'Buyer Network' means all exchange equipment, transmission equipment, network terminating equipment, line plant, power plant and ancillary equipment, owned or operated by the Buyer.

5.5   In this paragraph, 'lawful user' is as defined in the *Copyright (Computer Programs) Regulations 1992 (SI 1992/3233)*.

Notwithstanding any other Condition, the Supplier grants to the Buyer non-exclusive, royalty free, world-wide rights to any Software supplied under the Contract to the effect that the Buyer has:

(*a*)   all the rights of a lawful user of the Software; and

(*b*)   the rights to copy, disclose and use for any purpose any Information which:

    (i)   has been derived by the Buyer from observing, studying or testing the functioning of the Software;

    (ii)   relates to the ideas and principles which underline any element of the Software; and

    (iii)   is not subject to the Supplier's (or its licensor's) copyrights in the United Kingdom.

5.6   For the avoidance of doubt, nothing in the Contract shall prevent the Buyer from selling or deploying products, systems and services that are developed by the Buyer using the Software.

6. FAULTY SUPPLIES

The Buyer may reject any Supplies that do not accord with the Contract within 45 days of their respective delivery. The Buyer shall not be liable for any fees or charges in relation to such Supplies. The Buyer shall be deemed to have accepted Supplies that are not so rejected.

7. SECURITY

7.1   The Supplier shall ensure that Contract Personnel conform to all security, safety and works regulations and such other local instructions, as may be notified by the Buyer whilst on any Buyer site or customer premises.

7.2   The Buyer may remove from and refuse entry and re-admission to a Buyer site or customer premises any person who is, in the reasonable opinion of the Buyer, not conforming with these requirements or not a fit person to be allowed on Buyer premises.

7.3   The Buyer may at its discretion, search any Contract Personnel or their vehicles, or equipment upon any Buyer site or upon entry to and departure from any Buyer site or customer premises. The Supplier shall use its best endeavours to ensure that Contract Personnel are aware of and comply with these requirements and that no Contract Personnel unwilling to comply will be employed on any Buyer site.

7.4   The Supplier shall (and shall ensure Contract Personnel shall) access only those parts of Buyer sites strictly necessary for the purposes of the Contract.

7.5   The Supplier shall ensure that no Buyer equipment, facilities or materials are used or removed from any Buyer site without the Buyer's written consent and shall immediately notify the Buyer of any known or suspected breach of security in relation to the Contract and give the Buyer full co-operation in any investigation.

7.6   The Supplier shall supply on request details (name, address, date of birth) of any Contract Personnel who might have access to a Buyer site or customer premises under the Contract.

7.7   The Buyer may examine any Information relating to the handling, processing, transportation and storage of information or property of or supplied by the Buyer and held by the Supplier under the Contract, which Information shall be kept by the Supplier for at least one year after the termination or expiry of the Contract.

7.8   The Buyer shall not be responsible for safeguarding any property or money of Contract Personnel.

8. ESCROW

8.1   The Supplier warrants that on the first delivery of each item of Software, and on each anniversary of such delivery where there has been any new release of that item during the preceding 12 month period, it shall place with NCC Global (www.nccglobal.com) ('Escrow Agent') in the United Kingdom a copy of the relevant source code, listings, programmer's notes and other documentation sufficient to enable the Buyer to maintain or have maintained the Software ('the Escrow Documents').

8.2   If the Supplier fails, or is in the Buyer's reasonable opinion unable or unwilling to maintain the Software, the Supplier shall at the Buyer's request deliver the Escrow Documents to the Buyer and the Buyer shall be entitled to use them for the purpose of maintaining the Software or having it maintained by a third party.

9. PRICING AND PAYMENT

9.1   The Contract Price and all other prices payable by the Buyer shall be:

(*a*)   as stated in Appendix 2; and

(*b*)   inclusive, where relevant, of all non-returnable packing, delivery to Site, any licence fees, installation, testing and commissioning and all other charges associated with Supplies but shall exclude VAT.

9.2   The Buyer shall pay invoices submitted in accordance with this Condition within 45 days from receipt of a valid invoice. An invoice shall not be valid until the Supplies to which it relates have been Accepted.

9.3   When payment becomes due, the Supplier shall forward invoices to: _____.

9.4   Each invoice shall specify: its date; the Contract Number; any order reference (purchase order number and any other required reference number or code required by the Buyer; the full Buyer description of the Supplies to which the invoice relates (as defined in the Contract); the portion of Supplies for which payment is due; and, if appropriate, the cumulative amount invoiced to date.

10. CONFIDENTIALITY

10.1   Subject to the Condition headed 'Licence', either party receiving Information ('the Recipient') from the other shall not without the other's prior written consent use such Information except for Contract purposes or disclose such Information to any person other than Buyer people or Contract Personnel who have a need to know. The Recipient shall return documentation containing such Information to the other party when no longer required for such purposes.

10.2   Paragraph 1 of this Condition shall not apply to Information that is:

(*a*)   published except by a breach of the Contract;

(*b*)   lawfully known to the Recipient at the time of disclosure and is not subject to any obligations of confidentiality;

(*c*)   lawfully disclosed to the Recipient by a third party without any obligations of confidentiality; or

(*d*)   replicated by development independently carried out by or for the Recipient by an employee or other person without access to or knowledge of the Information.

10.3   The Supplier shall ensure that any sub–contractor is bound by similar confidentiality terms to those in this Condition.

10.4   Without prejudice to any prior obligations of confidentiality it may have, the Supplier shall ensure that no publicity relating to the Contract shall take place without the prior written consent of the Buyer.

11. INTELLECTUAL PROPERTY INDEMNITY

11.1   The Supplier indemnifies the Buyer against all actions, claims, proceedings, damages, costs, and expenses arising from any actual or alleged infringement of Intellectual Property Rights or breach of confidentiality by the Buyer's possession or use of any of the Supplies anywhere in the world provided such possession or use is in accordance with the rights and licences granted pursuant to the Contract.

11.2   The Buyer shall notify the Supplier in writing of any such allegation received by The Buyer and shall not make any admissions unless the Supplier gives prior written consent.

11.3   At the Supplier's request and expense, The Buyer shall permit the Supplier to conduct all negotiations and litigation. The Buyer shall give all reasonable assistance and the Supplier shall pay the Buyer's costs and expenses so incurred.

11.4   The Supplier may, at its expense, modify or replace the Supplies to avoid any alleged or actual infringement or breach. The modification or replacement must not affect the performance of the Supplies.

11.5   This indemnity shall not apply to infringements or breaches arising directly from the combination of the Supplies with other items not supplied under the Contract.

12. FORCE MAJEURE

12.1   Neither party shall be liable to the other party for any delay in the performance of the Contract directly caused by any event beyond its reasonable control ('the *Force Majeure* Period') provided such party shall have first given the other party written notice within seven days after becoming aware that such delay was likely to occur.

12.2   If the Supplier is so delayed and the *Force Majeure* Period exceeds 28 days, the Buyer shall have the option by written notice to the Supplier to terminate the Contract forthwith in whole or in part and have no liability for the whole or part so terminated.

12.3   For the avoidance of doubt, the provisions of this Condition shall not affect the Buyer's right to terminate the Contract under Paragraph 4 of the Condition headed 'Termination'.

13. TERMINATION

13.1   If the Supplier commits a material breach or persistent breaches of the Contract (or any other contract with the Buyer related to the Supplies), and in the case of a breach which is capable of remedy, fails to remedy the breach within seven days (or such longer period as the Buyer may at its option agree in writing) of written notice from the Buyer to do so then the Buyer shall have the right:

(*a*)   at any time to terminate the Contract forthwith as a whole or (at the Buyer's option) in respect of any part of the Contract to be performed; and

(*b*)   to recover from the Supplier all directly resulting losses and expenses (including, without limitation, the additional cost of completing Supplies, or having Supplies completed by another Supplier, to a similar standard).

13.2   The Buyer shall have the right at any time to terminate the Contract forthwith and to recover from the Supplier all directly resulting losses and expenses (including, without limitation, the additional cost of completing the Supplies, or having the Supplies completed by another Supplier, to a similar standard) if the Supplier shall become insolvent or cease to trade or compound with its creditors; or a bankruptcy petition or order is presented or made against the Supplier; or where the Supplier is a partnership, against any one partner, or if a trustee in sequestration is appointed in respect of the assets of the Supplier or (where applicable) any one partner; or a receiver or an administrative receiver is appointed in respect of any of the Supplier's assets; or a petition for an administration order is presented or such an order is made in relation to the Supplier; or a resolution or petition or order to wind up the Supplier is passed or presented or made or a liquidator is appointed in respect of the Supplier (otherwise than for reconstruction or amalgamation).

13.3   The Buyer may at any time on written notice terminate the Contract forthwith if the ownership or control of the Supplier is materially changed to (in the Buyer's reasonable opinion) the Buyer's detriment.

13.4   The Buyer may at any time on written notice terminate the Contract forthwith. Where the Buyer terminates the Contract under this paragraph 4 and does not have any other right to terminate the Contract, the following shall apply:

(*a*)   The Buyer shall subject to subparagraph (*b*) below, pay the Supplier such amounts as may be necessary to cover its reasonable costs and outstanding and unavoidable commitments (and reasonable profit thereon) necessarily and solely incurred in properly performing the Contract in relation to Applicable Supplies (as defined below) prior to termination.

(*b*)   The Buyer shall not pay for any such costs or commitments that the Supplier is able to mitigate and shall only pay costs and commitments that the Buyer has validated to its satisfaction. The Buyer shall not be liable to pay for any Applicable Supplies that, at the date of termination, the Buyer is entitled to reject (including any Supplies for which the Buyer may have issued a Certificate of Commercial Service) or has already rejected. The Buyer's total liability under sub-paragraph (*a*) above shall not in any circumstances exceed the price that would have been payable by the Buyer for Applicable Supplies if the Contract had not been terminated.

(*c*)   In this paragraph 4, 'Applicable Supplies' means Supplies in respect of which the Contract has been terminated under this paragraph, which were ordered by the Buyer under the Contract before the date of termination, and for which payment has not at that date become due from the Buyer.

(*d*)   Sub-paragraphs (*a*) and (*b*) above encompass the total liability of the Buyer for termination pursuant to this Paragraph 4, and the Buyer shall be liable for no other costs, claims, damages, or expenses consequent upon such termination.

13.5   Each right of the Buyer under this Condition is without prejudice to any other right of the Buyer under this Condition or otherwise.

14. INDEMNITY

Without prejudice to any other rights or remedies available to the Buyer, the Supplier shall indemnify the Buyer against all loss of or damage to any Buyer property to the extent arising as a result of the negligence or wilful acts or omissions of the Supplier or Contract Personnel in relation to the performance of the Contract; and all claims and proceedings, damages, costs and expenses arising or incurred in respect of:

(*a*)   death or personal injury of any Contract Personnel in relation to the performance of the Contract, except to the extent caused by the Buyer's negligence;

(*b*)   death or personal injury of any other person to the extent arising as a result of the negligence or wilful acts or omissions of the Supplier or Contract Personnel in relation to the performance of the Contract;

(*c*)   loss of or damage to any property to the extent arising as a result of the negligence or wilful acts or omissions of the Supplier or Contract Personnel in relation to the performance of the Contract; or

(*d*)   under *Part 1* of the *Consumer Protection Act 1987* in relation to Supplies.

15. LIMITATION OF LIABILITY

15.1   Subject to Paragraph 3 of this Condition, neither party shall be liable to the other under the Contract for any indirect or consequential loss or damage.

15.2   Subject to Paragraph 3 of this Condition the total liability of either party to the other under the Contract shall not exceed the greater of either:

(*a*)   £_____; or

(*b*)   125% of the total of all sums paid or due to the Supplier for Supplies.

15.3   Paragraphs 1 and 2 of this Condition shall not apply to loss or damage arising out of or in connection with:

(*a*)   death or personal injury; or

(*b*)   the wilful failure of either party to perform its contractual obligations; or

(*c*)   paragraph d) of the Condition headed 'Indemnity'; or

(*d*)   the Condition headed 'Intellectual Property'; or

(*e*)   the payment of liquidated damages; or

(*f*)   Buyer's obligation to pay the Contract Price.

16. INSURANCE

16.1 The Supplier shall at its own expense effect and maintain for the Contract Period such insurances as required by any applicable law and as appropriate in respect of its obligations under the Contract. Such insurances shall include third party liability insurance with an indemnity limit of not less than £_____ for each and every claim.

16.2 If the Supplier cannot provide evidence of such insurance to the Buyer on request, the Buyer may arrange such insurance and recover the cost from the Supplier.

16.3 The Supplier shall notify the Buyer as soon as it is aware of any event occurring in relation to the Contract which may give rise to an obligation to indemnify the Buyer under the Contract, or to a claim under any insurance required by the Contract.

16.4 This Condition shall not be deemed to limit in any way the Supplier's liability under the Contract.

17. CONTRACT CHANGE PROCEDURE

The Contract may only be varied by written agreement between each party's Commercial Contact who shall each respond in writing within ten days of receipt of a proposal for a variation from the other.

18. NOTICES

Notices required under the Contract to be in writing shall be delivered by hand, post or facsimile transmission to the Commercial Contact of the recipient and shall be deemed to be given upon receipt (except notices sent by facsimile transmission, which shall be deemed to be given upon transmission).

19. ASSIGNMENT AND SUB-CONTRACTING

19.1 The Supplier shall not, without the Buyer's written consent, assign or subcontract the whole or any part of the Contract. Any consent, if given, shall not affect the Supplier's obligations or liabilities under the Contract.

19.2   The Supplier shall allow the Buyer access to its subcontractors for technical discussions provided that the proposed agenda for such discussions and the outcome shall be promptly notified to the Supplier. The Buyer will notify any changes or proposals identified during such discussions to the Supplier who will process them in accordance with the Contract.

20. GENERAL

20.1   The headings to the Contract provisions are for reference only and shall not affect their interpretation.

20.2

(a)   No delay, neglect or forbearance by either party in enforcing any provision of the Contract shall be deemed to be a waiver or in any way prejudice any rights of that party.

(b)   No waiver by either party shall be effective unless made in writing or constitute a waiver of rights in relation to any subsequent breach of the Contract.

20.3   The Contract governs the relationship between the parties to the exclusion of any other terms and conditions on which any quotation or tender response has been given to the Buyer.

20.4   The Contract is governed by English law and subject to the non-exclusive jurisdiction of the English courts.

20.5   The Supplier shall not be, nor in any way represent itself as, an agent of the Buyer and shall have no authority to enter into any obligation on behalf of the Buyer or to bind the Buyer in any way.

20.6   Except as expressly set out in the Contract:

(a)   no assignment of or licence under any Intellectual Property Right or trade mark or service mark (whether registered or not) is granted by the Contract; and

(b)   no right is conferred on any third party.

20.7   The following provisions of the Contract shall survive its termination or expiry in addition to those provisions relating to intellectual property and those which by their content or nature will so survive.

- Licence;
- Confidentiality;
- Indemnity;
- Intellectual Property Indemnity; and
- Quality of Supplies.

Appendix 1

(Provision of Maintenance Services)

1. It is important to be clear what the support requirements are before contracting. This condition is a suitable standard for many cases. However, where defined customer requirements exist, they should be used instead of the relevant parts of this condition.

The requirements of Condition 3.1 may be replaced by the following in less critical cases:

(*a*) The mean time to restore shall not be greater than five hours.

(*b*) The mean outstanding time for problems shall not be greater than 20 weeks.

(*c*) The mean time to fix shall not be greater than ten weeks.

(*d*) [X%] of the problems shall be answered in ten weeks.

The Supplier shall supply maintenance services for the Software in accordance with the following:

Installation

Maintenance services shall include the installation of the Software and of subsequent releases of the Software by the Supplier on [*Buyer's licensed processors*] at no charge to the Buyer for a period of [X] years from the date of Acceptance of the Software.

Help–Desk

During Monday to Friday 8 am to 6 pm excluding Bank Holidays (hereinafter referred to as 'normal working hours') the Supplier shall provide a Hot–line or Help–Desk service manned by competent staff able to provide technical support and advice for the Software. The Supplier shall provide support outside normal working hours should the Buyer so require on terms and conditions to be agreed.

Meetings/Boards

The Supplier shall provide representatives with appropriate qualifications and decision–making powers to attend regular technical and management review meetings/boards with the Buyer.

The Supplier shall be prepared to undertake the maintenance of the Software for a period of [X] years from the Acceptance date. However, the Buyer shall have the option to have the maintenance undertaken either by itself or by a third party.

The documentation provided with any updates of the Software shall be defined and subject to the Buyer's agreement. As a minimum such documentation shall identify:

- the reason for the update (i.e. all faults cleared etc.);
- all new features and functions provided along with the invocation instructions;
- any impact upon the reliability of the Software;
- installation instructions for the update; and
- the update's compatibility with previous releases of the hardware and the Software.

The Supplier shall ensure all faults in the Software shall be classified and handled as follows.

Failures shall be classified as to the severity of effect that they have on the working system. The severity classification shall be used to determine the response time for returning the system to its fully operational state. The severity classifications shall be:

Severity Class A

Emergency. Any hardware or Software problem resulting in serious loss or degradation of service or serious loss of functionality.

Severity Class B

Urgent. Any hardware or Software problem that reduces system security or data integrity, or which represents a serious threat to service.

Severity Class C

Non-urgent. Low level hardware, Software or procedural problem requiring resolution in defined time scales.

Severity Class D

Low. Other low level hardware, Software or procedural problem.

The following targets shall be adopted by the Supplier for returning the system to its fully operational state:

Severity Class A – within two hours of receipt of a report from the Buyer.

Severity Class B – within four hours of receipt of a report from the Buyer.

Severity Class C – within five days of receipt of a report from the Buyer.

Severity Class D – by the next Software release.

The Buyer shall determine the severity classification of failures as they arise.

Failures shall also be classified as to the priority that should be given to the permanent rectification of the underlying fault. The criteria for prioritisation shall be agreed with the Buyer and shall include at least:

- the frequency of occurrence of the failures;
- the severity of the failures; and
- the maintenance effort needed to deal with the failures.

The priority classifications shall be:

Priority Class 1 – Very High;

Priority Class 2 – High;

Priority Class 3 – Medium;

Priority Class 4 – Low; and

Priority Class 5 – Very Low.

The priority classification given to failures shall be reviewed from time to time as more information becomes available as to the frequency of occurrence of the failures.

The following targets shall be adopted by the Supplier for providing a tested correction for the fault:

Priority Class 1 – within five days of receipt of a report from the Buyer;

Priority Class 2 – within ten days of receipt of a report from the Buyer;

Priority Class 3 – within one month of receipt of a report from the Buyer;

Priority Class 4 – within two months of receipt of a report from the Buyer; and

Priority Class 5 – by the next software release.

If the Supplier fails to meet any of the timescales for returning the system to its fully operational state, the buyer may invoke the Escalation Procedure, as set out below:

ESCALATION LEVEL	LEVEL OF SEVERITY		
	Severity A	*Severity B*	*Severity C*
The Supplier's Help Desk Supervisor or Account Representative	Within four hours of the Buyer reporting the problem	Within eight hours of the Buyer reporting the problem	Within ten days of the Buyer reporting the problem

ESCALATION LEVEL	LEVEL OF SEVERITY		
	Severity A	*Severity B*	*Severity C*
The Supplier's Technical Support Manager	Within six hours of the Buyer reporting the problem	Within 24 hours of the Buyer reporting the problem	Within 21 days of the Buyer reporting the problem
The Supplier's Technical Director/Managing Director	Within eight hours of the Buyer reporting the problem	Within one week of the Buyer reporting the problem	

The Supplier shall use the failure data to calculate the Mean Time Between Failures of Software incidents by severity.

The Supplier shall determine the root cause of each defect in the Software. This is essential for all *Severity A* and *Priority 1* defects. Other defects can be analysed on a sample basis to be agreed with the Buyer.

The Supplier shall record where the Software defects were discovered and where they were introduced and shall use the Information to improve the performance of the Software. The sources of introduction shall include at least include:

● specification;

● design;

● coding;

● testing; and

● maintenance

The Supplier shall classify the type of Software defects reported by the Buyer or the Supplier.

The maintenance service described in this condition shall be provided at no cost to the Buyer by the Supplier for 12 months following Acceptance of the Software. Thereafter the service, if the Buyer should require it, shall be chargeable at £ _____ per annum for a minimum of _____ years.

Appendix 2

(Software, Licence Types and Pricing)

Appendix 3

(Training – To be completed to suit the needs of the organisation)

Chapter B4
Professional Services Agreement – Supplier

At a glance

- Drafted by the supplier and favours the supplier – see CHAPTER B5 for the equivalent Buyer contract.

- Used where a supplier provides services, but not goods, to a customer. For sale of goods see CHAPTER B1.

- Consultancy contracts are rarely 'standard' as the services differ widely – this is an example only.

Commentary

- Clause 1 requires that the parties agree in writing in advance the work which will be done. Such document agreeing the work to be done is called a project document here but this title is for convenience only. If there is no project document, clause 1.2 provides that time sheets will be completed. Some projects will be charged on the basis of the time spent on the matter and others on a fixed fee basis.

- Clause 2 addresses payment. It allows the consultant to charge reasonable expenses in addition to the fee. Buyers' contracts such as those in CHAPTER B3 and CHAPTER B5 may provide that only limited expenses may be claimed.

- Clause 3.3 provides for a liquidated damages payment if the customer terminates the contract early. Any such sum must be a genuine pre-estimate of the supplier's losses in such a case otherwise the clause will be void under common law as comprising a 'penalty clause'. However it is sensible to consider including liquidated damages because then the parties know reasonably certainly what sum will be claimed for an early termination.

- Clause 4.5 provides that the supplier will own all copyright and other intellectual property rights in the materials it generates under the contract. The *Copyright, Designs and Patents Act 1988* has the effect that unless there is agreement to the contrary the author of copyright works such as computer software, web page designs etc.

will own the rights (or their employer, if they are employed). Thus consultants retain copyright unless the agreement says so even if the buyer is paying for the work. The buyer simply receives a licence to use the rights. Buyers wanting ownership therefore need to reverse this position by a contract term. This Chapter is drafted from the supplier's perspective however so the supplier retains copyright and it is preferable to state this expressly rather than relying on the default position under the copyright legislation. Where registered or unregistered design right or database right may be generated then the position is the reverse – the party paying (the commissioner) – will own the rights unless the agreement says otherwise. In practice it is best if the contract makes such ownership rights very clear. There will be contracts where no material protected by rights is generated but it is sensible to have a clause such as this just in case.

- Clause 5 provides limited warranties such as that the services will be provided with due care and skill. This should be contrasted with the contract in CHAPTER B5 – the equivalent buyer's contract for procuring services where much more stringent warranties to the disadvantage of the supplier are proposed.

- This precedent is based on provision of computer consultancy services, hence references to computer software. Other agreements would not need such references nor require clauses relating to ownership of copyright in software etc.

- Schedules set out the variables of the agreement such as the nature of the work to be done and the fees.

Precedent – Professional Services Agreement – Supplier
B4.3

_____Limited

Professional Services Agreement

Agreement Reference ....

....

BACKGROUND

Supplier has agreed to provide consultancy services to the Customer under the terms and conditions of this Agreement.

1. CONSULTANCY SERVICES

1.1   All professional services provided by the Supplier to the Customer shall be governed by the terms of this Agreement. At the commencement of the services the Supplier may submit to the Customer a statement of work and/or other similar document describing the services to be provided by the Supplier (such documents being collectively referred to as a 'Project Document') which shall specify the services to be performed and the fees payable. All Project Documents will reference this Agreement by number and be subject to the terms set out herein. The Customer shall notify the Supplier Project Manager immediately if the Customer does not agree with the contents of the Project Document. Upon the completion of the services described on the applicable Project Document, the Customer shall sign and return one copy of the Project Document to the Supplier. The parties may, from time to time, mutually agree upon and execute new Project Documents. Any changes in the scope of services to be provided hereunder shall be set forth in the Project Document, which shall reflect the changed services, schedule and fees.

Alternatively, for projects not using Project Documents, the Supplier shall submit timesheets to the Customer from time to time. The Customer shall sign such timesheets to indicate its acceptance of the professional services described on such timesheet.

1.2   All daily rates are based on an eight hour day, inclusive of travel time. Any services requested that are in excess of an eight hour day shall be charged at the prorated hourly rate, as applicable. Scheduled service dates shall be mutually agreed upon and subject to availability of the Supplier's personnel or the Supplier's authorised representative. Except as may be otherwise agreed to in writing by the Supplier Project Manager, time shall not be of the essence in the performance of any professional services, but the Supplier shall use all reasonable endeavours to complete services within the estimated time frames.

2. PAYMENT

2.1   The Customer shall pay to the Supplier the fees set forth in the applicable Project Document or as may be otherwise agreed between the parties. The Supplier will invoice the Customer monthly in arrears for services rendered in the previous month and for reasonable out-of-pocket expenses incurred in providing those services.

2.2   Invoiced amounts shall be due and payable within thirty (30) days of receipt of invoice. The Customer shall pay interest on overdue amounts at a rate equal to two percent (2%) above the base lending rate of National Westminster Bank plc as may be set from time to time. In the event that the Customer's procedures require that an invoice be submitted against a purchase order to payment, the Customer shall be responsible for issuing such purchase order before the services are rendered.

3. CUSTOMER'S OBLIGATIONS

3.1 To enable the Supplier to perform its obligations hereunder the Customer shall:

(*a*) co-operate with the Supplier;

(*b*) provide the Supplier promptly with all information and documentation reasonably required by Supplier;

(*c*) make computer time and resources available as necessary;

(*d*) give at its own expense reasonable access to hardware and software;

(*e*) make appropriate staff available who are familiar with the Customer's computer systems;

(*f*) provide suitable working space and facilities; and

(*g*) comply with such other requirements as may be set out in any Project Document or otherwise agreed between the parties.

3.2 The Customer shall be liable to compensate the Supplier for any additional expense incurred by the Supplier through the Customer's failure to follow the Supplier's reasonable instructions, or through the Customer's failure to comply with clause 3.1.

3.3 Notwithstanding the generality of the foregoing, in the event that the Customer unlawfully terminates/cancels the agreed-to services, the Customer shall be required to pay to the Supplier as agreed damages and not as a penalty the full amount of any third party costs to which the Supplier has committed and in respect of cancellations on less than five working days' written notice the full amount of the services contracted for as set out in the applicable Project Document, without prejudice to the Supplier's other rights. The Customer agrees this is a genuine pre-estimate of the Supplier's losses in such a case. For the purposes of this clause, the Customer's failure to provide the Supplier with adequate manpower or comply with its other obligations under clause 3.1 to enable the Supplier to perform its obligations shall be deemed to be a cancellation of the services and subject to the payment of the damages set out in this clause.

3.4 In the event that the Customer or any other third party, not being a sub-contractor of the Supplier, shall omit or commit anything which prevents or delays the Supplier from undertaking or complying with any of its obligations under this Agreement or any Project Document ('Customer's Default'), then the Supplier shall notify the Customer as soon possible and:

(*a*)   the Supplier shall have no liability in respect of any delay to the completion of any project resulting from the Customer's Default;

(*b*)   if applicable, the project timetable will be modified accordingly; and

(*c*)   the Supplier shall notify the Customer at the same time if it intends to make any claim for additional documented costs incurred as a result of Customer's Default and the payment of such costs and expenses shall be subject only to receipt of an itemised statement of expenditure.

3.5   Change control. Should either party request any alteration to this Agreement or an agreed Project Document insofar as it relates to services, such requests and any subsequent alterations will be subject to the change control procedures set out in the *Supplier Request for Change* form. Until such time as any alteration is formally agreed between the parties in accordance with such change control procedures, the parties will, unless otherwise agreed, continue as if such alteration had not been requested. The Supplier shall be entitled to make a reasonable charge for investigating a proposed alteration requested by the Customer. An 'alteration' includes any proposed amendment to this Agreement or any Project Document whether in whole or in part. For each such alteration which is agreed by the Supplier and the Customer, this Agreement or any relevant Project Document, as the case may be, shall be amended to the extent necessary to give effect to that alteration.

4. RIGHTS IN MATERIAL

4.1   The Supplier will specify Materials if any to be delivered to the Customer. 'Materials' are defined as being literary works or other works of authorship (such as programs, program listings, programming tools, documentation, reports, drawings and similar works) that the Supplier may deliver to the Customer as part of the consultancy services the Supplier provides.

4.2   The Supplier will deliver one copy of the specified Materials to the Customer. The Supplier grants the Customer a non-exclusive, worldwide licence to use, execute, reproduce, display, perform, and distribute, within its company only, a copy of the Materials. The Supplier will unless otherwise specified on the Schedule, retain ownership of all copyright, patent and other intellectual property rights in the Materials. Such licence shall be on the terms of the Supplier's Software Licence Agreement save as varied by this Agreement and its schedule.

4.3   The Customer shall reproduce the copyright notice and any other legend of ownership on any copies made under the licences granted in this Clause.

4.4   Except as may be otherwise agreed by the Supplier in writing, the Supplier shall have no obligation to provide support services for the Materials.

4.5   The Supplier retains all intellectual property rights in all pre-existing Supplier materials used in the Materials supplied to the Customer. The Supplier grants to the Customer a non-exclusive, non-transferable licence to use the same for the Customer's internal use only. The Customer may make one copy of such materials for archival or backup purposes only and shall include all existing copyright and other proprietary notices in such copy. No title to ownership of such materials or any of its parts, nor any applicable intellectual property rights therein such as patents, copyrights and trade secrets, are transferred to the Customer. Except to the extent expressly permitted under applicable law, the Customer shall not reverse engineer, reverse compile or reverse assemble the Materials or any pre-existing materials of the Supplier in whole or in part.

4.6   The Customer shall be responsible for promptly obtaining and providing to the Supplier all Required Consents necessary for the Supplier to access, use and/or modify software, hardware, firmware and other products used by the Customer for which the Supplier shall provide services hereunder. A Required Consent means any consents or approvals required to give the Supplier and its sub-contractors the right or licence to access, use and/or modify (including creating derivative works) the Customer's or a third party's software, hardware, firmware and other products used by the Customer without infringing the ownership or licence rights (including patent and copyright) of the providers or owners of such products.

4.7   The Customer agrees to indemnify, defend and hold the Supplier and its affiliates harmless from and against any and all claims, losses, liabilities and damages (including reasonable attorneys' fees and costs) arising from or in connection with any claims (including patent and copyright infringement) made against the Supplier, alleged to have occurred as a result of the Customer's failure to provide any Required Consents.

4.8   The Supplier shall be relieved of the performance of any obligations that may be affected by the Customer's failure promptly to provide any Required Consents to the Supplier.

4.9   Except as otherwise provided herein, no licence including any licence by implication, estoppel or otherwise, or any intellectual property right including but not limited to patents, copyrights, trade secrets and trademarks is transferred to the Customer.

5. WARRANTY; DISCLAIMER OF OTHER TERMS

5.1   The Supplier warrants that the services performed under this Agreement will be performed using reasonable skill and care, and of a quality conforming to generally accepted industry standards and practices.

5.2 Warranties. Except as expressly stated in this agreement and its schedules and without prejudice to clause 5.1 above, there are no warranties, express or implied, by operation of law or otherwise offered by the Supplier to the Customer in relation to the licensed software or user documentation or services to be provided. The express warranties contained in this agreement and its schedules shall not be expanded, diminished or affected by and no obligation or liability will arise or grow out of the Supplier's rendering of technical, programming or other advice or service in connection with any licensed software and user documentation provided hereunder.

5.3 Indemnity. The Supplier will indemnify the Customer against injury (including death) to any persons or loss of damage to any property, which may arise out of the default or negligence of the Supplier, its employees or agents in consequence of the Supplier's obligations under this Agreement and against all claims, demands, proceedings, damages, costs, charges and expenses whatsoever in respect thereof and in relation thereto.

5.4 Limitation. Except in respect of injury, including death to a person, due to negligence for which no limit applies, the Supplier's liability arising out of this Agreement, regardless of the form of the action, whether in contract or tort, will not exceed the fee paid by the Customer in relation to the services or software to which the cause of action relates.

5.5 Referrals. The Supplier may direct the Customer to third parties having products or services which may be of interest to the Customer for use in conjunction with the Services. Notwithstanding any Supplier recommendation, referral or introduction, the Customer will independently investigate and test third party products and services and will have sole responsibility for determining suitability for use of such products and services. The Supplier shall have no liability with respect to the Supplier relating to or arising from use of third party products and services.

5.6 Exclusion of Consequential Loss. In no event shall the Supplier be liable for:

(*a*) any incidental, indirect, special or consequential damages, including but not limited to loss of use, revenues, profits or savings, even if the Supplier knew or should have known of the possibility of such damages and even if an exclusive remedy fails of its essential purpose;

(*b*) claims demands or actions against the Customer by any person; or

(*c*) loss of or damage to customer's data from any cause.

5.7 No Exclusion for Death or Personal Injury. Nothing in this Agreement or its schedules shall exclude or limit the Supplier's liability for death or personal injury caused by its negligence.

6. INDEMNIFICATION

The Customer shall indemnify and hold the Supplier harmless against any claim brought against the Supplier alleging that any Materials or other products or services provided by the Supplier in accordance with the Customer's specifications infringes a patent, copyright or trade secret or other similar right of a third party.

7. PROTECTION OF PROPRIETARY INFORMATION

7.1   Definition. For purposes of this provision 'Proprietary Information' means any information and data of a confidential nature, including but not limited to proprietary, technical, developmental, marketing, sales, operating, performance, cost, know-how, business and process information, computer programming techniques and all record bearing media containing or disclosing such information and techniques, which is disclosed pursuant to this Agreement.

7.2   Nondisclosure. Each party ('Receiving Party') shall hold the other party's ('Originating Party') Proprietary Information in confidence and protect it from disclosure to third parties and shall restrict its use as provided in this Agreement. Each Receiving Party acknowledges that unauthorised disclosure of Proprietary Information may cause substantial economic loss to the Originating Party or its licensors. The Receiving Party shall inform its employees of their obligations under this provision and instruct them so as to ensure such obligations are met.

7.3   Limitation. The obligation of non-disclosure shall not apply to information that:

(*a*)   was in the possession of or known by the Receiving Party prior to its receipt from the Originating Party;

(*b*)   is or becomes public knowledge without fault of the Receiving Party;

(*c*)   is provided to the Receiving Party without restriction on disclosure by a third party, who did not violate any confidentiality restriction by such disclosure;

(*d*)   is made available on an unrestricted basis to the Receiving Party by the Originating Party or someone acting under the Originating Party's actual control;

(*e*)   is independently developed by the Receiving Party without reference to the Proprietary Information and without violation of any confidentiality restriction; or (*f*)   is disclosed by the Receiving Party pursuant to statute, regulation or the order of a court of competent jurisdiction, provided the Receiving Party has previously notified the Originating Party in order to permit the taking of appropriate protective measures.

7.4   Survival. This clause 7 shall survive termination of this Agreement.

8. TERMINATION

8.1   Duration. This Agreement shall continue unless and until terminated as provided below.

8.2   Termination for Default. Without prejudice to other remedies, either party may terminate this Agreement for material default if, upon written notice, the other party, in the case of a remediable breach, fails to cure the matters set forth in said notice within thirty (30) calendar days from the date of said notice.

8.3   Termination for Liquidation. If either party shall convene a meeting of its creditors or if a proposal shall be made for a voluntary arrangement within *Part I* of the *Insolvency Act 1986* or a proposal for any other composition scheme or arrangement with (or assignment for the benefit of) its creditors or if the other party shall be unable to pay its debts within the meaning of *Section 123* of the *Insolvency Act 1986* or if a trustee, receiver, administrative receiver or similar officer is appointed in respect of all or any part of the business or assets of the other or if a petition is presented or a meeting is convened for the purpose of considering a resolution or other steps are taken for the winding up of the other or for the making of an administration order (otherwise than for the purpose of an amalgamation or reconstruction) then the other party may terminate this Agreement immediately upon written notice to said party.

Customer shall pay to the Supplier the fees set forth in the applicable Schedule A to the relevant agreement or as may be otherwise agreed between the parties.

9. GENERAL PROVISIONS

9.1   Publicity. Neither party shall reveal the terms of this Agreement to any third party without the prior written consent of the other, except to its professional advisers. The Supplier may in publicity materials refer to the Customer as being a customer of the Supplier. This provision shall survive expiration, cancellation or termination of this Agreement.

9.2   Export. Customer shall not, without the prior written consent of the Supplier, export, directly or indirectly, any computer software generated under this Agreement or otherwise licensed by the Supplier to the Customer whether under this or any other agreement between the parties, to any country outside of the United Kingdom. The Customer also shall obtain any and all necessary export licences for any such export or for any disclosure of such software or its documentation to a foreign national where the Supplier has approved such export.

9.3   Notices. Any notice required or permitted by this Agreement to either party shall be deemed to have been duly given if in writing and delivered personally or sent by first class post to the party's address first written above, by registered or certified mail, postage prepaid, to the party's address first written above or by facsimile transmission.

9.4   Assignment. The Customer shall not assign its rights or obligations or delegate its duties hereunder without the prior written consent of the Supplier. Any attempted assignment or delegation in contravention of this Clause shall be void and of no effect.

9.5   Nonwaiver. The waiver by either party hereto of any default or breach of this Agreement shall not constitute a waiver of any other or subsequent default or breach.

9.6   Non-Solicitation. During the term of this Agreement and for a period of twelve months thereafter neither party shall solicit or permit any subsidiary or associated undertaking to solicit the employment of any employee, agent or sub-contractor of the other who is directly involved in the performance of this Agreement. If either party breaches this clause with respect to an employee of the other, the breaching party shall pay to the other party by way of agreed damages and not as a penalty an amount equal to the wages or salary (together with all associated employer costs) paid by the other party in respect of such employee for twelve months preceding the date of the breach. For the solicitation of an agent or sub-contractor of the other, the breaching party shall pay all damages actually incurred by the non-breaching party.

9.7   Use of Supplier Trademarks. The Customer shall not use the name, trade mark or trade name of the Supplier in any manner without the prior written approval of the Supplier.

9.8   Independent Contractors. The Supplier and the Customer are contractors independent of each other, and neither has the authority to bind the other to any third person or act in any way as the representative of the other, unless otherwise expressly agreed to in writing by both parties. The Supplier may, in addition to its own employees, engage sub-contractors to provide all or part of the services being provided to the Customer. The engagement of such sub-contractors by the Supplier shall not relieve the Supplier of its obligations under this Agreement or any applicable Schedule.

9.9   Data Protection. The Customer agrees that the Supplier or any Related Company may process personal data (for example contact details) provided by the Customer in connection with this Agreement ('Customer Data') for the purpose of this Agreement and/or for the purposes connected with the Customer's or any Related Company's business relationship with the Supplier. The Customer shall ensure it obtains all similar data protection consents needed from its employees and contractors and others whose personal data it supplies to the Supplier to give effect to this clause and hold the Supplier harmless for any loss arising from breach by the Customer of this provision. Such processing may also included transferring Customer Data to other Related Companies world-wide and its storage in a centralised database. For the purposes of this clause Related Company shall mean any holding company from time to time of the Supplier and/or any subsidiary from time to time of the Supplier or any such holding company (for which purposes the expressions 'holding company' and 'subsidiary' shall have the meanings given in *Section 736* of the *Companies Act 1985* including for these purposes bodies incorporated outside the United Kingdom.

9.10 Governing Law and Severability. This Agreement shall be governed by and construed in accordance with the laws of England and the parties submit to the jurisdiction of the English courts. If any provision of this Agreement is held invalid or unenforceable under any applicable law or be so held by applicable court decision, the parties agree that such invalidity or unenforceability shall not affect the validity and enforceability of the remaining provisions of this Agreement and further agree to substitute for the invalid or unenforceable provision a valid or enforceable provision which most closely approximates the intent and economic effect of the invalid provision within the limits of applicable law or applicable court decisions.

9.11 *Force Majeure.* Neither party shall be liable for non-performance or delays from causes beyond its reasonable control including but not limited to strikes (of its own or other employees), fires, insurrection or riots, embargoes, container shortages, wrecks or delays in transportation, inability to obtain supplies and raw materials, or requirements or regulations of any civil or military authority. In the event of the occurrence of any of the foregoing, the date of performance shall be deferred for a period equal to the time lost by reason of the delay. The affected party shall notify the other in writing of such events or circumstances promptly upon their occurrence.

9.12 Entire Agreement. This Agreement and its schedules set forth the entire agreement and understanding between the parties as to the subject matter hereof and merges all prior discussions between them, save that a confidentiality or non-disclosure agreement between the parties shall continue. Neither of the parties shall be bound by any conditions, definitions, warranties, understandings or representations with respect to such subject matter other than as expressly provided herein or as duly set forth on or subsequent to the date of acceptance hereof in writing and signed by an authorised representative of the party to be bound thereby.

9.13 No Third Party Rights. Nothing in this Agreement is intended to, nor shall it, confer any right on a third party whether under the *Contracts (Rights of Third Parties) Act 1999* or otherwise.

Professional Services Agreement Reference

Schedule A

COMPANY NAME:

ADDRESS:

REGISTERED OFFICE ADDRESS:

DESCRIPTION OF SERVICES:

LOCATION WHERE SERVICES ARE TO
BE RENDERED: _____

CONSULTANCY RATES (EXCLUDING EXPENSES):

Title	Daily Rate	No. of Days	Total Fee (exl. VAT)

The above quoted prices remain valid provided the customer calls of the
services by DD/MM/YYYY.

SIGNATURES

We indicate by our signatures that we accept the terms and conditions of this agreement.

Signed by _____   Signed by _____

Name: _____   Name: _____

Title: _____   Title: _____

Date: _____   Date: _____

For and on behalf of _____   For and on behalf of Customer
Limited

Chapter B5
Professional Services
Agreement – Buyer

At a glance B5.1

- Drafted from the perspective of a buyer buying services from a service provider/consultant.
- For provision of services by supplier please refer to CHAPTER B4.
- Includes strong protection for the buyer.
- For purchase of goods use CHAPTER B2 and for licensing of software use CHAPTER B3.

Commentary B5.2

- These conditions are to be used by buyers, not suppliers. They are drafted from the perspective of the buyer. For conditions for suppliers use CHAPTER B4.

- The agreement sets up a structure under which individual purchase orders can be placed for the ordering of services which in each case would reference this contract.

- Under clause 3.2.4 the agreement says the Deliverables will meet the Specification. It is important therefore that the buyer does ensure an adequate specification is drawn up which reflects its needs and requirements.

- Some buyers have problems with suppliers constantly changing the personnel assigned to undertake the services. Clause 4 is designed to provide protection in this respect.

- Clause 5 sets out provisions as regards the fees for the services. Under clause 5.6 the fees are fixed once the initial agreement has been reached under the relevant purchase order. However the parties could agree to vary any of these provisions by agreement in writing and document the differences from the standard contract on the purchase order concerned.

- Clause 7 includes acceptance tests/criteria. There may be some services where this is not appropriate, such as provisions for training.

However if there are any deliverables such as computer software, web site designs, drawings etc. then the buyer will want a chance to check the deliverables before they are accepted. Suppliers offering acceptance testing normally give themselves a right to submit the work for re-testing if the tests are failed. Buyers will usually want, as in this precedent, a 'cut off point' after which the deliverables can be rejected and the contract terminated and monies refunded. Often payment of a final tranche of monies due is payable on final acceptance.

- Clause 10 provides that intellectual property rights in the materials/deliverables will be owned by the buyer when they are created. Some suppliers will want to retain such ownership and only give a licence. Others will only want ownership to pass on payment. In other services contracts no intellectual property protected items will result.

- Attachment 2 is a change control. Procedures the parties use to ensure all alterations to the requirements of what is to be produced can be documented.

- Attachment 3 is an individual confidentiality undertaking. It is recommended that this is used with the confidential information sign.

- Attachment 5 is an expenses policy which some buyers are able to impose on their suppliers, depending on the parties' respective negotiating position.

Precedent – Professional Services Agreement – Buyer

B5.3

THIS SERVICES AGREEMENT is made on _____
_____ (the 'Commencement Date')

BETWEEN:

ABC LIMITED a company incorporated in England and Wales (registered no. _____), and whose registered office is at _____
_____ ('the Buyer'); and

[   ] a company incorporated in England and Wales (registered no. _____) and whose registered office is at _____
_____ ('the Company').

1. DEFINITIONS

In this Agreement the following words will have the following meanings:

- **'Acceptance Certificate'** means a document signed by an authorised representative of the Buyer confirming that the Acceptance Criteria have been met.

- **'Acceptance Criteria'** means the evaluation and/or tests defined in the Work Package that the Deliverables must pass in order for the Services to be deemed as completed.

- **'Agreement'** means these terms and conditions comprising preamble, attachments and Clauses 0 to 20 together with the terms of any applicable Purchase Order.

- **'Business Day'** means a day other than a Saturday, Sunday or bank holiday in the United Kingdom.

- **'Company Material'** means documents, notes, information, software, know-how, or other like material owned or licensed by the Company prior to the commencement of this Agreement, or obtained (whether created, purchased or licensed) by the Company separately from and otherwise than in connection with the Services.

- **'Company Personnel'** means any employee or contractor supplied by the Company to provide the Services.

- **'Confidential Information'** means any information that is marked as or is manifestly confidential and is disclosed (whether before or after the date of this Agreement, in writing, verbally or otherwise and whether directly or indirectly) by or on behalf of the Disclosing Party to the Receiving Party in connection with the Services.

- **'Deliverables'** means the items described in a Work Package or as otherwise agreed by the parties in writing from time to time to be delivered by the Company as part of the Services.

- **'Disclosing Party'** means the party to this Agreement disclosing the Confidential Information.

- **'Expenses'** means costs and expense incurred in the provision of the Services, which have been agreed in advance by the Buyer and conform to the Expenses policy as detailed in Attachment 5.

- **'Fees'** means the charges, expenses and fees, as set out in a Work Package and agreed in a Purchase Order, payable by the Buyer for the performance of the Services.

- **'Force Majeure'** means any of the following events and the effects thereof if and only to the extent that such event is not caused by, and the effects are beyond the reasonable control of, the affected party including: war or civil war (whether declared or undeclared) or armed conflict, invasion and acts of foreign enemies, blockades

241

and embargoes; acts of Government or local authority or regulatory body; civil unrest, commotion or rebellion; any act, or credible threat, of terrorism; lightning, earthquake or extraordinary storm or weather conditions; nuclear, chemical or biological contamination; explosion, fire or flooding; non-availability of power; general strikes or other industrial action of general application.

- **'Buyer Group Company'** means a subsidiary of the Buyer or a holding company of the Buyer, or another subsidiary of a holding company of Buyer.

- **'Intellectual Property Rights'** means all patents, topography rights, design rights, trade marks, copyrights, rights in databases and computer data, generic rights, and all other intellectual property rights of a similar nature in any part of the world and all applications and rights to apply for the protection of any of the foregoing.

- **'Key Personnel'** means the personnel supplied by the Company and listed in the Work Package who will contribute to the provision of the Services.

- **'Project Plan'** means a plan listing the specific Deliverables and acceptance tests and the dates when both parties have agreed they are due to start and for completion.

- **'Purchase Order'** means the standard Buyer document which refers to the Work Package and provides a unique reference number and maximum value payable by the Buyer to the Company, which will be concluded in accordance with Clause 0;

- **'Receiving Party'** means the party to this Agreement to whom the Confidential Information is disclosed.

- **'Services'** means the services specified in any Work Package and confirmed in a Purchase Order including but not limited to Work and Deliverables.

- **'Specification'** means the detailed statements and documents setting out the functionality and requirements of each component of the Deliverables as detailed or referred to in a Work Package or Purchase Order.

- **'Term'** means the duration of this Agreement as specified in Clause 2.

- **'Variation'** means any change or variation to this Agreement or any Work Package that is agreed pursuant to the change control procedure set out in Attachment 2.

- **'Work'** means any Deliverable, idea, method, invention, discovery, design, business process or method, communication, analysis, drawing, composition, database, writing, computer software, computer data or any other similar item (in any media) which is produced by the Company and/or the Company Personnel in connection with performing the Services.

- **'Work Package'** means the standard form of work package set out in Attachment 1 agreed by the Company and the Buyer prior to the commencement of the Services being supplied to the Buyer. A Work Package shall not be valid unless referenced by Purchase Order and signed by an authorised representative of each party.

2. STRUCTURE AND TERM

2.1   This Agreement will govern the provision of Services by the Company pursuant to one or more Purchase Orders.

2.2   If the parties agree that Company will provide specific Services, then such Services will be documented in the standard form of Work Package. The Work Package will, at a minimum, set out the following information.

(*a*)   Buyer contact person.

(*b*)   Services to be performed including but not limited to, a description and Specification of the Deliverables and a Project Plan.

(*c*)   The Company's Fees for the Services and method of calculation (e.g., hourly, daily or otherwise).

(*d*)   Names of Key Personnel performing the Services.

2.3   The Work Package will be deemed to have been agreed by the Buyer only after a Purchase Order has been issued and the Work Package has been signed by the relevant authorised Buyer representatives.

2.4   Unless the parties expressly amend the terms of this Agreement in a Work Package in relation to the subject matter of the Work Package, to the extent there is any conflict between this Agreement and a Work Package, the terms of this Agreement shall prevail. The parties agree however that the terms of this Agreement and a Work Package shall always prevail over the terms of any Purchase Order except that no Fees identified in a Work Package shall be due to the Company unless a Purchase Order to the value of the Fees has been issued by the Buyer.

2.5 The term of this Agreement will commence on the Commencement Date and, unless terminated earlier pursuant to Clause 6, shall continue in force for an initial term of 12 months and thereafter until terminated by notice pursuant to Clause 6.

3. COMPANY WARRANTIES AND OBLIGATIONS

3.1   In consideration of the Fees, the Company agrees to carry out the Services and provide the Deliverables in accordance with the terms of this Agreement.

3.2   The Company warrants, represents and undertakes that:

(*a*)   it will provide the Services promptly and with all due skill, care and diligence, in a good and workmanlike manner and otherwise in line with best practice within its industry ('Best Industry Practice');

(*b*)   the Company Personnel will possess the qualifications, professional competence and experience to carry out such services in accordance with Best Industry Practice. For the avoidance of doubt, the Company shall be responsible for any training of the Company Personnel that may be required to enable the Company Personnel to perform the Services, and the Buyer shall not be liable for any charges, fees or expenses in relation to any such training;

(*c*)   the Services will not in any manner or way infringe or violate any Intellectual Property Rights, trade secrets, or rights in proprietary information, nor any contractual, employment or property rights, duties of non-disclosure or other rights of any third parties;

(*d*)   the Deliverables shall upon delivery conform in all material respects to the Specification;

(*e*)   upon termination of this Agreement, any Work Package or Purchase Order, the Company shall afford all reasonable assistance to any incoming supplier and where requested promptly provide them with all necessary documentation and assistance to ascertain the status of the Deliverables and the Work required to complete them in accordance with the Specification and the Project Plan; and

(*f*)   it has full capacity and authority to enter into this Agreement and that it has or will obtain prior to the Commencement Date, any necessary licences, consents, and permits required of it for the performance of the Services.

3.3   The Buyer engages the Company to provide the Services and the Company agrees to provide the Services in accordance with this Agreement.

3.4   The Company will procure that where required, the Company Personnel will provide the Services at such places and between such hours as set out in the Work Package.

3.5   The Company will provide the Buyer with such progress reports, evidence or, information concerning the Services as may be requested by the Buyer from time to time.

3.6   The Company will be responsible for maintaining such insurance policies in connection with the provision of the Services as may be appropriate or as the Buyer may require from time to time.

3.7   The Company will procure that the Company Personnel take all reasonable steps to safeguard their own safety and the safety of any other person who may be affected by their actions, and the Company agrees to indemnify and keep indemnified the Buyer from all and any liabilities, obligations, costs and expenses whatsoever arising from any loss, damage, or injury caused to the Buyer or any third party by the Company Personnel in this regard.

3.8   The Company will procure that the Company Personnel co-operate with the Buyer's employees, officers and agents and comply with the instructions of the Buyer in providing the Services, including without limitation, any applicable internal Buyer policies notified to the Company or the Company's Personnel.

3.9   The Company will be responsible for implementing any required disciplinary action with respect to any of the Company Personnel.

4. COMPANY PERSONNEL

4.1   Where required and documented in the Work Package, identified parts of the Services shall be performed by the Key Personnel.

4.2   The Company shall make no change to such Key Personnel without the prior approval of the Buyer which shall not be unreasonably withheld or delayed. If the Buyer approves of or requires a change to the Company Personnel in accordance with this Agreement, the Company shall submit to the Buyer the names and full *curricula vitae* of any proposed substitute and shall permit the Buyer to interview any proposed substitute. The Buyer may in its absolute discretion refuse to accept any proposed substitute, in which case the Company shall as soon as reasonably possible submit to the Buyer further names and full *curricula vitae* of proposed substitutes until a substitute is accepted.

4.3   The Buyer may, in its sole discretion, require termination of the involvement of any Company Personnel performing the Services ('Individual') by providing written notice to the Company with immediate effect. The Company will provide a suitable replacement for such an Individual without delay in accordance with the process set out in clause 4.2.

4.4   To the extent that the Work Package requires Company Personnel to be dedicated to the provision of the Services on a full-time basis, the Company will procure that such Company Personnel are fully dedicated to performing the Services and do not work for third parties other than the Buyer until the Work Package is complete.

4.5   Neither party shall, during the term of this Agreement and for a period of six (6) months after the termination howsoever caused, directly or indirectly solicit or entice away or endeavour to solicit or entice away from the other party any employee of the other party who has been engaged in the provision of Services for the performance of this Agreement. Nothing in this Agreement is intended to prevent any person from seeking employment by responding from to a *bona fide* recruitment advertisement placed by (or on behalf of) the new employer.

4.6 Neither party will be liable to the other for any charges or fees, whether transfer fees or otherwise, where a person takes up any employment having responded to a bona fide recruitment advertisement.

4.7 If any Company Personnel are unable due to illness or other incapacity or for any other reason to supply the Services on any day on which the Company is required to provide the Services, the Company will notify or will procure that the relevant Company Personnel will notify the Buyer as soon as practicable.

4.8 The Buyer will be under no obligation to pay the Company in respect of any periods during which any Company Personnel are unable to carry out the Services due to illness or other incapacity in the event that the fees have been calculated on a time and materials basis.

4.9 If applicable, time sheets for hours or time worked by the Company Personnel will be submitted weekly to the person designated in the Purchase Order as the Buyer contact for approval. All such timesheets will be submitted by the Company with the relevant invoice.

4.10 The Company will procure that Company Personnel performing the Services will not provide any services that are the same as or similar to the Services to any direct or indirect competitor of the Buyer during the period beginning on the Commencement Date and ending on the date which is six (6) months after the latest expiration date of any Purchase Order or Work Package relating to Services with which such Company Personnel have been involved.

4.11 During the period beginning on the Commencement Date and ending on the date which is six (6) months after the latest expiration date of any Purchase Order or Work Package, the Company shall not attempt to discourage any person, firm or company or any supplier who is at the date of cessation or has at any time during the continuance of this Agreement been a client, customer or supplier of the Buyer from dealing with the Buyer.

5. FEES AND PAYMENT TERMS

5.1 The Fees and Expenses for the Services will be as specified in the Work Package provided that such Fees and Expenses are agreed and set out in the applicable Purchase Order. If such Fees are not set out in a Work Package then the Fees and Expenses set out in Attachment 4 and Attachment 5 will apply and the Buyer's then current expenses policy (as the same is notified to the Company from time to time) will apply.

5.2 VAT (where applicable) will be payable by the Buyer in addition to the Fees subject to presentation to the Buyer by the Company of a valid VAT invoice. The Buyer agrees to settle correctly presented, valid and undisputed VAT invoices at the end of the month following the month in which the Invoice is received.

5.3 The Company will invoice the Buyer monthly in arrears or as otherwise specified in accordance with the Purchase Order, as per the Buyer's standard terms of payment.

5.4 The Buyer will not be responsible for any expenses, charges or fees other than the Fees and Expenses set out in the Purchase Order.

5.5 If the parties agree that the Company is to provide services or resources in addition to those specified in a Purchase Order, then such agreement will be reflected in a further Purchase Order, which on execution will be deemed incorporated into this Agreement.

5.6 Once a Work Package has been agreed by the Buyer the Fees for the Services will be fixed.

6. TERMINATION

6.1 The Buyer may terminate this Agreement, a Purchase Order or any Work Package for any reason by providing 15 days prior written notice to Company.

6.2 The Buyer may terminate this Agreement, a Purchase Order or any Work Package with immediate effect by providing written notice to the Company if:

(a) the Company becomes insolvent, has a receiver or manager appointed, commits an act of bankruptcy or commences to be wound up (except for amalgamation or reconstruction);

(b) the Company or the Company Personnel commit any material or persistent breaches of this Agreement;

(c) the Company unreasonably fails or refuses after written warning to procure that the Company Personnel provide the Services properly required of them in accordance with this Agreement;

(d) the Company or the Company Personnel acts or omits to act in a manner calculated or likely to bring the Buyer or any Group Company into disrepute;

(e) the Company fails to meet any Acceptance Criteria on three consecutive occasions; or (*f*)   the Company or the Company Personnel fails to comply with any applicable internal Buyer policies.

6.3   Upon termination of this Agreement or any Purchase Order or Work Package for whatever reason, the Company will deliver, and procure that the Company deliver, to the Buyer's offices or such other location as the Buyer may direct:

(*a*)   all Work whether complete or partially complete;

(*b*)   all books, documents, papers, materials, equipment, customer lists, technical information and data, reports; and

(*c*)   any other property (including copies, summaries and excerpts) in whatever form or medium relating to the business of Buyer or any Group Company,

which are in the possession or control of Company or the Company Personnel at the time of termination.

7. ACCEPTANCE

7.1   The Services will be deemed to have been accepted by the Buyer when the Acceptance Criteria specified in a Work Package have been met and an Acceptance Certificate has been issued. Where no Acceptance Criteria are specified in a Work Package, the Services will be deemed accepted 180 days after delivery of the Deliverables to the Buyer, provided the Buyer has raised no earlier objections, issues or concerns regarding the Services.

7.2   Subject to any alternative acceptance procedure agreed in a Work Package, where a Deliverable is rejected under clause 7.1, the Company shall have two opportunities to resubmit the non-performing Deliverable but should it continue to fail to perform to the Buyer's satisfaction, the Buyer shall have the right to reject that Deliverable and recover any Fees associated with the same that it has paid to the Company and no further Fees shall be due to the Company.

8. STATUS AND LIABILITIES

8.1   Neither the Company nor any Company Personnel will have authority to act as agent for the Buyer or to contract on the Buyer's behalf.

8.2   The Company Personnel will at no time be deemed to be employed, or otherwise engaged by the Buyer.

8.3   The Company will be responsible for paying the Company Personnel and for making any deductions required by law in respect of income tax and National Insurance contributions or similar contributions relating to the provision of the Services. The Company agrees to indemnify the Buyer and any Buyer Group Companies in respect of any claims that may be made by the relevant authorities against the Buyer or any Buyer Group Companies in respect of tax demands or National Insurance or similar contributions relating to the provision of the Services by the Company.

8.4   The Company will, and will procure that the Company Personnel will, comply with all applicable laws, statutes, rules, orders and regulations in providing the Services, including all immigration and employment requirements imposed by any applicable jurisdiction, and the Company will indemnify and hold harmless the Buyer or any Buyer Group Companies from damages arising out of any failure to do so.

9. CONFIDENTIALITY

9.1   Each party undertakes to keep the other party's Confidential Information confidential and to use the other party's Confidential Information solely for purposes related to this Agreement.

9.2   The Receiving Party will not disclose, copy, reproduce or distribute the Disclosing Party's Confidential Information to any person, except:

(*a*)   with the prior written consent of Disclosing Party;

(*b*)   to its employees, professional advisors, consultants and authorised representatives (including to such persons representing its group undertakings), but only to the extent that disclosure is necessary for the purposes related to this Agreement; or

(*c*)   where disclosure is required by law, by a court of competent jurisdiction, by the rules of any stock exchange or by another appropriate regulatory body, provided that all reasonable steps to prevent such disclosure will be taken, the disclosure will be of the minimum amount required, and the Receiving Party consults the Disclosing Party first on the proposed form, timing, nature and purpose of the disclosure.

9.3   The obligations under clauses 9.1 and 9.2 will not apply to Confidential Information:

(*a*)   to the extent it is or becomes generally available to the public other than through a breach of this Agreement;

(*b*)   which the Receiving Party can show by its written or other records was in its lawful possession prior to receipt from the Disclosing Party and which had not previously been obtained from the Disclosing Party or another person under an obligation of confidence; or

(c) which subsequently comes into the possession of the Receiving Party from a third party who does not owe the Disclosing Party an obligation of confidence in relation to it.

9.4 The Company will procure that all Company Personnel execute the form deed of confidentiality undertaking attached hereto as Attachment 3 prior to commencing any Services.

10. INTELLECTUAL PROPERTY

10.1   Subject to the exceptions in clauses 10.2 and 10.3 below, the Company agrees and will procure that the Company Personnel agree that Intellectual Property Rights in the Work will vest in the Buyer on its creation and the Company hereby assigns, and agrees to procure that the Company Personnel will assign, to the Buyer with full title guarantee (by way of present and future assignment) such rights throughout the world for as long as such rights shall last. The Company further agrees to procure that the Company Personnel will agree to do such acts and sign such documents as will be necessary to give effect to the matters contemplated by this clause 10.

10.2   Clause 10.1 will not apply if and to the extent:

(a) the Intellectual Property Rights belong to a third party other than the Company Personnel; or

(b) prior to this Agreement, such copyright formed part of any Company Material.

10.3   The Company retains all Intellectual Property Rights, whether owned or licensed, in Company Material, provided that where any Company Material is delivered as part of the Services the Company hereby grant to the Buyer or any Buyer Group Company a world wide, non–exclusive, perpetual, irrevocable, royalty free licence to use or modify Company Material unless and to the extent that a licence in respect of some or all of the Company Material concerned is granted subject to a separate agreement between the parties.

10.4   The Company hereby waives and agrees to procure that the Company Personnel waive all moral rights the Company or the Company Personnel has or may have under the *Copyright Designs and Patents Act 1988* or otherwise in all Works.

10.5   The Company undertakes to defend the Buyer and all Buyer Group Companies from and against any claim or action that the use or possession of any Deliverable infringes the Intellectual Property Rights of a third party ('IPR Claim') and shall fully indemnify and hold the Buyer and all Buyer Group Companies harmless from and against any losses, damages, costs (including legal fees) and expenses incurred by the Buyer and/or any Buyer Group Company or awarded by a court of competent jurisdiction against the Buyer and/or any Buyer Group Company as a result of or in connection with such an IPR Claim. The Company shall be promptly informed by the Buyer or the relevant Buyer Group Company in writing and furnished with a copy of each communication, notice or other action relating to the alleged infringement and the Buyer or the relevant Buyer Group Company shall provide the Company with all reasonable authority, information and reasonable assistance (at the Company's expense) necessary for the Company to defend or settle such an IPR Claim provided always that in doing so the Company shall not take any step which the Buyer or a Buyer Group Company reasonably believes to be detrimental to its commercial interests.

10.6   The foregoing indemnity shall remain in effect notwithstanding any termination of this Agreement.

10.7   If any IPR Claim is made, or in either party's reasonable opinion is likely to be made, against the Buyer or any Buyer Group Company, the Company shall, with minimal disruption to the Buyer and the Buyer Group Companies, at its option, promptly and at its own expense either:

(*a*)   procure for the Buyer and the Buyer Group Companies the right to continue using and possessing Work; or

(*b*)   modify or replace the infringing part of the Work (without prejudice to the representations and warranties made as to such Work and without diminishing or curtailing any of the required Specification, functions, facilities or the performance of the Services) so as to avoid the infringement or alleged infringement.

10.8   In the event that the Buyer or any Buyer Group Companies are not reasonably satisfied with any modification or replacement Work provided by the Company pursuant to this clause 10, the Buyer may terminate this Agreement and, without prejudice to its other rights and remedies, receive a refund of all sums paid under the Agreement to the Company.

10.9   The Company's indemnity obligations hereunder shall not apply to the extent that the infringement arises out of any modification of the Work made by any one other than the Company or the Company Personnel or the combination, operation or use of the Work with other computer software if such infringement was directly caused by such combination, operation or use of the Work with other computer software.

11. OTHER AGREEMENTS

This Agreement together with any Work Package or Purchase Order(s) executed in accordance with clause 2 will supersede all other agreements or discussions whether written or oral between the Buyer and the Company and comprise the entire agreement between the parties with respect to the subject matters described herein.

12. VARIATIONS

No changes or variations to this Agreement or any Work Package shall be effective unless agreed in writing pursuant to the change control procedure set out in Attachment 2.

13. PUBLICITY

The Company shall not disclose in its publicity material or otherwise the existence of this Agreement or the terms of its relationship with the Buyer without the prior written consent of the Buyer.

14. ASSIGNMENT

The Company will not sub-contract or assign its obligations hereunder to any third party without the Buyer's prior written consent.

15. WAIVER

The failure of either party to enforce or to exercise any term of this Agreement does not constitute a waiver of such term and will in no way affect that party's right later to enforce or to exercise it.

16. THIRD PARTY RIGHTS

A person not party to this Agreement shall have no rights under the *Contracts (Rights of Third Parties) Act 1999* to enforce its terms.

17. FORCE MAJEURE

If either party is prevented or delayed in the performance of any of its obligations under this Agreement by Force Majeure that party shall forthwith serve notice in writing on the other party specifying the nature and extent of the circumstances giving rise to Force Majeure, and shall, subject to service of such notice, have no liability in respect of the performance of such of its obligations as are prevented by Force Majeure during the continuation of the events, and for such time after they cease as is necessary for that party, using all reasonable endeavours, to recommence its affected operations in order for it to perform its obligations.

18. SEVERABILITY

In the event that any provision of this Agreement or any part of any provision shall be determined to be partially void or unenforceable by any court or body of competent jurisdiction or by virtue of any legislation to which it is subject or by virtue of any other reason whatsoever, it shall be void or unenforceable to that extent only and no further and the validity and enforceability of any of the other provisions or the remainder of any such provision shall not be affected thereby.

19. NOTICES

Any notice or other communication to be given under this agreement shall be in writing and signed by or on behalf of the Party giving it and may be served by leaving it or sending it by fax, delivering it by hand or sending it by first class post to the address and for the attention of the relevant Party set out in clause 19.2 (or as otherwise notified from time to time under this agreement). Any notice so served by hand, fax or post shall be deemed to have been received:

- in the case of delivery by hand, when delivered;
- in the case of fax twelve (12) hours after the time of confirmation of despatch;
- in the case of post, at the expiration of two (2) Business Days or (in the case of air mail) five (5) Business Days after the envelope containing the same was delivered into the custody of the postal authorities;

provided that where, in the case of delivery by hand or by fax, such delivery or transmission occurs after 6pm on a Business Day or on a day which is not a Business Day, service shall be deemed to occur at 9a.m. on the next following Business Day.

The addressees of the parties for the purpose of clause 19.1 are as follows:

Party: _____

Buyer: _____

Address: _____

_____

Fax No: _____

Attention Of: _____

Party: _____

Buyer: _____

Address: _____

_____

Fax No: _____

Attention Of: _____

20. APPLICABLE LAW

This Agreement will be construed in accordance with the laws of England and Wales and the parties agree to submit to the exclusive jurisdiction of the Courts of England and Wales.

EXCECUTED by the parties on the date first above written:

SIGNED by for and behalf of   _____

[BUYER] Limited

Print Name: _____

Date: _____

SIGNED by for and behalf of   _____

[SUPPLIER] Limited

Print Name: _____

Date: _____

Attachment 1

Standard Work Package

(Specimen Work Package)

Project Number/Description/Primavera ID:

This Work Package is issued in accordance with the Professional Services Agreement ('the Agreement') between [XXXXXX] ('the Company') and [XXXXXX] Limited ('the Buyer') executed on [COMMENCE-MENT DATE] and is subject to the terms and conditions contained therein.

PART 1. STATEMENT OF WORK

Description of Services: _____

_____

_____

_____

Deliverables:
The Deliverables under this
Work Package are: _____

_____

_____

The Deliverables will be
produced in the following
formats.

1. Documentation: _____

2. Project Reports: _____

3. Prototypes: _____

4. Project Definition: _____

Additional Buyer Requirements:

Overview and Aim of the
Project: _____

pecific Project Objectives: _____

Start Date: _____

End Date: _____

Fee (Fixed Fee/Rates)
(if different from the agreement): _____

PART 2. PROJECT PLAN

Delivery Dates: _____

_____

_____

_____

Other Key Milestones: _____

_____

_____

_____

Company: Key Personnel: _____

_____

Key Contact: _____

Project Manager: _____

Buyer's Personnel: Key Contact: _____

Delivery Manager: _____

Project Sponsor: _____

PART 3. ADDITIONAL/SPECIAL TERMS (IF ANY)

Note: Intellectual Property (the parties should specify here if any or all intellectual property rights are to vest in the Company)

For the purposes of this Work Package, the following provisions shall take precedence over the provisions of the Agreement:

- Clause [   ] shall be amended as follows:

_____

_____

_____

_____

- Clause [   ] shall be amended as follows:

_____

_____

_____

_____

Payment Terms (if different from the Agreement)

_____

_____

_____

_____

Confidentiality Requirements (over and above those contained within the Agreement)

1. _____
2. _____
3. _____
4. _____

Acceptance Testing (if applicable)

Name (and date) of party who is to prepare the schedule of acceptance criteria:

_____

Name (and date) of party who is to prepare the schedule of acceptance test procedures:

_____

Period(s) allowed for agreeing/ rejecting acceptance criteria and acceptance test procedures:

_____

ne (and date) of party responsible for preparing acceptance test data:

_____

Period allowed for acceptance testing (using acceptance test data):

_____

Acceptance Criteria

_____

_____

Additional Resources (if applicable)

_____

_____

Signed for & on behalf of the Buyer:	**Signed for & on behalf of the Company:**
Signature: _____	Signature: _____
Name: _____	Name: _____
Title: _____	Title: _____
Date: _____	Date: _____

Acceptance Certificate

I hereby acknowledge the services described in this Work Package have been delivered to the Buyer and the Acceptance Criteria have been met.

_____   _____
Signature   Date

For and on behalf of the Buyer.

Attachment 2

Change Control Procedure

1. INITIATION OF CHANGE CONTROL PROCEDURE

1.1   The Buyer and the Company shall discuss Variations proposed by either party and such discussion shall result in either a written request for a Variation by the Buyer; or a written recommendation for a Variation by the Company.

1.2　　Where a written request for a Variation is received from the Buyer, the Company shall, unless otherwise agreed, submit a Change Control Note ('CCN') to the Buyer within five (5) Business Days.

1.3　　A written recommendation for a change by the Company shall be submitted as a CCN direct to the Buyer at the time of such recommendation.

1.4　　Each CCN shall conform to the pro-forma set out below.

PRO-FORM CCN

Title of the Variation
Originator and the date of request or recommendation for the Variation:
Reason for the Variation:
Impact analysis indicating the impact of the Variation on the following: (a)　the Services, Company Software, Buyer Environment and other aspects of the Work; (b)　the Project Plan; (c)　the Charges; (d)　the contractual documentation; and (e)　staff resources.
Full details of the Variation including any Specifications and user facilities:
Price, if any, of the Variation:
Timetable for implementation together with any proposals for Acceptance of the Variation:
Schedule of the cost of the Variation:
Date of expiry of validity of the CNN (which shall not be less than [xx] working days:
Provision for signature by the Buyer and the Company:

2. APPROVAL OR DISAPPROVAL OF CCN

For each CCN submitted the Buyer shall, within the period of validity of the CCN:

(*a*) allocate a sequential number to the CCN;

(*b*) evaluate the CCN and as appropriate either:

    (i) request further information;

    (ii) approve the CCN; or

    (iii) notify the Company of the rejection of the CCN.

If approved, two copies of the approved CCN will be signed by or on behalf of the Buyer and the Company. The signing of the CCN will signify acceptance of a Variation by both the Buyer and the Company.

Attachment 3

Form Deed of Confidentiality Undertaking

Name and Address

_____

_____

_____

_____

RE: CONFIDENTIALITY UNDERTAKING – SERVICES AGREEMENT BETWEEN [XXXXXX] AND THE BUYER

Dear Sir or Madam:

1. In connection with the Services Agreement executed by _____ Limited ('the Buyer'), and [XXXXXX] ('the

Company'), I acknowledge that the Buyer may make available certain of its confidential information, for the purpose of my performing the functions described in that agreement ('the Purpose'). This letter relates to information that the Buyer or any of its group undertakings (including each of their respective officers, employees, advisers, agents and representatives) may supply in connection with the Purpose ('the Information').

2.   In consideration of the disclosure of the Information to me, I agree and undertake to:

(*a*)   use the Information solely to the extent necessary for the Purpose;

(*b*)   take all reasonable steps necessary to prevent unauthorised publication or disclosure of the Information; and

(*c*)   hold the Information in strict confidence and not disclose, copy, reproduce or distribute any Information to any person, other than as permitted by the Buyer, or to those of the Buyer's employees who need access strictly for the Purpose, and on the basis that they themselves will not disclose, copy, reproduce or distribute it to any person who is not so authorised (together, the 'Authorised Recipients').

3.   The above undertakings will not apply to Information which:

(*a*)   at the time of supply is in the public domain;

(*b*)   subsequently comes into the public domain, except through breach of the undertakings set out in this letter;

(*c*)   is already in my lawful possession or that of an Authorised Recipient (as evidenced by written records);

(*d*)   subsequently comes lawfully into my possession or that of an Authorised Recipient from a third party who does not owe the Buyer an obligation of confidence in relation to it; or

(*e*)   is required to be disclosed by law, regulation, the rules of any stock exchange or any governmental or competent regulatory authority, as long as I consult with the Buyer first on the proposed form, timing, nature and purpose of the disclosure.

4.   On request, I agree to destroy or return to the Buyer any documents or other materials (including any note, analysis, memorandum or other material that I prepare) containing Information and any copy which may have been made, and take reasonable steps to expunge all Information from any computer, word processor or other device containing Information.

5.   I understand that no right or licence is granted to me in relation to the Information except as expressly set out in this letter, and the Buyer will retain all rights, title and interest to its Information.

6.   I acknowledge and agree that the undertakings set out in this letter will survive completion of the Purpose.

7.   I acknowledge and agree that if I breach this letter in any manner the Buyer will be entitled to terminate either my provision of the Services or the Services Agreement immediately, at the Buyer's sole discretion.

8.   If any provision of this letter is held to be invalid or unenforceable, that provision will (so far as it is invalid or unenforceable) be given no effect and will be deemed not to be included in this letter, but without invalidating any of the remaining provisions.

9.   I confirm that I am acting in this matter as principal and not as an agent or broker for any other person.

10.   I agree that this letter and the relationship between the parties will be governed by, and construed in accordance with, English law, and each party submits to the exclusive jurisdiction of the English courts.

Yours faithfully,

_____

Print Name: _____

Date _____

Agreed and accepted

_____

_____ Limited

Print Name: _____

Date _____

Attachment 4

(Non) Work Package Rates

XXXXXX Rate Chart for Buyer	
Rate	£

All Prices GBP exclusive of VAT

Attachment 5
Expenses

The aim of this document is to explain what expenses are allowed and how to claim.

The basic guidelines are simple:

- All Expenses must be 'wholly, exclusively and necessarily' incurred in the proper performance of the provision of the Services related to Buyer.

- All Expenses incurred must be reasonable, and substantiated with written receipts.

- All Expenses must be planned in a Forecast by the Company and submitted to the Buyer in advance with each Forecast for Consultancy, and the Company shall ensure such Forecast Expenses are approved by the Buyer Project Manager and are covered by a Purchase Order, otherwise the Buyer will not be obliged to reimburse the Company for such expenses.

ALLOWABLE EXPENSES:

Note: Basis

No handling charge – all expenses charged at cost. All receipts to be provided. In the isolated case of an unreceipted expense claim, full supporting detail must be provided as to the cause of the claim, or reimbursement may be delayed or withheld. Entertainment and time used whilst travelling are non–chargeable.

Exceptions to Basis

- Company car mileage shall be charged at ___ p per mile, for mileage incurred whilst engaged on execution of the Services (unreceipted expense).

- Overnight accommodation with breakfast: max £__ per night.

- Subsistence (refreshments/meals/out-of-pocket expenses): max £__ per day.

- Taxi/bus /airfares charged at cost; rail fares charged at cost for standard class travel.

- Venue costs (room hire, equipment hire, food etc) in the implementation of the programmes – chargeable at cost.

Chapter B6
Terms and Conditions for Sale of Goods by Export

At a glance

- Drafted from point of view of supplier.

- For terms and conditions of a purchaser who imports, please refer to CHAPTER B7.

- Ensures it is clear which of the Incoterms 2000 are used – FOB, Ex works, DDP, DDU etc. can all be used (see CHAPTER A3 for further information).

Commentary

B6.2

- These conditions are a short and simple set to apply where a supplier sells goods for export. Where the supplies will be to another UK customer then modifications need to be made (e.g. reference to Incoterms 2000 would not then be appropriate). In such a case, CHAPTER B1 could be used instead.

- Export control legislation needs to be considered particularly if sensitive technology or goods which can be used in the arms industry are involved or if the sale is to a territory where exports can cause problems, such as Yemen, North Korea, Vietnam, Cuba or Iraq.

- Clause 2 provides that payment is by letter of credit. Often letters of credit are rejected by the bank because of an error on the documentation. This clause requires the Customer to pay any such bank charges which then arise, which can be considerable.

- Under clause 4 time for delivery is not of the essence, because these conditions are drafted for the benefit of the supplier.

- Clause 5 deals with when ownership of the goods sold will pass, and risk. These issues may be implied by the Incoterm used so the clause states that the default provisions in the agreement apply unless otherwise required by the Incoterm under which the parties have agreed the goods will be supplied.

- The terms state that English law applies and that the parties submit to the non-exclusive jurisdiction of the English courts in connection with any dispute.

Precedent – Terms and Conditions for Sale of Goods by Export

B6.3

ABC Limited

[Address]

[Tel] [Fax]

[E-mail]

Terms and Conditions of Sale

1. TERMS

These terms and conditions apply to all supplies of goods by the Supplier to Customers. They prevail over any terms supplied by the Customer. No prior statements or correspondence forms part of this Agreement and the Customer accepts it has not relied on any representations in entering into this Agreement.

In these terms:

(*a*)   'Supplier' means ABC Limited of [address].

(*b*)   'Bespoke Goods' means Goods or parts of Goods specifically made or customised for the Customer.

(*c*)   'Customer' means the customer buying the Goods who is named on the Order.

(*d*)   'Goods' means the products to be sold by the Supplier to the Customer named on the Order.

(*e*)   'Order' means the Customer's purchase order for the Goods or, if none, described in the confirmation of order of Supplier or otherwise agreed in writing by the parties.

(*f*)   'Price' means the charge to be paid by the Customer to the Supplier for the Goods.

2. SUPPLY AND PAYMENT

The Supplier sells the Goods to the Customer on the terms of this Agreement in consideration of the payment by the Customer of the Price. Payment for the Products shall be in UK pounds sterling and shall be made by confirmed, transferable, irrevocable without recourse letter of credit providing for payment at sight allowing partial deliveries and collections and issued by a reputable first class bank acceptable to the Supplier. The Customer shall also pay any handling and shipping or other incidental costs and expenses the Supplier has incurred or will incur in relation to the Goods. Prices are exclusive of VAT or other sales taxes which are payable in addition by the Customer and are to be paid in full without deduction of taxes, charges or duties imposed. The parties shall collaborate to take advantage of any double taxation treaties in force. Where there is an error on the letter or credit, or for whatever reason the Supplier's bank rejects the letter or credit, the Customer shall pay all the bank charges and other costs of the Supplier in relation to such error and ensure that a correct letter of credit is issued forthwith. The Supplier shall not offer any credit to the Customer. The Distributor shall not pledge the credit of the Supplier. The Customer shall open each letter of credit within seven (7) days after the Customer's receipt of the Supplier's acceptance of the order and it shall remain open for at least 30 days or such longer period as may be agreed by the parties in relation to individual letters of credit. The terms of the letter of credit may be specified by the Supplier from time to time and payment for Goods shall be made in full without deduction, set off or counterclaim. For payment of the price as to time and amount, time shall be of the essence.

The Price includes packaging charges. Delivery charges shall be paid where so specified in clause 3 below. The Price shall remain fixed for the Order unless otherwise agreed in writing by the parties. Where credit has been agreed in writing between the parties, all invoices shall be paid by the Customer within 30 days of the date of invoice. No right of set off shall arise. Supplier may charge interest at 3% above base rate from time to time of National Westminster Bank plc on all late payments of invoices. Once an Order is placed the Customer may not cancel or alter such Order without the prior written consent of the Supplier.

3. DELIVERY CHARGES

Delivery charges shall, where supply is specified on the Order as on the basis that Supplier shall deliver to the Customer, be stated on the Order and are payable by the Customer. Supply shall be on the Incoterm 2000 specified on the Order – DDP, CIF, ex works etc.

4. DELIVERY

The Supplier shall deliver the Goods to the address specified on the Order, unless otherwise agreed in writing. Time for delivery specified on the Order, if any, is an estimate only and time shall not be of the essence. Where a carrier delivers Goods which the Customer believes are not the quantity or kind ordered or which are damaged, the Customer must notify Supplier by telephone immediately on receipt and confirm this in writing within seven (7) days of delivery otherwise the Supplier accepts no liability for this. Where on investigation the Supplier agrees the incorrect quantity was delivered or the Goods were damaged, the Supplier shall ensure the correct quantity is supplied and the Customer will return any over supply, and/or the Supplier shall replace the damaged Goods with undamaged Goods and this shall be the Customer's only remedy in such a case. The Customer shall return any damaged Goods at its own expense to the Supplier. Where the Supplier, after inspection, agrees the Goods were damaged it shall refund to the Customer the carriage costs of such return, but not otherwise.

5. PASSING OF TITLE

Title to the Goods shall pass to the Customer unless otherwise required by the Incoterm under which the parties have agreed the Goods will be supplied, or, if no such agreement exists, when payment is made to the Supplier for those Goods. Until payment is made the Customer shall not resell the Goods or combine them with other Goods and shall ensure they are kept separately from other goods and are clearly marked as the Supplier's property. The Supplier may, until such time as payment is made, enter the Customer's premises to retrieve its Goods. Risk in the Goods shall pass on delivery unless otherwise required by the Incoterm under which the parties have agreed the Goods will be supplied.

6. INTELLECTUAL PROPERTY RIGHTS AND SERVICES

The Supplier owns all copyright, design and registered design rights, trade mark and other intellectual property rights in the Goods and in Bespoke Goods. The Customer shall not register any intellectual property right or claim any such right in the Goods or the Bespoke Goods and shall keep any rights notice of the Supplier's on the Goods or Bespoke Goods and notify the Supplier if it discovers any infringement of the Supplier's such rights by a third party. In particular, the Customer acknowledges that it has no right or licence by virtue of having purchased the Goods or Bespoke Goods or otherwise itself to manufacture the Goods or Bespoke

Goods. It shall ensure its employees, agents, customers and contractors are aware of Supplier's such intellectual property rights. Where the Customer requests specific modifications or additions the Customer shall ensure the Supplier is given all information it requires to make such modifications and the Customer shall fully indemnify the Supplier against any loss or liability arising from the Supplier following the Customer's instructions and/or performing such services or making Bespoke Goods. Any manufacturing data, product or other confidential or commercial information supplied by the Supplier to the Customer, whether marked as confidential or not, shall be held in strict confidence by the Customer and only used for the purposes for which it was supplied.

7. LIABILITY

The Supplier shall use all reasonable endeavours to ensure:

(i)   the Goods comply with their description on the Order; and

(ii)   are of satisfactory quality and/or fit for their purpose; and

(iii)   are delivered to the Customer.

Where the Supplier fails to use such reasonable endeavours, the Customer shall notify the Supplier within seven (7) days of delivery in writing and the Supplier's sole obligation shall be to repair, replace or supply the Goods. Save as provided in this clause, the Supplier's liability to the Customer is otherwise excluded, including, without limitation, implied conditions to the fullest extent permitted by law. Supplier limits its liability to the Price of the Goods in relation to any claim relating to Goods supplied and excludes all liability for consequential, indirect loss, loss of profit revenue and goodwill. The Supplier shall not be liable for any delay or failure caused by circumstances beyond its reasonable control, including, without limitation, liability arising from failures by subcontractors, manufacturers, terrorist activity, Government action or Acts of God. However, nothing in these terms shall exclude the Supplier's liability for death and personal injury caused by its negligence. Where a Customer's modification to the Goods or combination of the Goods with other Goods or other Customer action, including without limitation, installation, results in a loss to, or liability of, the Supplier, the Customer shall fully indemnify and hold harmless the Supplier against all such loss and liability.

8. STANDARDS

It is the responsibility of the Customer to ensure that the Goods comply with any safety or other standard and for the product or market in which the Goods will be used or resold or used and that the Goods will not infringe the intellectual property rights of any person in the market in which the Customer intends to sell the Goods. Whilst the Supplier shall use its reasonable endeavours to assist Customers, where further information in this respect is required, the Supplier reserves the right to levy a charge, which will be estimated to the Customer in advance, for any significant research or investigations required to satisfy the Customer's detailed enquiries in relation to such matters, and does not accept liability for statements made in providing such assistance. The Customer shall fully indemnify and hold the Supplier harmless against all loss and liability, including legal fees on an indemnity basis, arising from claims by the Customer's customer arising from non-compliance of the Goods with any local law or intellectual property right.

9. GENERAL

This Agreement is subject to English law and the Supplier and the Customer agree to submit to the non-exclusive jurisdiction of the English courts in relation to any dispute. Notices shall be served on the Supplier at the address above and the Customer at the address on the Order. The failure to enforce a right under this Agreement shall not amount to a waiver of it by the Supplier. Where any provision of this Agreement is held to be void, the other provisions of this Agreement shall continue notwithstanding to apply.

Chapter B7
Terms and Conditions for Purchase of Goods and Services (by Import)

At a glance — B7.1

- These terms are for use by a buyer, not a supplier.

- They are to be used where a UK buyer is buying either good or services from abroad by way of import.

- These terms are not suitable for suppliers to use when selling goods or services.

Commentary — B7.2

- These terms and conditions are prepared from the standpoint of the buyer of the goods, not the supplier. They therefore include provisions favourable to buyers such as ensuring goods are of good quality and can be rejected if unsuitable. The terms also can be used where services are used.

- The terms are designed where goods are imported from abroad and thus in particular address issues of foreign imports, intellectual property including trade mark issues, and other related areas of law.

- They are not to be used where goods are sold, rather than purchased. Sellers will have terms which favour them which should be used instead.

- Clause 13 provides that the buyer will own the intellectual property rights in any customised work undertaken. If this is not provided then by default under English law most rights will remain with the supplier, even though the buyer is paying.

Precedent – Terms and Conditions for Purchase of Goods and Services (Import)

B7.3

_____Limited

[Address]

[Tel] [Fax]

[E-mail]

Terms and Conditions of Purchase of Goods and Services – Import

Draft 1

1. CONDITIONS

These conditions shall apply to all orders for the purchase of goods and services by us from our suppliers and sub-contractors from outside the UK. Any qualification of these Conditions by you or any other Conditions which you seek to impose will be inapplicable unless expressly accepted in writing, signed by us. We agree to buy the goods or services specified on the order from you on the terms set out below. Only written orders on our official purchase order form and signed by an authorised person are valid. Reference must be made to our purchase order number in all correspondence, invoices and delivery notes enclosed with the goods. Failure to include such a delivery note may result in our incurring additional costs, which you shall pay. If further documentation is required this will be stated on the order or on annexed delivery instructions.

2. ORDER NUMBER

Any delivery against this order must be accompanied by an advice and/or packing note quoting the order number. If your invoice does not quote our order number payment will be subject to delay.

272

3. DEFINITIONS

(*a*)   'Goods' means machinery, apparatus, materials, instruments, articles, parts and things of all kinds to be provided or work to be done under the order.

(*b*)   'Services' means the services you will perform for us described on our purchase order.

(*c*)   'We' means _____ Limited of _____ _____, Tel _____, Fax _____ _____, E-mail _____.

(*c*)   'You' means the supplier of goods or services or our sub–contractor whose name and address appears on our purchase order.

4. IDENTIFICATION

All goods supplied against our drawings must be marked with our drawing number except where such a number cannot physically be incorporated. Packages containing goods supplied against our drawings, part numbers or catalogues must be marked with the appropriate reference.

5. PRICES

Prices shall remain firm as quoted by you for the whole of this order and shall not be subject to variation unless we agree in writing and unless we also have been given 28 days' notice of such proposed variation. If we do not accept the variation we shall be entitled to cancel the whole or any part of the order, at our discretion, without prejudice to our other rights and remedies. Any deposit or sum paid by us in advance shall immediately be repaid by you. Any value added tax shall be deemed included in the price except where specified separately on the order. Value added tax shall be stated separately on the invoice.

6. INVOICES

Invoices which do not refer to our purchase order number will be rejected. All invoices must be received by the fourth of the month following the date of despatch of the Goods or performance of the Services, otherwise payment will be delayed. All statements of account shall be rendered by you to us by the ninth of each month.. Unless otherwise agreed invoices are due for payment 60 days from the date of invoice where the terms of this agreement in relation to this invoice are met. We reserve the right to charge interest at 3% above National Westminster Bank plc base rate from time to time on all sums overdue hereunder.

The price shall be deemed to include all materials, expenses and costs except where expressly stated on the purchase order.

Payment shall be in UK pounds sterling unless otherwise stated on the purchase order and shall be made by the payment means specified on the purchase order, or, where not so specified, by letter of credit. Prices are exclusive of VAT or other sales taxes which are payable in addition by us. You agree to collaborate to take advantage of any double taxation treaties in force.

7. PACKING MATERIAL

Packing cases, skids, drums and other packaging are to be supplied free of charge by you to us. Empty packaging where relevant will be returned at your expense upon request to you by us, but we can accept no liability for their return in safe condition. Returnable containers must be stencilled with your name and address together with an addressed reversible label.

The type of packing material shall be such as will adequately protect the goods in transit for storage at our premises or those of our customer. You will mark the goods in accordance with our instructions. Such instructions shall not obviate the need for you to mark the goods according to their nature such as 'Fragile'.

8. DELIVERY

Unless otherwise specified on the purchase order, you shall deliver the Goods to us or provide Services to us at the address on the purchase order. Title to, and risk in the Goods shall pass on delivery. Where terms on the order such as FOB, ex works etc. are used these shall be construed in accordance with Incoterms 2000. The Goods and/or Services must be delivered or provided not later than the delivery date on the purchase order or otherwise agreed in writing by us or where delivery is to be by instalments not later than the agreed date. Time shall be of the essence. Where additional goods or work are delivered or modifications are made you shall not be entitled to extra time for delivery except where agreed in writing with us in advance. You shall only be entitled to payment for the quantity of goods specified on the purchase order which comply with these terms and the purchase order.

We shall be under no obligation to accept delivery of Goods or provision of Services before the agreed date. Should we agree to accept early delivery we shall be entitled to withhold payment in respect of such deliveries until the agreed date. We shall be entitled to reject all the Goods or Services if any part is not delivered by the agreed date or any agreed extension of such date. The time for delivery shall be extended by a reasonable period if delay in delivery is caused by industrial dispute or by circumstances beyond your control, provided that you have notified us immediately on becoming aware of the likelihood of any such delay and we agree such extension and provided, where relevant, our own customer accepts an extension. The delays of your approved sub-contractors or suppliers shall not be treated as a cause beyond your reasonable control. Any failure by you to make delivery occasioned otherwise than by *force majeure*, entitles us to damages in addition to or by way of alternative to compensation. If due to industrial dispute or circumstances beyond our control we are unable to accept delivery on the agreed date you will arrange for storage and the reasonable cost of such storage shall be borne by us. No responsibility can be accepted by us for Goods received damaged. In such cases you will be notified and required at our option to credit or exchange the Goods.

9. INSPECTION

The Goods will be subject to inspection by us and/or our customer after delivery and any rejected Goods may be returned to you at your expense. We shall also examine Services provided. We will advise you of any rejects and you will be given reasonable opportunity to advise disposition. We reserve the right to inspect at your works any material or equipment the subject of the order at any stage in the process of manufacture.

10. DEFECTS AFTER DELIVERY AND WARRANTY

All Goods and Services supplied by you to us shall be of first class material and workmanship throughout and in accordance with the contract, the description on the purchase order, their specification, if any, and otherwise as represented to us by you. You will only use new parts, not second hand or reconditioned parts, unless agreed by us. You shall use materials in providing the Goods or Services, such as paint, which comply with our requirements set out on the purchase order, specification or other document. All Goods shall be of reasonable commercial quality and you shall be responsible for ensuring they are fit for their intended use where stated or where such use is clear. You shall comply with any contractual requirements of our customer set out on our purchase order and shall indemnify us for any loss suffered by us arising from any breach of these terms, including, without limitation, where such breach causes us to breach our contract with a customer. All Services shall be provided with reasonable skill and care by competent staff. You will make good by repair, or at our option by the supply of a replacement, defects which under proper use appear in the Goods and Services within a period of 36 months after supply and/or installation at the ultimate location where the Goods will be used or such alternative period as may be specified on the purchase order, without prejudice to our other rights and remedies. The repaired or new Goods or Services will be delivered by you free of charge as provided in Clause 8 above. You shall hold product liability insurance relevant to damages caused by default in the quality of the Goods or Services.

Work under this agreement may not be sub-contracted without our prior written consent. Where we agree to sub-contracting it shall be sub-contracted on the same terms as this agreement, in particular, but without limitation, in relation to ownership of intellectual property rights and quality and you shall ensure your sub-contractors contract on such terms.

Any international standards to which the goods must comply shall be stated on the purchase order and shall be the latest such standards.

11. REJECTIONS AND TESTING

We shall be entitled to reject any Goods or Services not in accordance with the contract within a reasonable time after they have been received. All such rejected Goods or Services must be replaced and the Goods or Services shall not be deemed to have been delivered until such rejected goods are replaced. No payment shall be made for any rejected Goods or Services. If you are unable to replace rejected Goods or Services within a reasonable time after being notified of their rejection we shall be entitled to cancel the order in respect of the rejected Goods or Services and obtain equivalent goods or services elsewhere and any extra expense to which we may be put shall be paid for by you, without prejudice to our other rights and remedies.

Where formal acceptance tests are to be undertaken by us or our customer or quality audits undertaken by such customer or us, these shall be specified on the purchase order. You shall provide us with test certificates indicating the character, scope and results of the tests performed. Where we or our customer require(s) a test to be carried out in our joint presence this shall be at a venue and on a date which is convenient to us or our customer at your expense. You shall provide all equipment and tools necessary for such tests. We shall be entitled to check all equipment used in such tests. In addition to tests specified in the order we are entitled to check the Goods otherwise comply with the contract. Where Goods fail a test they shall be retested only where we agree. We will not normally demand a retest for slight defects. The passing of an acceptance test does not remove any right for us to claim any breach of contract or warranty under this agreement.

Our signature of your delivery note shall, notwithstanding any notice on such note, not comprise acceptance of the Goods or Services nor an acknowledgement that they comply with the contract.

12. INTELLECTUAL PROPERTY RIGHTS INDEMNITY

You will indemnify us against any claim of infringement of patent, registered design, design right, trade mark, copyright, database right or any other intellectual property right by the use or sale of any article or material supplied by you to us and against all costs and damages, including legal fees, which we may incur in any action or threatened action for such infringement or for which we may become liable in any such action, provided always that this indemnity shall not apply to any infringement which is due to your having followed a design or instruction furnished or given by us or to the use of such article or material in a manner or for a purpose or in a foreign country not specified by us or disclosed to you, or to any infringement which is due to the use of such article or material in association or combination with any other article or material not supplied or approved by you. We will give you immediate notice of any such claim and permit you to defend the same and to conduct any litigation that may ensue and all negotiations for a settlement of the claim.

13. OWNERSHIP OF INTELLECTUAL PROPERTY RIGHTS AND TOOLS

We shall own all intellectual property rights in tools, gauges, dies, jigs, fixtures, patterns of drawings, computer software, plans, diagrams or other materials specially made by you for us ("Tools") for the purposes of this order automatically on their creation. You waive all moral rights therein. You shall not register any rights in such Tools and shall not use them except for the purposes of performance of your obligations under this agreement. Where you have incurred costs in purchase of physical materials or parts for such Tools and the purchase order does not specify that we obtain ownership of the physical property in the Tools as part of the price, we shall own such physical property where we pay you its written-down value as appearing in your accounts at the date we exercise such right. You will give us credit for any payment made for Tools towards the original cost of purchase or manufacture.

Where we supply tools of the kind specified above, including without limitation, patterns, measuring devices and packaging, to you so you can perform the contract, they remain our property and should be returned to us immediately on request and only used for the purposes of the contract. We shall supply a list of such tools to you. You shall store our tools separately from your property and name them as our property. We shall have a right of entry to your premises to recover them. You shall maintain, insure and store them at your expense and to our required standards. You will not modify, move or alter them without our consent. You will inform us when they cease to produce acceptable products or when additional tools, models etc are required.

Where samples are to be produced you shall send them to us free of charge as soon as possible or by the date on the order, if any. We shall examine them and notify you of any alterations required and where another sample shall be sent. The acceptance of the sample shall not limit your guarantee obligations. We shall notify you within two (2) weeks of our receipt of the sample as to whether it is acceptable.

You shall not use our name in any publicity or claim any connection with us without our prior consent in writing. You shall put any patent numbers, names or other signs we or our customer requires on the Goods.

You shall keep confidential all information you obtain about us whether as to our customers, products, supplies or other commercially sensitive material without limit as to time and not disclose or use this save as expressly required for the purposes of this Agreement.

14. HEALTH AND SAFETY

All goods shall have all necessary safety devices fitted. You are responsible for compliance with the *Health and Safety at Work Etc. Act 1974* in relation to Goods and Services and will indemnify us against any liability, costs, losses or expenses we may sustain if you fail to do so.

When you are working at our premises or the premises of our customer in the performance of any services or installation of the goods you shall ensure your staff comply with our or our customer's reasonable requirements at the premises.

15. GENERAL

Headings to the Clauses in these Conditions are for convenience only and shall not affect the construction thereof.

If any provision in these Conditions (or part thereof) shall be found to be invalid or unenforceable, the invalidity or unenforceability of such provision (or part thereof) shall not affect any other provision (or the other part of the provision).

Our failure to insist on strict performance of any of your obligations shall not be construed as a waiver and shall not affect our right to require strict performance of all your obligations.

These terms are personal to you and may not be assigned or transferred by you. We may assign and/or sub-contract our obligations under this agreement.

These Conditions shall be governed by and construed in accordance with the laws of England and you agree to submit to the non-exclusive jurisdiction of the English courts where disputes arise.

_____ Ltd – Conditions of Purchase (Import).

Section C:
Business-to-consumer
Contracts

Chapter C1
Consumer Contracts –
Distance Selling

Preliminary issues of incorporation   C1.1

It should be stressed at the outset that distance selling terms and conditions should be presented to a potential buyer prior to the conclusion of the contract, otherwise they will not be binding. If the initial contact is with the consumer through, for example, a direct mail shot or media advertising, then the terms and conditions should be contained in that initial contact, or, at the very least, reference to the terms and conditions should be made in that contact if the potential supplier is not inclined to spell them all out immediately. In particular, this may be the case where the initial contact is by radio or television, or over the telephone. If the supplier wishes to incorporate the terms and conditions by reference only, the initial contact, in whatever form it is made, should state something on the lines of:

> 'This contract is made subject to our terms and conditions. Copies are available on request from . . .'

Precedent – Specimen Distance Selling Contract

C1.2

1.   This contract is for the supply and delivery of the items specified herein.

> **Comment**:
>
> The particular items to be supplied will be specified here. The *Consumer Protection (Distance Selling) Regulations 2000 (SI 2000/2334)* also require the contract to describe the main characteristics of the goods, such as 'inkjet business cards', or 'arum lily white'.
>
> Provision may be made for the products listed to be identified by code and for the quantity of each particular product being ordered.

2. We will endeavour to deliver all products ordered within 28 days of receipt of order, but delivery time cannot be guaranteed.

Comment:

The Regulations provide that the supplier is to perform the contract within 30 days from the day following the day the consumer sent the order. By stating that delivery time cannot be guaranteed, the supplier is taking advantage of the further provision in the Regulations that the 30 day period applies 'unless the parties agree otherwise'.

3. The products displayed here are illustrative only and the actual product delivered may differ in some respects.

Occasionally, particularly if the item to be supplied has not actually been manufactured, or if an enhanced version of an existing product is expected, the supplier might wish to take advantage of some such clause as this. It should be noted, though, that, while it is not infrequently used, its success cannot be guaranteed. While it might avoid any allegation that the goods supplied do not conform to their description, it is less clear that such a clause will avoid *s 1* of the *Trade Descriptions Act 1968*. This provides that an offence arises if goods are falsely described. Importantly, the offence can arise regardless of any intention or blame on the part of the supplier.

Case Example: *Norman v Bennett [1974] 1 WLR 1229.*

A supplier can always qualify any description, but the rule laid down in this case is that any such qualification must be as 'bold, precise and compelling' as the description itself. This would mean that any such statement as above must be in immediate proximity to the product or the product description, so that the customer sees them simultaneously.

4. Your payment must be enclosed with this order. Payment can be by personal cheque drawn on an UK bank and must be crossed 'A/C payee only' if not already so crossed. Payment may also be made by debit, credit or charge card by completing the following details . . .

Comment:

It should be added that, under *s 75* of the *Consumer Credit Act 1974*, the credit card company is as liable as the supplier in the event of there being a misrepresentation or breach of contract by the supplier, where the cash price of the relevant item is at least £100 and not more than

£30,000. Note, however, this applies only to credit cards, i.e. cards where the debt can be paid off in instalments. It does not apply to charge cards, such as American Express, where the debt is to be paid off in one sum.

Alternatively, the supplier might provide for payment by instalments, in which case account should also be taken of the *CCA 1974*. When the Act applies, the supplier must be licensed by the Office of Fair Trading; if not, the agreement can be enforced only by an order from the OFT itself.

Various formalities must also be observed as to the form and content of the contract and the provision of copies. Breach of these requirements means that the agreement can be enforced only on a court order and, in some cases, not at all.

A supplier can avoid these provisions, however, if the agreement is exempt from control under the provisions of the *Consumer Credit (Exempt Agreements) Order 1989 (SI 1989/869)*. The relevant exemption refers to agreements where the credit is repayable in not more than four instalments over not longer than one year.

5.   Credit account applications are granted subject to status and to checks made through credit reference agencies. If you do not wish us to contact such agencies, please advise us accordingly.

Comment:

The supplier will make use of such a clause if he offers a credit account against which customers can charge their purchases.

6.   You have a right to cancel this agreement at any time up to seven working days from the day after your receipt of the goods. In the event of cancellation by you, the goods must be returned to us at your expense or you can arrange for us to collect the goods at your expense. You may cancel your order by sending or delivering us a letter, by fax or e-mail. We cannot accept verbal cancellations unless these are confirmed by any of the methods just specified.

Comment:

The *Consumer Protection (Distance Selling) Regulations 2000 (SI 2000/2334)* give a right to the seven-day cooling-off period and require that this is stated in the contract. In relation to the last sentence, the supplier does not have to say that the goods have to be returned if this is not the case, but must indicate if collection or return is required at the customer's expense. The supplier is always free to bear the costs himself.

The statement that verbal cancellation cannot be accepted arises from the Regulations saying that notification of cancellation must be in writing or in another 'durable medium available and accessible to the supplier'. This does seem to allow cancellation notification left on an answerphone.

The Regulations do not preclude a supplier from offering better terms, of which the following is an example.

> 'Any item ordered will be accepted for return for any reason within 30 days of receipt by the customer. If you are not completely satisfied with the product, we will provide a complete refund and provide you with a reply-paid label for the return of the product'.

7.   We guarantee that this product will be free of any defects rendering it unfit for its purpose or not of satisfactory quality for 12 months from the date of purchase. In the event of a breach of this guarantee, we will repair or replace the product free of charge, whichever the customer shall choose. This does not affect your statutory rights.

Comment:

While this term is not compulsory, the *Consumer Protection (Distance Selling) Regulations 2000 (SI 2000/2334)* do require a supplier to state if he provides any guarantee.

Again, this is essentially a voluntary undertaking. The last sentence is, however, required by the *Consumer Transactions (Restrictions on Statements) Order 1976 (SI 1976/1813)*, in precisely those circumstances where such a voluntary undertaking is given. It has the effect of reminding the customer that he always has his rights against the supplier under the *SGA 1979*, or the *SGSA 1982*.

It should also be realised that the rights which a consumer, as opposed to a business customer, has under those Acts to goods which are of satisfactory quality and reasonably fit for their purpose cannot be excluded or limited, and that any term in the contract to such effect is illegal by virtue of the above Order.

8.   While we use only reputable carriers, and ensure that the goods are packed securely, we cannot accept any liability for any dam-

age or deterioration in the goods which occurs, for whatever reason, while the goods are in transit to you.

Comment:

The *SGA 1979* allows the parties to make their own provision as to who bears the risk of damage or deterioration in goods sent to the customer. This clause takes advantage of this. This clause could not, however, be used if clause 6 above is also used, unless clause 7 was stated to be subject to clause 8.

---

9.   The property in the goods remains with the supplier until payment has been received in full.

Comment:

This again takes advantage of the provision in the *SGA 1979* relating to the passing of property. If this provision is not used, property, and hence the full rights of ownership, will pass once the goods have been ascertained by the supplier and put in transit (see A2.16 above). If property is retained by the supplier as recommended, then the goods remain his and can be repossessed.

---

10.   The price of this product is £117.50 inc VAT at the standard rate.

Comment:

The *Consumer Protection (Distance Selling) Regulations 2000 (SI 2000/2334)* require the price to be stated 'including all taxes'. This appears to rule out saying '£100 plus £17.50' even though the calculation of the total price is straightforward. In fact, it is not even necessary to say that the price given does include VAT. It is enough for the purposes of the Regulations that it does include VAT.

---

11.   Please add £3.50 postage charges to the value of the goods ordered when calculating the overall amount you have to pay.

Comment:

The *Consumer Protection (Distance Selling) Regulations 2000 (SI 2000/2334)* require the contract to indicate any delivery costs which may be payable. If no delivery costs are payable, this does not have to be stated, but of course the supplier can indicate this if he wishes. The supplier can also indicate that delivery costs will be imposed on certain levels of order by value.

---

12. To place your order with us, please fax, phone or e-mail on or at the following freephone numbers or address.

13. The cost of your calling us on the number given will be [state cost] and the call will last for approximately [state period].

> **Comment**:
>
> Under the *Consumer Protection (Distance Selling) Regulations 2000 (SI 2000/2334)*, the cost of contacting the supplier must be stated if this is more than the 'basic rate'. Accordingly, if it is necessary to make the call by a premium rate number, the costs of doing so must be stated. The costs of communication need only be stated if they exceed the basic rate, though there is nothing to stop a supplier from giving the costs of communication not exceeding the basic rate.

14. Should the goods you have ordered for any reason become unavailable, we reserve the right to offer you goods of an equivalent or better value. You may return any such replacement goods at our cost by use of a reply-paid label.

> **Comment**:
>
> There is no requirement in law to offer replacement goods when the intended goods become unavailable, but the *Consumer Protection (Distance Selling) Regulations 2000 (SI 2000/2334)* state that a supplier must state in the contract if his policy is to provide substitutes. He must also state that he will bear the cost of returning any substitute goods supplied.

15. By entering this contract, you agree to accept monthly deliveries for a period of 12 months.

> **Comment**:
>
> The Distance Selling Regulations require such a statement if the contract is one for the supply of goods permanently or recurrently.

16. Please Note: We cannot accept orders from those under [specify an age here appropriate to the product in hand] without the countersignature of a responsible adult.

> **Comment**:
>
> Depending on the nature of the product concerned, this provision is required by the *Consumer Protection (Distance Selling) Regulations 2000*

(*SI 2000/2334*) inasmuch as it requires the supplier to ensure compliance with 'the principles governing the protection of those who are unable to give their consent such as minors'.

17.   We may contact you in the future with further offers, or supply your details to carefully selected third parties. Please tick the boxes alongside if you do not wish to hear from us [   ] or from third parties[   ].

Comment:

This is not required by the *Consumer Protection (Distance Selling) Regulations 2000 (SI 2000/2334)*, but arises from the *Data Protection Act 1998*, and its requirement that all data be processed 'fairly'. The Act does not state that there must be a tick box, nor specify whether this can be an 'opt in' or 'opt out' box. It remains possible to comply with the Act by asking consumers to write, phone, fax or e-mail with their preference.

18.   {Name of supplier and address}.

Comment:

The Regulations only require an address if advance payment is to be made.

19.   As part of our continuing service to you, the customer, we have established a helpline whose address is . . . {Insert address}. It can be contacted between 8am and 5.30pm on the following numbers . . . {Insert number}.

Comment:

The *Consumer Protection (Distance Selling) Regulations 2000 (SI 2000/ 2334)* do not require any kind of complaint procedure to be established, but, if one is established, its 'geographical address' must be given. Accordingly, it would not be enough simply to give a phone, fax or e-mail address, but these can be given in addition to the geographical address. It does not seem necessary to use the word 'complaints'. So long as an address is given to which complaints can be made, that suffices. Alternatively, the following can be used:

'Should you require our help or advice in making the best use of your purchase, please contact our helpline on . . .'

The *Consumer Protection (Distance Selling) Regulations 2000 (SI 2000/ 2334)* require an indication of any after-sales services provided by the supplier, though they do not go so far as requiring there to be an such service.

Electronic commerce requirements   **C1.3**

The following additional requirements are imposed under the *Electronic Commerce (EC Directive) Regulations 2002 (SI 2002/2013)*. In the requirements set out below, 'information society service' means 'any service normally provided for remuneration, at a distance, by means of electronic equipment for the processing (including digital compression) and storage of data, and at the individual request of a recipient of a service'. The Regulations expressly state that these requirements are in addition to those imposed by the *Consumer Protection (Distance Selling) Regulations 2000 (SI 2000/2334)*.

General information

A person providing an information society service shall make available to the recipient of the service and any relevant enforcement authority, in a form and manner which is easily, directly and permanently accessible:

- the name of the service provider;

- the geographic address at which the service provider is established;

- the details of the service provider, including his electronic mail address, which make it possible to contact him rapidly and communicate with him in a direct and effective manner;

- where the service provider is registered in a trade or similar register available to the public, details of the register in which the service provider is entered and his registration number, or equivalent means of identification in that register;

- where the provision of the service is subject to an authorisation scheme, the particulars of the relevant supervisory authority;

- where the service provider exercises a regulated profession:

  - the details of any professional body or similar institution with which the service provider is registered;

  - his professional title and the Member State where that title has been granted;

  - a reference to the professional rules applicable to the service provider in the Member State of establishment and the means to access them; and

C1: Consumer Contracts – Distance Selling   **C1.3**

- where the service provider undertakes an activity that is subject to value added tax, his VAT registration number.

Where a person providing an information society service refers to prices, these shall be indicated clearly and unambiguously and, in particular, shall indicate whether they are inclusive of tax and delivery costs.

Commercial communications

A service provider shall ensure that any commercial communication provided by him and which constitutes or forms part of an information society service shall:

- be clearly identifiable as a commercial communication;
- clearly identify the person on whose behalf the commercial communication is made;
- clearly identify as such any promotional offer (including any discount, premium or gift) and ensure that any conditions which must be met to qualify for it are easily accessible, and presented clearly and unambiguously; and
- clearly identify as such any promotional competition or game and ensure that any conditions for participation are easily accessible and presented clearly and unambiguously.

Unsolicited commercial communications

A service provider shall ensure that any unsolicited communication sent by him by electronic mail is clearly and unambiguously identifiable as soon as it is received.

Conclusion of contracts

Unless parties who are not consumers have agreed otherwise, where a contract is to be concluded by electronic means a service provider shall, prior to an order being placed by the recipient of a service, provide to that recipient in a clear, comprehensible and unambiguous manner:

- the different technical steps to follow to conclude the contract;
- whether or not the concluded contract will be filed by the service provider and whether it will be accessible;
- the technical means for identifying and correcting input errors prior to the placing of the order; and
- the languages offered for the conclusion of the contract.

291

Unless parties who are not consumers have agreed otherwise, a service provider shall indicate which relevant codes of conduct he subscribes to and give information on how those codes can be consulted electronically.

The above requirements shall not apply to contracts concluded exclusively by exchange of electronic mail or by equivalent individual communications.

Where the service provider provides terms and conditions applicable to the contract to the recipient, the service provider shall make them available to him in a way that allows him to store and reproduce them.

Placing of the order

Unless parties who are not consumers have agreed otherwise, where the recipient of the service places his order through technological means, a service provider shall:

- acknowledge receipt of the order to the recipient of the service without undue delay and by electronic means; and

- make available to the recipient of the service appropriate, effective and accessible technical means allowing him to identify and correct input errors prior to the placing of the order.

For the purposes of the first bullet point above:

- the order and the acknowledgement of receipt will be deemed to be received when the parties to whom they are addressed are able to access them; and

- the acknowledgement of receipt may take the form of the provision of the service paid for where that service is an information society service.

The foregoing requirements shall not apply to contracts concluded exclusively by exchange of electronic mail or by equivalent individual communications.

Right to rescind contract

Where a person:

- has entered into a contract to which these Regulations apply; and

- the service provider has not made available means of allowing him to identify and correct input errors as required above, he shall be entitled to rescind the contract unless any court having jurisdiction in relation to the contract in question orders otherwise on the application of the service provider.

Presentation of contract terms   **C1.4**

For the most part, the *Consumer Protection (Distance Selling) Regulations 2000* (*SI 2000/2334*) require the foregoing terms to be provided to the consumer 'in good time' prior to the conclusion of the contract. Their presence in a direct mail catalogue, newspaper, or on the Internet would suffice. Where a consumer is called by phone, there is the further requirement laid down in the Regulations that the identity of the supplier and the commercial purpose of the call must be made clear to the consumer at the outset. This would appear to apply whether or not the consumer requested the call.

Terms to be in writing   **C1.5**

The above requirements could be met purely by the provision of verbal information. The Regulations go on to say, however, that certain information must be provided in writing 'or in another durable medium which is available and accessible' to the consumer. This would appear to allow use of a fax; e-mail and perhaps also an answerphone message.

Deadlines for presenting terms   **C1.6**

This information is to be supplied before the conclusion of the contract, or 'in good time'. This must be no later than the time of delivery when delivery is not to third parties. This is a reference to those cases where one person, perhaps by way of gift, orders goods to be delivered to a third party's home. In such cases, the written or other durable information must be provided simply in good time.

What must be provided:

The information which actually must be in writing or in another durable medium is:

- the identity of the supplier and, where advance payment is required, the supplier's address;

- a description of the main features of the goods;

- price, including all taxes;

- any delivery costs;

- the existence of the right to cancel;

- how the right to cancel is exercised;

- the geographical address of the supplier's business to which complaints can be sent; and

- information about guarantees and after-sales service.

In practical terms, while these are the only terms which actually have to be in writing or some durable medium, all the terms specified earlier will be in such form.

Contracts outside the Regulations   C1.7

The *Consumer Protection (Distance Selling) Regulations 2000 (SI 2000/2334)* do not cover:

- land contracts except rental agreements;
- building construction contracts where the contract also provides for the disposition of an interest in the land, except for a rental agreement;
- contracts relating to financial services;
- contracts made through a vending machine or automated commercial premises;
- contracts made with a telecommunications operator via a public pay-phone; or
- auction contracts.

Internet-related aspects   C1.8

At the same time, it should be recognised that communication via the Internet poses special issues and these should be recognised both in the contract and in the procedures established to deal with business sales.

Acknowledgment of order

The supplier's system should be so set up that, where an order is sent by e-mail, an acknowledgement of order is immediately sent back to the consumer by e-mail. This reply should:

- clearly spell out the goods or services which have been ordered;
- the price and the method of payment;
- a reference number for the contract;
- delivery date;
- place of delivery (that is, if the goods are to be sent to the consumer's home or are to be collected by him);
- an e-mail address for queries and also a phone number;
- the geographical address of the supplier's place of business;
- any registration numbers appropriate to the supplier's business;
- the supplier's website address; and

- arrangements for cancellation and refunds.

The reply should also indicate that it should be printed off and retained by the consumer.

Privacy statement

The reply should further contain a privacy statement on these lines: 'This e-mail and any attachment are confidential and intended solely for the use of the individual to whom it is addressed. If you are not that individual, please pass it to that individual and notify us at the above e-mail address.'

The reply should also state, if it is in fact the case, that the e-mail reply has been swept for the presence of all known computer viruses.

Internet-related terms   C1.9

Failure in transmission

The contract should state: 'We cannot be held responsible, and accept no liability for, any failure in transmission by you and where, for whatever reason, your transmission is corrupted, fails to arrive, or arrives after an undue delay, or is received in an unintelligible form.' This provision should not only appear in the terms and conditions, but it should appear on the order page, so that it is clearly conveyed to the consumer before any contract is made with them. Since, furthermore, this is a term which precedes the formation of any contract, it will not be subject to the provisions of the *UCTA 1977* or the *Unfair Terms in Consumer Contracts Regulations 1999 (SI 1999/2083)*.

Avoiding premature offer

It should be clearly stated on the order page, that any display of goods or services is not an offer, but nothing more than an invitation to treat. If the website amounts to an offer, then the consumer can accept that offer, at the price stated, and thus give rise to a binding contract. If the website is, however, just an invitation to treat, then the consumer makes the offer which the supplier can then accept or reject in his absolute discretion.

Case Example:

The Kodak website offered digital cameras at £100 instead of £330. More than 5000 customers E-mailed an acceptance, and received an automated E-mail reply confirming the offer and accepting it. This created a binding contract.

The website should specifically state: 'Nothing contained in this website amounts to an offer to supply the goods or services, and any order from a customer can be refused at our absolute discretion.'

Chapter C2
Hire Purchase Contracts

Definition   C2.1

In law, a hire purchase agreement is a bailment, or leasing of goods, with an option to purchase them.

> **Case Example**: *Helby v Matthews [1895] AC 471.*
>
> In this case, the court recognised the basic structure of the modern hire purchase agreement – a contract of bailment or lease whereby ownership is retained by the supplier of goods (the bailor), and the hirer (or bailee) obtains mere possession coupled with an option to buy the goods on payment of the agreed sum, usually nominal, on exercising that option.

Hire purchase v conditional sale   C2.2

A contract of hire purchase is to be distinguished from a condition sale.

> **Case Example**: *Lee v Butler [1893] 2 QB 318.*
>
> It was held that where the buyer commits himself at the outset to buy the goods, and agrees to pay the purchase price in instalments, that is a conditional sale agreement. The difference between this and a hire purchase agreement is that, as pointed out above, the latter is an agreement to hire goods with an option to purchase. In a condition sale agreement, in contrast, the buyer commits himself at the outset to make the purchase. In practice, of course, there is no real difference in the agreements.
>
> **Case Example**: *Forthright Finance Ltd v Carlyle Finance Ltd [1997] 4 All ER 90.*
>
> It was held that a contract is a contract of conditional sale if the buyer is obliged to pay all the instalments, even though the contract provides an option not to take the title.

Case Example: *Close Asset Finance v Care Graphics Machinery Ltd [2000] CCLR 43.*

By contrast, in a contract of hire purchase, a party has an option to buy, and is not legally obliged to acquire title, even if the option price is nominal and one that a person would almost certainly pay, given the amount of the previous instalments.

Regulated hire purchase agreements   C2.3

The *Consumer Credit Act 1974*, regulates hire purchase agreements where the amount of credit extended does not exceed £25,000. This amount can be varied by Order made under *CCA 1974*, so the current level should always be checked. The current level was set by the *Consumer Credit (Increase of Monetary Limits) (Amendment) Order 1998 (SI 1998/996).*

Copy requirements   C2.4

The most common situation is where the customer selects the goods to be obtained on hire purchase, and signs a form setting out the details of the agreement. It is then up to the dealer, or a third party finance house, to accept the offer contained in the form signed by the customer.

First and second copies

On signing the offer document, the customer becomes entitled to a copy of it.

A second copy must be delivered to the customer within seven days of the agreement being made. This will occur when the other side signs the agreement and posts it to the customer. If a finance company is involved, what happens is that the finance company itself buys the goods from the dealer, and itself enters into the hire purchase agreement with the customer.

It is less common for all the relevant parties to sign the agreement at the same time. If this is case, though, the document signed by the customer is the complete contract, and he is entitled to just one copy.

Consequences of failure to comply

If the copy requirements are not complied with, under the *CCA 1974* the agreement cannot be enforced against the consumer unless the court grants an enforcement order. An enforcement order may be made conditional on such terms as the court thinks fit.

Exempt agreements

C2.5

A number of agreements are outside the remit of the *CCA 1974*, however, even if the credit advanced is within the current limit of £25,000. Under the *Consumer Credit (Exempt Agreements) Order 1989 (SI 1989/869)*, an agreement will be exempt if the number of repayments is not more than four, and are to be made within 12 months.

Status of customer

C2.6

For an agreement to be within the jurisdiction of the *CCA 1974*, and hence regulated by that Act, the customer must be an 'individual'. This is defined by *s 189(1)* of the *CCA 1974* to include a partnership and any other unincorporated body of persons which does not consist entirely of bodies corporate. Given also the fact that an individual can be a sole trader, and hence in business, it should be realised, therefore, that business customers can also be within the Act.

Form of regulated agreement

C2.7

Since the form and content of a regulated hire purchase agreement is subject to the provisions of the *Consumer Credit (Agreements) Regulations 1983 (SI 1983/1553)*, there is little room for variation.

Precedent – Specimen Hire Purchase Contract

C2.8

1. Hire Purchase Agreement regulated by the Consumer Credit Act 1974.

    This is an agreement under which we [as owners] agree to hire out to you [as customer] the goods described below.

Comment:

There then follows a description of the goods and a full financial statement. This statement will give:

- the total cash price;
- the amount of any deposit;
- any further charges payable;
- the total amount payable;
- the Annual Percentage Rate of Charge;
- the number of payments (monthly, or such other period as applies);
- the date of the first payment;
- a statement as to the day when the subsequent payments are made (e.g. 15th day of each month) and the amount of each payment; and
- the final payment (if this is different).

There must also be a statement of the name and postal address of both parties.

2. TERMINATION: YOUR RIGHTS

You have a right to end this agreement. If you wish to do so, you should write to the person authorised to receive your payments. We will then be entitled to the return of the goods and to [the installation charge plus half the rest of the total amount payable under this agreement, that is] [half the total amount payable under this agreement, that is][1] [£amount][2]. If you have already paid at least this amount plus any overdue instalments, you will not have to pay any more, provided you have taken reasonable care of the goods.

[1] This is to be inserted where the amount calculated in accordance with the *Consumer Credit Act 1974* applies. Under the Act, where the customer terminates the contract, which he can do at any time before the final payment is due, he will be liable, unless the agreement itself provides for a smaller payment, to pay the amount by which one half of the total price exceeds the total of sums paid and sums due. If any installation charges are to be paid in the agreement, the Act specifies that these must be paid in addition to the foregoing sum. If the agreement does in fact provide for a smaller sum to be paid on cancellation, the passages in both square brackets are to be deleted.

[2] The amount to be inserted here is the amount calculated in accordance with the Act (see footnote [1]) or the lesser amount specified in the agreement.

The capital letters at the head of this clause are not mandatory but, if capitals are not used, there should instead be some other prominent form of lettering, such as underlining, or the use of large or bold print.

The courts are unwilling to hold that a customer has voluntarily terminated agreement unless the full consequences of doing so are considered to have been fully appreciated by that consumer.

Case Example: *Bridge v Campbell Discount Co Ltd [1961] 2 All ER 97.*

The House of Lords held that a party had not terminated the contract but was writing to advise the other side that he was compelled to break the contract when he wrote: 'Owing to unforeseen personal circumstances I am sorry but I will not be able to pay any more payments on the Bedford Dormobile. Will you please let me know when and where I will have to return the car. I am very sorry regarding this but I have no alternative'.

---

3.   Names and addresses of two witnesses to customer's signature:

Signature: _____

Address: _____

               _____

Signature: _____

Address: _____

               _____

Comment:

This provision is optional, since there is no legal requirement for witnesses.

---

4. REPOSSESSION: YOUR RIGHTS

If you fail to keep to your side of this agreement but you have paid [the installation charge plus one third of the rest of the total amount payable under this agreement, that is] [one third of the total amount payable under this agreement, that is][1] [£amount][2], the creditor may not take back the goods against your wishes unless he gets a court order.

Comment:

[1] The creditor should insert what is appropriate in the square brackets.

[2] The creditor should insert here the amount calculated in accordance with the *CCA 1974*.

Note. The capital letters at the head of this clause are not mandatory but, if capitals are not used, there should instead be some other prominent form of lettering, such as underlining, or the use of large or bold print.

Section 90 of the *CCA 1974* refers to what it calls 'protected goods'. These are goods where, as the above wording indicates, the customer has paid one third or more of the total price of the goods and all installation charges. *Section 91* provides that if the owner repossess the goods without a court order, then the agreement is then terminated, and the customer can recover all sums paid by him under the agreement.

The provisions of the *CCA 1974* in relation to protected goods apply only where the customer is in breach of the hire purchase contract. To that extent, therefore, the wording of the above clause, which is required by the *Consumer Credit (Agreements) Regulations 1983 (SI 1983/1553)* is slightly misleading, since it suggests that a court order is required in all cases where repossession is sought. It might, for example, be sought where the customer has become insolvent or decided to move abroad. Often, agreements give a right to repossess in such cases, but becoming insolvent or moving abroad is not a breach of the agreement, rather a triggering event.

The reference to the total amount payable is a reference to the total sum payable under the agreement including any sum which may be payable on the exercise of an option to purchase, but does not include any sum payable as a penalty or as compensation or damages for breach.

A court order is also required by *s 92* of the *CCA 1974* before the owner can enter land to take possession of goods, whether or not the goods are protected. A breach of this provision entitles the customer to sue for damages.

5. DECLARATION BY CUSTOMER

By signing this agreement you are declaring that:

(*a*)   your name and address as contained in this agreement are correct;

(b)   all the information you have given us whether in this contract or in the course of negotiation are correct;

(c)   you accept that we rely on that information when deciding whether or not to make this agreement.

Comment:

This provision is not a statutory requirement. Effectively, it gives the owner a right to sue for breach or for misrepresentation in the event of any inaccuracies.

---

6.   This is a Hire Purchase Agreement regulated by the Consumer Credit Act 1974. Sign it only if you want to be legally bound by its terms.

Signature of Customer(s): _____

Date(s) of Signature: _____

The goods will not become your property until you have made all the payments. You must not sell them before then.

Comment:

The date of signature can be left out if the agreement is not cancellable (see clause 7 below) and if the date on which the agreement became executed is inserted into the agreement instead. An agreement becomes executed on the application of the second signature, this being the point at which an offer is accepted. In most cases, the owner will be the last to sign. The above details are required by the *Consumer Credit (Agreements) Regulations 1983 (SI 1983/1553)* which also requires them to be within a signature box. The owner's signature must be outside the box, and the date of the signature shall also be outside the box, though the date may be omitted in the circumstances described immediately above.

It is stated that the goods must not be sold prior to property in them passing. This does not necessarily mean, however, that a sale or disposition before then will not pass property to a third party. *The Hire Purchase Act 1964* provides that a third party, other than a dealer, taking a motor vehicle in good faith when that vehicle is still subject to a hire purchase agreement or condition sale agreement (where, in this latter case, the credit does not exceed the current limit of £25,000) will receive a good title.

Importantly, as pointed out above, the customer might be a business, and hence would be capable of passing a good title to goods subject to a hire purchase agreement under other provisions recognised by the *Factors Act 1889* and the *Sale of Goods Act 1979*. A factor, or mercantile agent, can also pass a title to a bona fide third party.

In addition, title can pass by operation of the doctrine of estoppel. It will always be a question of fact as to whether the circumstances show that there has been an estoppel, that is to say that a person – by his conduct – should be estopped or prevented from denying what he has led another person to believe is the case.

Case Example: *Central Newbury Car Auctions Ltd v Unity Finance Ltd [1957] 1 QB 371.*

A car was obtained on hire purchase from the claimant and driven away with the registration book. The defendant then declined the proposal for a hire purchase agreement, the car being sold to a third party. It was held that the car still belonged to the auction house. Its allowing the customer to have possession did not amount to a representation that he had the right to sell. The registration book was not a document of title and indeed contained a warning that the person in whose name the vehicle was registered might not necessarily be the owner.

Case Example: *Moorgate Mercantile Leasing Ltd v Twitchings [1976] 3 WLR 66.*

Moorgate were a finance company which owned a car which was let on hire purchase to a customer. Before completing the payments, the customer sold it to a car dealer. Both Moorgate and the dealer were members of Hire Purchase Information (HPI) Ltd which operates a register of hire purchase agreements available for inspection by members. Moorgate had carelessly failed to register the agreement, the result being that HPI told the dealer that no such agreement was outstanding. The dealer accordingly claimed that Moorgate were estopped from denying that the customer was the owner of the car. The claim failed; Moorgate had made no representations to the dealer.

The only statement to the dealer was that made by HPI, namely that there was no hire purchase agreement relating to the car in question. That statement was true and had, in any case, not been made by Moorgate since HPI was not its agent. It was true that Moorgate had been careless, but this was not the same as 'negligence' unless Moorgate were in breach of a duty to take care. Moorgate were not obliged to join HPI, nor under a duty of care to register agreements. No estoppel could therefore be made out, and Moorgate were entitled to succeed in their claim against the dealer. Since this case, however, HPI have written into its terms of membership an absolute duty to register, so that if the facts of this case were to recur, the result might well be different.

7. YOUR RIGHT TO CANCEL

Once you have signed this agreement, you will have for a short time a right to cancel it. Exact details of how and when you can do this will be sent to you by post from us.

Comment:

This clause *must* be boxed. Instead of capital letters, however, the requirement as to prominence can again be met in other ways, such as underlining or the use of bold print.

Section 67 of the *Consumer Credit Act 1974* provides that an agreement is cancellable if:

- the negotiations leading up to the agreement included oral representations made when in the presence of the customer by or on behalf of the owner; and

- the customer signed the agreement at premises other than those of the owner.

The first of these requirements will be fulfilled in almost every case where the agreement is made after the prospective customer has spoken face-to-face either with the owner or an agent acting for the owner. A dealer who sells the goods to the finance house, as is typically the case in a hire purchase contract, would be the agent of the finance house. The requirement would not be met if negotiations were conducted entirely by phone, fax, over the Internet, or through the post.

The second requirement is met if signature by the customer takes place away from the owner's premises or those of the agent. This would cover signature by the customer in his home, or at his own business premises.

The cancellation period is five days from the day after the customer has received his second copy of the agreement.

The copy requirements in the case of cancellable agreements are set out in *ss 62–64* of the *CCA 1974* as follows.

- If the agreement is personally presented to the customer, and it becomes executed on signature by him, a copy of the agreement must be given to him at the same time.

- The position is the same in the more likely case when the agreement is presented personally to him and the agreement does not

> become executed on his signature (meaning that the other side has yet to sign).
>
> - If an un-executed agreement is sent to the customer for signature, a copy must be sent at the same time.
> - When both signatures have been applied, so that the agreement becomes executed, a copy must be sent or delivered to the customer by post within the seven days following the application of the second signature.
>
> Where the agreement is cancellable, the required copies must contain a cancellation notice (see below) and must be sent by post within the seven days following the day when the last signature was applied.
>
> If the requirements as to copies are not complied with, the agreement can be enforced only on a court order.

8. YOUR RIGHT TO CANCEL

Once you have signed this agreement, you will have for a short time a right to cancel it. Exact details of how and when you can do this will be sent to you by post.

> **Comment**:
>
> The above is mandatory, when the agreement is cancellable, and is required by the *Consumer Credit (Agreements) Regulations 1983 (SI 1983/1553)*. The block capitals can, however, be replaced by other forms of prominence.

Certain wording is required when the notice of cancellation rights is sent separately through the post.

> # 9. IMPORTANT – YOU SHOULD READ THIS CAREFULLY
>
> STATUTORY NOTICE RELATING TO A REGULATED HIRE PURCHASE AGREEMENT.
>
> YOUR RIGHT TO CANCEL.
>
> You recently made a hire purchase agreement [1] with [2]. You have a right to cancel if you wish by sending or taking a WRITTEN notice of cancellation to [3]. You have FIVE DAYS starting with the day after

you received this notice. You can use the form provided. If you cancel the agreement, any money you have paid, [goods given in part-exchange (or their value) and property given as security][4] must be returned to you. You will not have to make any further payment.

If you already have any goods under the agreement, you should not use them and should keep them safe. (Legal action may be taken against you if you do not take proper care of them). You can wait for them to be collected from you and you need not hand them over unless you receive a written request. [If you wish, however, you may return the goods yourself][5]. [You are warned that it would be dangerous and could be in contravention of Health and Safety legislation for you to attempt to disconnect and return the goods yourself][6].

[You will not, however, be required to hand back any goods supplied to meet an emergency or which have already been incorporated, for example in your home. But you will still be liable to pay for emergency goods or services or for any goods which have been incorporated by you or one of your relatives][7]

[Note: Your notice of cancellation will not affect [your contract for life assurance] [your contract for insurance] [your contract of guarantee] [your contract to open a current account] [your contract to open a deposit account].[8] [The place where your financial obligations consequent upon cancellation of this agreement are shown is [9]][10]][11].

Comment:

[1] Owner to insert reference number, code or other identification details.

[2] Owner to enter its name.

[3] Creditor to insert name and address of person to whom notice may be given.

[4] Words in square brackets to be omitted if inapplicable.

[5] Owner to include the words in the first set of square brackets unless the words in the second set are applicable; e.g. in a case where the subject matter of the agreement is liquefied petroleum gas of greater than 150 litres water capacity.

[6] Creditor to omit words in square brackets if not applicable.

[7] Creditor may omit words in square brackets where inapplicable.

[8] Creditor to omit words in square brackets if not applicable.

[9] Creditor to insert clear reference to the place where these obligations appear.

[10] Creditor may include words in square brackets were applicable.

[11]   Creditor to omit words in square brackets where inapplicable.

The above wording is prescribed by the *Consumer Credit (Cancellation Notices and Copies of Documents) Regulations 1983 (SI 1983/1557)*. Capital letters can be replaced by other forms of prominence.

In those cases where the notice of cancellation rights is included in the copies of agreements, the first paragraph under YOUR RIGHT TO CANCEL should read: 'Once you have signed, you will have for a short time a right to cancel this agreement. You can do this by sending or taking a WRITTEN notice of cancellation to [1].

[1]   Creditor to insert name and address of person to whom notice may be given, or an indication of the person to whom notice may be given, together with a clear reference to the place in the document where his name and address appear.

Again, the capital letters can be replaced by any other form of prominent lettering.

10. CANCELLATION FORM

(Complete and return this form ONLY IF YOU WISH TO CANCEL THE AGREEMENT.)

To: _____ [1]

I/we hereby give notice that I/We wish to cancel agreement [2].

Signed: _____

Date: _____

Name: _____

Address: _____

Comment:

[1]   Owner to insert name and address of person to whom notice of cancellation can be given.

[2]   Owner to insert reference number, code or other identification details.

Again, the capital letters can be replaced by any other form of prominent lettering.

This cancellation form is applicable whichever of the forms set out in clause 9 above is used. It is important to remember, however, that the customer does not have to use the cancellation form provided. *Section 69(1)* of the *CCA 1974* states that any written notice of cancellation which, however expressed, and whether or not the cancellation form provided, is effective to cancel the contract if it indicates an intention to withdraw from the contract.

11. IMPORTANT: YOU SHOULD READ THIS CAREFULLY

YOUR RIGHTS

The *Consumer Credit Act 1974* covers this agreement and lays down certain requirements for your protection which must be satisfied when the agreement is made. If they are not, we cannot enforce the agreement against you without a court order.

The Act also gives also gives you a number of rights. You have a right to settle this agreement at any time by giving notice in writing and paying off all amounts payable under the agreement which may be reduced by a rebate.

If you would like to know more about the protection and remedies provided under the Act, you should contact either your local Trading Standards Department or your nearest Citizens' Advice Bureau.

Comment:

This is required by the *Consumer Credit (Cancellation Notices etc) Regulations 1983 (SI 1983/1557)*. Instead of upper case, the above words can be in any other prominent form.

Further terms C2.9

The above are the terms which are required to appear in the agreement. There will, of course, be other terms which the owner will wish to incorporate and these are considered below.

Incorporating these further terms

Section 61(1)(b) of the *Consumer Credit Act 1974*, however, does say that the contractual document must embody all the terms of an agreement other than implied terms (though these can be included if the owner

wishes). In this context, *s 189(4)* provides that an agreement embodies a
contract term if it refers to it, thus allowing incorporation by reference.
Breach of this provision renders an agreement improperly executed and
hence enforceable only on a court order.

(I) PAYMENT

All payments must be made not later than the date stipulated in this agreement. If this provision is not complied with, we reserve the right to
charge interest at the rate charged for credit under this agreement. Interest
will be calculated on a daily basis from the date the amount falls due until
such time as it is received and will run both before and after any judgment
(such obligation to be independent of and not to merge with any judgment). If you are making payments by post, we advise the use of recorded
or registered delivery. Should you not make use of such services, the onus
is on yourself to prove despatch and receipt of the payment by ourselves.

Comment:

The passage in brackets above avoids the fact that the law does allow
for interest to be payable up to judgment date, but not after it, unless
there is a provision in the agreement allowing for post-judgment
interest.

Case Example: *Director General of Fair Trading v First National Bank plc
[2002] 1 All ER 97.*

The Director General sought a declaration that this provision was
unfair, and hence unenforceable, under the provisions of the *Unfair
Terms in Consumer Contracts Regulations 1994 (SI 1994/3159)* (these
have been replaced, without any relevant difference by the *Unfair
Terms in Consumer Contracts Regulations 1999 (SI 1999/2083)*). *Reg
3(2)(b)* excludes from the scope of the Regulations a term which
defines the main subject matter of the contract or which concerns the
adequacy of the price or remuneration, as against the goods or services
sold or supplied. The House of Lords accepted that the disputed clause
was not within this provision, and hence subject to the fairness test
imposed by the Regulations.

It then ruled that the clause was not unfair. It said that the provision
could not be said to cause a significant imbalance in the parties' rights
and obligations to the detriment of the consumer to an extent which
was contrary to the requirement of good faith, this being the test laid
down by the Regulations. The essential bargain was that the bank
would make funds available to be repaid, over a period, with interest.

Neither party could suppose that the bank would willingly forgo any part of its principal or interest.

The House of Lords pointed out that the customer did have certain remedies open to him under the *CCA 1974*, but that there was no requirement for the agreement to indicate their presence. It indicated that this was a matter which the Director General could bring to the attention of the Department of Trade and Industry which could amend the requirements as to the form and content of agreements. At the time of writing, no action has been taken.

It should be noted that *s 92* of the *CCA 1974* says that a customer cannot be obliged to pay interest on sums outstanding at a rate exceeding the contractual rate of interest.

(II) OWNERSHIP OF THE GOODS HIRED

The goods hired to you under this agreement remain our absolute property until such time as you have fulfilled all conditions, relating to payment or otherwise, necessary for property to vest in yourself.

Comment:

For the ability of a customer to pass title regardless of any such clause, see the above 'Specimen of a Hire Purchase Contract' at C2.8.

(III) CUSTODY OF GOODS

You must maintain the goods in good condition and repair at your own expense. Should you have been provided with the goods by a third party, you must not allow that third party to retain the goods or to have any lien over them. You will at all times be responsible for any loss or damage incurred by the goods, fair wear and tear excepted, even if such loss or damage arises because of events beyond your reasonable control.

Comment:

This clause cannot in fact prevent the customer from giving a lien over the goods, since a third party is not bound by the agreement, but the giving of a lien would amount to a breach of contract, thus allowing the owner to terminate under further provisions of the contract (see below).

> This clause can also be used in conjunction with *s 80* of the *CCA 1974*. This allows the owner, where the agreement requires the customer to keep the goods under his control, to require the customer, following notice in writing, to advise the owner within seven working days of the whereabouts of the goods.

(IV) YOUR DETAILS

You must notify us in writing of any change in your address within seven days of such change taking effect.

> **Comment**:
>
> It is of obvious importance for the owner to know the whereabouts of the customer, and hence of the goods. Failure to inform the owner of a change of address would be a breach of contract and hence allow the owner to terminate the agreement (see below).

(V) INSPECTION OF THE GOODS

You must allow us or a representative of ours to inspect the goods on due notice and at all reasonable times.

> **Comment**:
>
> It is likely that, in the vast majority of cases, the owner would never want to exercise this right, but it could be useful in the case of high value goods, such as cars.

(VI) INSURANCE

You must keep the goods insured under a fully comprehensive policy of insurance at your own expense. You must notify us of any loss or damage to the goods and hold any moneys payable under the policy in trust for us. You irrevocably authorise us to collect the moneys from the insurers. If a claim is made against the insurers we may at our absolute discretion conduct any negotiations and effect any settlement with the insurers and you agree to abide by such settlement.

Comment:

The customer, as hirer of the goods, has an insurable interest in the goods although he is not the actual owner. By using this clause, the customer is committed to taking out the widest possible level of cover. Although he may be the person to receive the insurance payment, he holds it in trust for the owner.

(VII) YOUR RIGHT TO END THE AGREEMENT

You have the right to terminate this agreement as set out in the TERMI-NATION: YOUR RIGHTS notice set out in this agreement. You must then at your own expense return to us the goods together with, in the case of a motor vehicle, the registration document, the road fund licence and any current test certificate.

Comment:

This builds on the statutory right of termination referred to above. The *CCA 1974* does not prevent the imposition of expenses where the customer does exercise his right to terminate.

(VIII) OUR RIGHT TO TERMINATE THE AGREEMENT

In the event of the happening of the following, we will have the right, after serving on you at your last known address, the right to terminate this agreement if:

* you fail to keep to any of the terms of this agreement, express or implied;

* you commit any act or bankruptcy or have a receiving or bank-ruptcy order made against you or you petition for bankruptcy, or are served with a creditor's demand under the Insolvency Act 1986 (or any re-enactment thereof), or go into administrative receiver-ship, or make a formal composition or scheme with your creditors, or call a meeting of them, or, other than for normal purposes of amalgamation and reconstruction, wind up your business;

* execution is levied or sought against any of your assets or income;

* the landlord of the premises where the goods are situated threatens or takes any steps to distrain on the goods.

- where you are a partnership, the partnership is dissolved;

- you have given false or misleading information in connection with your entry into this agreement;

- the goods are destroyed or the insurers treat a claim under the policy referred to in (vi) above; or

- you fail to notify us of any change of address or you move to live permanently outside the United Kingdom.

If we do terminate this agreement, then subject to the provisions covered by REPOSSESSION: YOUR RIGHTS contained in this agreement, we may resume possession of the goods. You will also have to pay all outstanding payments and such further amount, as appropriate, as will make up one half of the total purchase price payable under this agreement. If you have failed to take reasonable care of the goods, you may be liable to compensate us for this.

Comment:

The foregoing clause gives the right to terminate in all cases, and is not concerned with whether any terms infringed are conditions or warranties.

It recognises, particularly in relation to partnerships and winding up, that the *CCA 1974* covers not just individuals, but also partnerships and any legal entity not consisting entirely of bodies corporate.

The reference to 'implied terms' ensures that the owner's right to terminate exists not just in relation to the terms expressly written in the agreement. The right will apply also in relation to any duties implied on the customer by law. The customer is, for example, under a common law duty to accept delivery of the goods (*National Cash Register Co v Stanley [1921] 3 KB 292*) and hence any breach of this implied duty would entitle the owner to terminate the agreement.

It limits the customer's liability to 50% of the purchase price. This limit is not mandatory, but is aimed at avoiding the rule against penalty clauses.

Case Example: *Bridge v Campbell Discount Co Ltd [1962] AC 600.*

The House of Lords ruled that a provision requiring the customer to pay 2/3 of the hire purchase price was not a liquidated damages clause, but an unenforceable penalty clause instead.

Owner's obligations before termination

It is important to realise that restraints are imposed by the *CCA 1974* on the owner when he seeks to invoke such a termination clause. *Sections 76, 87* and *98* of the Act require the issue of notices on the customer to be in the form specified by the *Consumer Credit (Enforcement, Default and Termination Notices) Regulations 1983* (*SI 1983/1561*). Where the customer is actually in breach of the agreement, he must be given at least seven days after service of the notice to make good the breach (*s 88(2), CCA 1974*).

Reference should also be made here to the discussion of Protected Goods under the REPOSESSION: YOUR RIGHTS clause above.

(VIII) EXPENSES

You will be required to pay on demand any expenses and legal costs which we incur for:

(*a*) finding your address if you change your address without notifying us, or of us finding the goods if they are not at your address; or

(*b*) taking such steps as, in our discretion, are considered necessary, including but without limitation any court action, to recover the goods or to obtain payment for them.

(IX) YOUR RIGHT TO A REBATE

You have a statutory right at any time to pay all amounts payable under this agreement, and any such early settlement may entitle you to a statutory rebate. Any notice you give to make use of this right must be in writing.

Comment:

This reflects the provisions of *s 94* of the *CCA 1974* and of the *Consumer Credit (Rebate on Early Settlement) Regulations 1983* (*SI 1983/1562*). If the agreement provides for a higher level of rebate than that provided for in the Regulations, the customer is entitled to the higher rebate (*Home Insulation Ltd v Wadsley [1988] CCLR 25*).

(X) LIMITATION OF LIABILITY

Except where you are dealing as a consumer as that term is defined in the *Unfair Contract Terms Act 1977*, your rights under the *Supply of Goods*

315

(Implied Terms) Act 1973, or under any other provision, whether statutory or existing by virtue of implication of law, are hereby excluded.

Comment:

The exclusion of consumers from this clause (broadly speaking those who are not taking the goods in the course of a business) recognises the fact that, under the *UCTA 1977*, terms implied as to description, quality and fitness for purpose cannot be excluded vis-a-vis such customers.

A person is deemed to be a consumer unless the contrary is proved (s 12(3), *UCTA 1977*).

Case Example: *R&B Custom Brokers Co Ltd v United Dominions Trust [1988] 1 WLR 321.*

The claimant company obtained a car from the defendant finance company. A term in the agreement excluded the implied terms as to the condition or quality of the car or its fitness for purpose. The car was the second or third which the claimant had acquired on credit terms. They were in business as shipping brokers and freight forwarding agents. This particular car had been obtained for business and personal use. The Court of Appeal ruled that the purchase was only incidental to the claimant's business activity and that a degree of regularity was required before that transaction could be said to be an integral part of the claimant's business. Since the car was, at the most, the third acquired on business terms, that degree of regularity was lacking. The company had, therefore, dealt as a consumer.

If the customer does not deal as a consumer, then the clause is valid if it can be shown by the owner to be reasonable. While it cannot be said with certainty that a total exclusion clause such as this one would fail the reasonableness test, it is always possible. Accordingly, the owner might like to replace the total exclusion with a limitation of its maximum liability to a specified sum, or a sum worked out by a given formula, such as limiting liability to the value of the contract.

It is also possible to attempt to have the best of both worlds by using a clause which provides for a total exclusion, but which adds that 'in the event of the foregoing being deemed by any court or arbitrator to be unreasonable, liability shall be accepted up to the value of the contract' or such other limitation as is deemed appropriate.

(XI) MISCELLANEOUS

This agreement is personal to you and may under no circumstances be assigned by you to any third party.

We may in our absolute discretion assign the agreement to any third party we think fit.

> **Comment**:
>
> The owner is allowed by virtue of the above to assign the agreement to a third party. This can take place when the business is sold or taken over, or when the owner factors his debts, i.e. sells them to another in return for payment of the right to collect debts which would otherwise be due to the owner.

Unregulated hire purchase agreements   C2.10

An agreement will fall outside the *CCA 1974* if the credit extended exceeds the current limit of £25,000, or the customer is not an individual, defined in *s 189(1)* of the Act as including a partnership or any other body not consisting entirely of bodies corporate.

Where an agreement is outside the Act, none of the requirements as to form will apply. There are no common law requirements as to the form and content, as to copies, or as to cancellation or termination. Nor is there any requirement that the contract must be in writing and signed, though, as a practical matter, both are usual and to be recommended.

Applicability of enactments   C2.11

The contract will be subject to the provisions of the *Supply of Goods (Implied Terms) Act 1973*, which implies into such contracts terms as to conformity with description, satisfactory quality and reasonable fitness for purpose. Similarly, the *Unfair Contract Terms Act 1977*, will apply in relation to exclusion clauses, and the *Unfair Terms in Consumer Contracts Regulations 1999 (SI 1999/2083)* will also be applicable.

Unauthorised dispositions   C2.12

The provisions relating to sales by a customer of goods subject to a hire purchase agreement will also apply (see the discussion attached to clause 6 above).

Termination   C2.13

The termination by breach of an unregulated hire purchase agreement will be governed by the terms of the agreement alone. It would be common, therefore, to find in such an agreement a clause similar to that of

(vii) above. Such a clause will, of course, be subject to the rules against penalties, and hence will be valid only if it represents a genuine pre-esti-mate of likely loss. If a clause is rejected as being a penalty, the owner will remain able to sue for damages representing his actual loss.

Where the agreement provides for termination by death, bankruptcy, liq-uidation, moving abroad and such like, the agreement may specify for the payment of minimum sums in the event of such events happening.

> **Case Example**: *Re Apex Supply Co Ltd [1942] Ch 108.*
>
> It was held that the occurrence of any such event could not be regarded as a breach of contract, and hence the rules as to penalty clauses were inapplicable.

In the event of voluntary termination by the customer, where the agree-ment provides for a minimum payment, and the customer gives notice of termination, returning the goods, the position at common law is that the minimum payment is to be made since there is no breach and the rules as to penalties cannot apply. The effect is that the customer may be better off if he breaks the agreement since he can then argue that the sum is payable on breach and is potentially a penalty.

The owner's right to repossess   **C2.14**

Where the agreement is not regulated, an owner's right to repossess in the event of a breach is wider than that allowed under the *CCA 1974* where the agreement is regulated. If the goods remain in the customer's posses-sion, the owner may repossess at any time.

If there has been a wrongful disposition of the goods, the owner can claim the goods from the person in possession. No court order is needed but if, as a matter of practicality, one has to be obtained (for example because access to the goods is physically impossible without trespassing), the owner can bring an action for wrongful interference under the provisions of the *Torts (Interference with Goods) Act 1977*. The Act gives the court a discretion not to order repossession and, where the goods have been bought by an innocent third party, and the provisions discussed above as to an innocent third party obtaining title apply, obviously no order can be made. In that case, there are two alternatives, which are:

- an order for the return of the goods, but giving the third party the option of paying damages; or

- damages.

The damages would be the unpaid balance of the total price payable under the agreement, the result effectively being that the obligations under the agreement have been transferred from the customer to the third party. The third party would be able to sue the customer for the amount paid.

If the owner does attempt to repossess the goods where the customer has paid a substantial amount under the agreement, a court may take the view that, in the interests of fairness, some relief should be granted to the customer. The point has never been decided but in *Snook v West Riding Investments Ltd [1967] 1 All ER 518, 527*, Lord Denning spoke of the customer's 'valuable equity' in goods subject to a hire purchase agreement.

Extortionate credit bargains C2.15

The provisions of the *CCA 1974* allowing the court to reopen an extortionate credit bargain are not restricted to regulated agreements. In this context, the Act covers any agreement between an individual (which includes a partnership and any other body not consisting entirely of bodies corporate), and where the credit bargain is extortionate. *Section 137* of the *CCA 1974* defines the credit bargain as meaning the credit agreement and, if appropriate any other transactions, setting out the total charge for credit. A credit bargain is, by virtue of *s 138*, extortionate if it requires payments which are 'grossly exorbitant' or which otherwise 'grossly contravenes ordinary principles of fair dealing'.

Conditional sale agreements C2.16

A conditional sale agreement differs from a hire purchase agreement in that the customer commits himself to the purchase at the outset, paying off the purchase price in instalments. In a hire purchase agreement, in contrast, the customer merely takes a lease of the goods with an option to purchase.

> **Case Example**: *Forthright Finance Ltd v Carlyle Finance Ltd [1997] 4 All ER 90.*
>
> In this case it was found that a contract is a contract of conditional sale if the buyer is obliged to pay all the instalments, even though the contract provides an option not to take the title.

Unauthorised dispositions C2.17

The position of the customer who takes goods under a conditional sale as regards any further disposition by him during the currency of the agreement is generally identical to that of the customer under a hire purchase agreement. The customer under a conditional sale agreement is, however, also a person who has agreed to buy, and hence, potentially, can also pass title to an innocent third party under *s 25* of the *Sale of Goods Act 1979*. The right to pass title under this provision is, however, restricted by the Act to those cases where the agreement is a regulated consumer credit agreement, meaning that the customer must be an individual (which includes a partnership and any body not consisting entirely of bodies corporate) and the credit advanced must not exceed the current limit of £25,000. If the agreement is not a regulated agreement, then the customer under a conditional sale agreement can pass a valid title as a buyer in possession who has bought or agreed to buy goods to an innocent third party.

Requirements as to regulated conditional sale agreements   **C2.18**

The provisions discussed in relation to regulated hire purchase agreements apply almost in their entirety to regulated conditional sale agreements. The only difference is that the agreement must be headed 'Conditional Sale Agreement regulated by the *Consumer Credit Act 1974*'.

The discussion as to unregulated hire purchase agreements above is equally apposite to unregulated conditional sale agreements.

Chapter C3
Online Terms and
Conditions of Sale

At a glance

C3.1

- Such contracts fall under the *Consumer Protection (Distance Selling) Regulations 2000 (SI 2000/2334)* as well as the ordinary law of contract.

- Specific detail must be presented in the online contract.

- There are special requirements to note as to mode of delivery and of time for performance.

- There is a general right to cancel a contract, but this is somewhat limited in the case of a contract for the provision of a service.

- There are obligations as to when the mandatory information is to be supplied.

- There are also obligations as to how this information is to be provided.

- There is room for choosing just where the information is located.

- Some of the information is to be presented in a written or 'durable medium'.

- The mandatory information is not exhaustive, however, and other contract terms can always be included.

- There are tight controls on the use of exclusion clauses, though there is more scope for their use in the case of service contracts.

- Service contracts are subject to much the same requirements as to information provided in written or durable form, though some exceptions apply.

Distance selling

C3.2

Online sales are a form of distance selling and, as such, are subject to the provisions of the *Consumer Protection (Distance Selling) Regulations 2000 (SI 2000/2334)*. It should be borne in mind, though, that the law of contract also applies, in particular the rules relating to offer and acceptance. The Internet copy would amount to an invitation to treat, not an offer, meaning that it is the consumer who makes the offer, which the supplier is entitled to reject in his absolute discretion. This could be important if, as has happened, the Internet advertisement states a much lower price for the goods than was intended.

Contract terms required by the Regulations   C3.3

There is no need for the on-screen contract to be presented as a formal document, but it must contain at least the following detail.

- **The identity of the supplier.**

  If payment is required in advance, the supplier's address must also be given. It seems permissible for the address to be a PO Box number, and not an actual geographical address.

- **A description of the main characteristics of the goods or services.**

- **The price of the goods or services including all taxes.**

  Although the *Consumer Protection (Distance Selling) Regulations 2000 (SI 2000/2334)* are not entirely clear on this point, it would appear permissible to quote the price in the form of £100 plus £17.50 VAT, as an alternative to quoting a VAT inclusive price. If the latter is chosen, there is no requirement actually to say that it includes VAT. It does not appear permissible to say '£100 plus VAT at the appropriate rate'.

- **There must be a statement of the relevant delivery costs.**

- **There must be a statement of the arrangements for payment, delivery or performance.**

  The arrangements for payment could embrace online means for paying, usually by entering credit card details, or by allowing for sums to be deducted straight from a bank account.

Requirements as to statement of performance   C3.4

The stated arrangements as to performance will show how delivery is to be made, for example by despatch to the consumer's home address or to a central collection point such as the nearest post office. It does not seem necessary to indicate just how the goods will be delivered (e.g. by mail, parcel post, courier), though these can be stated and often are. These provisions in the contract as to performance can be linked to further provisions in the *Consumer Protection (Distance Selling) Regulations 2000 (SI 2000/2334)* as to the time of performance.

Time of performance **C3.5**

Unless the contract says otherwise, the supplier must perform the contract within a maximum of 30 days from the day after the consumer sent his order. If, therefore, the supplier expects to provide the goods six weeks from the order, the arrangements for performance should state this. If, though, he expects no problem with performing within 30 days, then nothing further need be said, though it is common for suppliers to indicate that the consumer should expect delivery within 28 days.

Notice must be given of the consumer's right to cancel. This should state that the consumer can cancel the contract at any time up to seven working days from the day after receipt of the goods. In addition, there must be an indication as to how the consumer can exercise his right to cancel and, if this is what the supplier wants, a statement that the goods must be returned at the consumer's expense on cancellation. Under the *Consumer Protection (Distance Selling) Regulations 2000 (SI 2000/2334)*, the notice of cancellation must be in writing or in another 'durable medium' available to and accessible by the supplier, which would thus include fax or E-mail and, arguably, a message left by answerphone. The contract must indicate the ways in which the consumer must provide the notice of cancellation.

The supplier always has the option of saying that the goods are to be returned or collected at his expense.

Long-term contracts **C3.6**

If the contract is one of unspecified duration, or for a duration of a year or more, then the supplier must give details of any contractual right to cancel. A supplier is, of course, always free to provide a right to cancel regardless of any issues as to duration, so long as this extra contractual right is not less generous than the right to cancel which the consumer, as described above, always has.

It should be noted that there is no right to cancel under the *Consumer Protection (Distance Selling) Regulations 2000 (SI 2000/2334)* (although the supplier can offer the right to cancel if he wishes) to contracts for the supply of software, audio or video recordings if these have been unsealed by the consumer.

There must be a statement of the cost of using the means of distance communication, unless the cost is charged at the appropriate standard rate. In practical terms, this provision has no application to Internet dealing since calls will either be free or at local rates.

There must be an indication as to how long the offer or price remains valid. If there is a definite close date, this should be stated. It would also seem possible to say that the offer is subject to availability. It also seems possible to say that an offer remains open until further notice. As a practical matter, the supplier should withdraw the details from the Internet site as soon as orders can no longer be fulfilled.

If the contract is for the supply of goods on a permanent or recurrent basis, the minimum duration of the contract if this is appropriate. For instance, the supply of records from an Internet record club might provide for records to be sent every four months. Unless the consumer can terminate the contract at any time, the duration of the contract must be specified.

If the agreed goods become unavailable, the supplier may wish to offer the consumer an alternative of equivalent quality and price. If he wishes to do so, and the option is his, this information must be provided along with a statement to the effect the supplier will pay the costs of return should the consumer cancel the contract.

The contract must give a 'geographical address' of the place of business of the supplier to which complaints can be addressed. It does not seem necessary for there to be a specific reference for 'complaints' in the contract. It would be enough if, for example, the address was given as one to which queries can be directed. Although the requirement is simply to give an address and not, for example, a telephone number, fax number or E-mail address, one or the other can and should be provided.

If the supplier offers any form of after sales service or guarantee, relevant information must be provided. There is no compulsion to offer a guarantee or after sales service.

The regulations state that regard must be had to the principles 'governing the protection of those who are unable to give their consent such as minors'. While a transaction through mail order could cope with this by requiring the signature of a parent or guardian, it is difficult to see how this can also be achieved in relation to Internet sales. It would seem better for supplies through this medium always to exclude minors.

Based on the above, a standard Internet contract could be as follows.

A Model Contract

C3.7

ABC Co Ltd, 123 Any Street, Any Town AA1 1AA

To supply 1 garden shredder at a total cost of £299 (add £6.50 delivery charges for all orders under £300).

[Complete here details of your credit card and billing address. If the address to which the goods are to be delivered differs, please also provide this address.]

The above equipment will be delivered to your address within 30 days.

While we are confident that your use of these goods will be trouble free, we are anxious to deal with any problems which might arise. Please address any queries to us at the above address or contact us on _____.

All goods and prices displayed here are subject to availability and are liable to be withdrawn at any time without notice.

IMPORTANT: Please note that you have a right to cancel this contract. You can do this at any time up to seven (7) days starting with the day after the goods are delivered to you. If you do wish to cancel, you must notify us in writing or its equivalent. Any cancellations by phone must be confirmed in writing within the permitted cancellation period. You will then be required to return the goods to us at your expense.

[Note: The supplier can always say here instead that he is prepared to accept the cost of return delivery and will, for instance, send a reply paid label or arrange for the collection of the goods himself.]

If you are under 18, we cannot accept your order.

[To comply with the Data Protection Act 1998, there should also be some such notice as the following.]

Please click here if you do not want us to send you further information or supply your details to third parties.

When the mandatory information is to be provided   **C3.8**

The details must all be provided 'in good time' prior to the conclusion of the contract. Presumably, 'in good time' means in such time as will allow the consumer to consider the terms before proceeding with the order.

For information regarding additional important requirements set out by the *Electronic Commerce (EC Directive) Regulations 2002 (SI 2002/2013)* see C1.3 above.

Offer and acceptance   **C3.9**

Since a contract is not concluded until the supplier accepts the offer, as by an e-mail confirmation, these terms and conditions should be made available before any acceptance takes place. It should also be realised that if the acceptance adds further terms beyond those presented to the consumer before the order, that will amount to a rejection of the consumer's order and be a counter-offer.

Form of presentation of required information   **C3.10**

All of the provisions above under the *Consumer Protection (Distance Selling) Regulations 2000 (SI 2000/2334)* must be provided in a 'clear and comprehensible manner appropriate to the means of distance communication'. This would require them to be easily legible, and not, for example, such that flash on and off the screen so that reading them is difficult. 'Comprehensible' does not appear to mean that the terms and conditions must be in English, since any language is comprehensible to those who speak it, and because a consumer faced with a language he does not speak is always free to ignore the offer. It presumably does require that, given the language can be understood, that the above provisions are expressed with due clarity.

Location of information   **C3.11**

It also seems possible for the provisions to be elsewhere than on the page containing details of the offer. If there is a link to the provisions, so long as this is clearly indicated, that would suffice. In principle, it is possible for the on screen page to indicate that the provisions are available from an address, perhaps itself postal, which will be sent to the customer by post. Since, however, the supplier must provide the relevant terms in good time before the contract is made, this would impose severe practical limitations, and this is an option which should not be considered.

Written and additional information   **C3.12**

The above requirements can be met by the simple display of the provisions on screen. The provisions referred to in C3.3–C3.5 above, however, must also be provided to the consumer in writing 'or in another durable medium' prior to the conclusion of the contract; or, at the latest and in good time, when the goods are delivered. To comply with both sets of requirements at the same time, a supplier is obviously well advised simply to present all the above provisions in writing, or other durable medium, prior to the conclusion of the contract, since this will obviously also satisfy the other requirement as to provision prior to the conclusion of the contract.

The reference to 'writing, or in another durable medium which is available and accessible' to the consumer would extend to printable or downloadable terms and conditions.

Optional terms   **C3.13**

The provisions referred to above are mandatory. The supplier is always free to add to them. To ensure that they are binding, they should either be presented in exactly the same way as the mandatory provisions are, or presented in a way which satisfies the contractual requirements as to incorporation. Thus, the on-screen order form can simply:

- say that full terms and conditions are available on request;
- provide a link to a page where they can be read; or
- state them in full with the other provisions on the order form.

Possible optional terms

Such further terms could include:

- 'The risk in the goods passes to you when the process of despatch to you begins.'
- 'Property in the goods does not pass to you before payment is made in full.'

The supplier may also wish to provide a guarantee, though this is for the moment optional. Should he wish to do so, it could be phrased as follows:

- 'Should these goods fail in normal use within 12 months of purchase, we will repair or replace them at our expense. This does not affect your statutory rights.'

This last sentence is required in such cases by the *Consumer Transactions (Restrictions on Statements) Order 1976 (SI 1976/1813)*. It refers to the fact that, quite apart from the guarantee, the consumer might also be able to sue under the *Sale of Goods Act 1979*.

Comment:

The contract should not make any attempt to exclude or limit the rights of a consumer to goods which are of the contract description, which are of satisfactory quality and which are reasonably fit for their purpose. This is because such provisions, when used in a consumer contract, are not only void under the *Unfair Contract Terms Act 1977*, but also give rise to a criminal offence under the *Consumer Transactions (Restrictions on Statements) Order 1976 (SI 1976/1813)*.

Special provisions as to the supply of services   C3.14

For the most part, the foregoing provisions apply as much to Internet contracts for the supply of a service as they do to the supply of goods. There are some points unique to service contracts, as set out below.

Written and additional information   C3.15

The requirements as to written and additional information as to the supply of goods apply equally to contracts of service, except where the services are supplied on just one occasion and are invoiced by the operator of the means of distance communication. This latter is defined as a person, public or private, whose business involves making available means of distance communication, and thus refers only to Internet Service Providers. Accordingly, contracting with an ISP for the provision of broadband services would come within the exception.

Address requirements   C3.16

Even in such a case, however, the supplier is required to take all necessary steps to ensure that a consumer is able to obtain the supplier's geographical business address and the place of business to which the consumer can address complaints. This would mean that the on–screen order form would refer to the provider as being ABC Ltd, 123 Anytown Lane, Anytown AA1 1AA. This should be also identified as the place for queries, or some other place so identified if the former is not the place for queries.

Cancellation   C3.17

Except in the case of services supplied on one occasion and the invoice comes from the operator of the means of distance communication, the right to cancel a contract for a service is restricted in certain circumstances, unless the parties have agreed otherwise in the contract.

Thus, the right to cancel will not apply if, with the consumer's agreement, performance of the contract began before expiry of the appropriate cancellation period. That period can vary depending on whether or not the supplier has complied with the normally applicable provisions above as to written and additional information. Where there has been compliance on or before the day on which the contract was concluded, the cancellation period ends seven working days from the day following conclusion of the contract. Where there has been no compliance, but the supplier has – within three months beginning the day after the contract was concluded – provided the consumer in writing or other durable medium the information referred to in C3.3–C3.5 above and also what might be called the 'warning notice' (see below), the period of cancellation is seven working days from the day after the consumer received the information. If neither of these alternatives applies (i.e. the supplier never makes the information available), the cancellation period is three months and seven working days from the day after conclusion of the contract.

The 'warning notice'

The 'warning notice' is a reference to the fact that the indication of the right to cancel will be lost if the supplier, with the consumer's agreement, begins performance of the service prior to the end of the cancellation service.

Form of 'warning notice'

The relevant clause could thus read:

> 'You have a right to cancel this contract at any time before seven working days has passed from the day after this contract was made. You can cancel by notice in writing or any other durable means (such as by fax). If, however, we start to perform our side of the contract with your agreement before you exercise this right to cancel, your right to cancel is lost'.

Optional terms   C3.18

Terms as to passing of property and risk have no relevance to contracts for the provision of services.

Exclusion and limitation clauses   C3.19

There is, however, scope for the use of exclusion or limitation clauses. The *Supply of Goods and Services Act 1982* imposes on those providing a service an obligation to use reasonable care and skill. A clause seeking to exclude or limit this obligation is not rendered automatically void by the *Unfair Contract Terms Act 1977*, still less is it made a criminal offence against the *Consumer Transactions (Restrictions on Statements) Order 1976 (SI 1976/1813)*. Instead, such a clause is valid if it can be shown to be reasonable under *UCTA 1977* or not judged unfair under the *Unfair Terms in Consumer Contracts Regulations 1999 (SI 1999/2083)*. There is, therefore, nothing to be lost by the use of such a clause as the following.

> 'The supplier accepts no liability for any failure, shortcomings or defects, howsoever arising, in the service provided, save only that full responsibility is accepted for death or personal injury caused by the supplier's negligence.'

The last words recognise that, under the *UCTA 1977*, it is not possible to avoid liability for death or personal injury caused by negligence.

A two tier clause   C3.20

The broad sweep of this clause may make it vulnerable under the UCTA 1977 and the *Unfair Terms in Consumer Contracts Regulations 1999 (SI 1999/2083)*, so the supplier could add the following:

> 'To the extent that the above clause is found by any court or arbitrator to be void, the supplier will accept liability in an amount not exceeding the contract price.'

This too may be judged unreasonable or unfair, but could well succeed so should be retained.

Checklist   C3.21

- Are you fully aware of the application to the contract of the *Consumer Protection (Distance Selling) Regulations 2000 (SI 2000/2334)* and of the *Electronic Commerce (EC Directive) Regulations 2002 (SI 2002/2013)*?
- Have you made sure that all the information required by those Regulations has been supplied?
- Are you sure that the relevant information will be supplied at the time and in the manner required by those Regulations?
- Have you made sure that your on-screen copy is couched in terms of an invitation to treat and not an offer?
- Have you set out how you intend to perform the contract?
- Are you fully aware of the rights of the consumer to cancel and how long the cooling off period lasts?
- Are you also aware of the limitations on the right to cancel?
- Has thought been given to providing alternative goods should the original ones become unavailable?
- Are you sure that you have considered any problems which might arise from applications from those under age?
- Is all the contractual information located or placed where it can be accessed in accordance with the Regulations?
- Have you made use of the fact that the Regulations allow you to add terms and conditions of your own choosing?
- In the drafting of any exclusion clauses, have you been fully aware of the restrictions imposed on their use?
- Have you complied with data protection rules?

Chapter C4
Online Terms and Conditions for the Supply of Software

At a glance   C4.1

- The *Consumer Protection (Distance Selling) Regulations 2000 (SI 2000/2334)* and the *Electronic Commerce (EC Directive) Regulations 2002 (SI 2002/2013)* apply to such contracts.

- The normal law of contract also applies, in particular the rules as to offer and acceptance.

- Such contracts can only be contracts for the supply of services.

- There are specific requirements as to what must go into the particular contract.

- Careful consideration must be given to calculating the delivery charges.

- Cancellation rights can easily be lost in this particular context. The provisions as to payment and countermanding payment are of particular importance here.

- Substitute software can be offered.

- There must be a specific geographical address given to which complaints can be addressed.

- Details of any after-sales service or guarantee are to be provided, though there is no compulsion to provide either or these.

- There are requirements as to the time and manner in which the mandatory information is presented.

- There is scope for deciding where the information is to be provided.

- Certain information is to be in writing or some other durable medium.

- Apart from the terms made mandatory by the *Consumer Protection (Distance Selling) Regulations 2000 (SI 2000/2334)*, the supplier is free to add his own terms and conditions. These could cover various matters such as systems support, copying restrictions, virus warnings and the like.

- There is scope for the use of exclusion or limitation clauses.

Issues   C4.2

In this context, where there is no question of a disk being supplied, the supply of software online can only be the provision of a service (see CHAPTER A4 SOFTWARE CONTRACTS – SPECIAL ISSUES).

Such sales are a form of distance selling and, as such, are subject to the provisions of the *Consumer Protection (Distance Selling) Regulations 2000 (SI 2000/2334)*. It should be borne in mind, though, that the law of contract also applies, in particular the rules relating to offer and acceptance.

Offers and invitations to treat   C4.3

The Internet copy would amount to an invitation to treat, not an offer, meaning that it is the consumer who makes the offer, which the supplier is entitled to reject in his absolute discretion. This could be important if, as has happened, the Internet advertisement states a much lower price for the item than was intended.

Contract terms required by the Regulations   C4.4

There is no need for the on–screen contract to be presented as a formal document, but it must contain at least the following detail.

(1) The identity of the supplier. If payment is required in advance, the supplier's address must also be given. It seems permissible for the address to be a PO Box number, and not an actual geographical address.

(2) A description of the main characteristics of the software.

(3) The price of the software including all taxes. Although the Regulations are not entirely clear on this point, it would appear permissible to quote the price in the form of £100 plus £17.50 VAT, as an alternative to quoting a VAT inclusive price. If the latter is chosen, there is no requirement actually to say that it includes VAT. It does not appear permissible to say '£100 plus VAT at the appropriate rate'.

(4) There must be a statement of the relevant delivery costs.

Determining delivery costs   C4.5

It is far from clear how this requirement will operate in this context if its assumed, as it seems proper to do, that the costs of downloading are delivery charges. Internet connections are invariably either freephone or at local rates. The supplier will not know this, nor will he necessarily know how long it will take the consumer to download the software. This problem is compounded if the supplier is outside the United Kingdom. It seems that the best the supplier can do is to give an approximate time for downloading and to say that the costs will depend on applicable connection rates.

(5) There must be a statement of the arrangements for payment, delivery or performance. The arrangements for payment could embrace online means for paying, usually by entering credit card details, or by allowing for sums to be deducted straight from a bank account.

The stated arrangements as to performance will be easily and automatically covered by the instructions for downloading.

Given the nature of this particular transaction, it is obviously unnecessary to give any dates for performance.

(6) Notice must be given of the consumer's right to cancel. This should state that the consumer can cancel the contract at any time up to seven working days from the day after conclusion of the contract.

Exercising the right to cancel   C4.6

In addition, there must be an indication as to how the consumer can exercise his right to cancel. Under the *Consumer Protection (Distance Selling) Regulations 2000 (SI 2000/2334)*, the notice of cancellation must be in writing or in another 'durable medium' available to and accessible by the supplier, which would thus include fax or E-mail and, arguably, a message left by answerphone. The contract must indicate the ways in which the consumer must provide the notice of cancellation.

Losing the right to cancel   C4.7

Given the nature of the envisaged contract, the right to cancel can easily be lost, since there is an exclusion from the right to cancel, unless the parties agree otherwise, where the supply of the particular service has begun with the consumer's consent. Since the act of downloading is instigated by the consumer, then it will begin with his consent.

To comply with the Regulations, the supplier, after giving the online instructions as to payment, should clearly indicate that the consumer can countermand his payment before beginning downloading by confirming the contract. The Regulations also require a statement to the effect that cancellation is not permitted once downloading has begun.

(7) There must be a statement of the cost of using the means of distance communication, unless the cost is charged at the appropriate standard rate. In practical terms, this provision has no application to Internet dealing since calls will either be free or at local rates.

(8) There must be an indication as to how long the offer or price remains valid. If there is a definite close date, this should be stated. It would also seem possible to say that the offer is subject to availability. It further seems possible to say that an offer remains open until further notice. As a practical matter, the supplier should withdraw the details from the Internet site as soon as orders can no longer be fulfilled.

(9) If the contract is for the supply of software on a permanent or recurrent basis, the minimum duration of the contract must be included if this is appropriate. For instance, the supply of software might be for downloading anti-virus software every time an update to cover new viruses is made necessary.

(10) If the intended software is unavailable, the supplier may wish to offer the consumer an alternative of equivalent quality and price. If he wishes to do so, and the option is his, this information must be provided.

(11) The contract must give a 'geographical address' of the place of business of the supplier to which complaints can be addressed. It does not seem necessary for there to be a specific reference to 'complaints' in the contract. It would be enough if, for example, the address was given as one to which queries can be directed. Although the requirement is simply to give an address and not, for example, a telephone or fax number, or E-mail address, one or the other can and should be provided.

(12) If the supplier offers any form of after sales service or guarantee, relevant information must be provided. There is no compulsion to offer a guarantee or after sales service.

(13) The *Consumer Protection (Distance Selling) Regulations 2000 (SI 2000/2334)* state that regard must be had to the principles 'governing the protection of those who are unable to give their consent such as minors'. While a transaction through mail order could cope with this by requiring the signature of a parent or guardian, it is difficult to see how this can also be achieved in relation to Internet sales. It would seem better for supplies through this medium always to exclude minors.

For information regarding additional important requirements set out by the *Electronic Commerce (EC Directive) Regulations 2002 (SI 2002/2013)* see C1.3 above.

Precedent – Standard Internet Contract for Software

C4.8

ABC Co Ltd

123 Any Street

Any Town

AA1 1AA

DETAILS

Agreement for the provision of anti-virus software at a total cost of £29.99. Please note: we cannot advise specifically on how much your connection charges will be for downloading. We would advise that downloading time depends on the quality of the line and the modem strength, but, under normal circumstances, downloading should not take more than 60 minutes.

CREDIT CARD DETAILS

Complete in the on-screen box details of your credit card and billing address. If the address to which the software is downloaded is different to the billing address, please also provide this address.

HELPLINE

While we are confident that your use of the software will be trouble free, we are anxious to deal with any problems which might arise. Please address any queries to us at the above address or contact us on: _____.

All services and prices displayed here are subject to availability and are liable to be withdrawn at any time without notice.

IMPORTANT: Please note that you have a right to cancel this contract. You can do this at any time up to seven days starting with the day after

335

the contract between us is concluded. You can cancel this contract at any time within the permitted period by clicking on the 'not confirmed' button placed beneath the payment box. Please note: If you commence downloading, then your right to cancel is lost.

If you are under 18, we cannot accept your order.

Please click here if you do not want us to send you further information or supply your details to third parties.

Form in which contract details must be presented   C4.9

The details must all be provided 'in good time' prior to the conclusion of the contract. Presumably, 'in good time' means in such time as will allow the consumer to consider the terms before proceeding with the order. Since a contract is not concluded until the supplier accepts the offer, as by an E-mail confirmation, these terms and conditions should be made available before any acceptance takes place.

Manner of presentation   C4.10

These provisions above must be provided in a 'clear and comprehensible manner appropriate to the means of distance communication'. This would require them to be easily legible, and not, for example, such that flash on and off the screen so that reading them is difficult. 'Comprehensible' does not appear to mean that the terms and conditions must be in English, since any language is comprehensible to those who speak it, and because a consumer faced with a language he does not speak is always free to ignore the offer. It presumably does require that, given the language can be understood, that the above provisions are expressed with due clarity.

Location of terms   C4.11

It also seems possible for the provisions to be elsewhere than on the page containing details of the offer. If there is a link to the provisions, so long as this is clearly indicated, that would suffice. In principle, it is possible for the on-screen page to indicate that the provisions are available from an address which will send them to the consumer by post. Since, however, the supplier must provide the relevant terms in good time before the contract is made, this would impose severe practical limitations, and this is an option which should not be considered.

Written and additional information C4.12

The above requirements can be met by the simple display of the provisions on screen. The provisions referred to in C4.4–C4.5 above, however, must also be provided to the consumer in writing 'or in another durable medium' prior to the conclusion of the contract; or, at the latest and in good time, when the goods are delivered. To comply with both sets of requirements at the same time, a supplier is obviously well advised simply to present all the above provisions in writing, or other durable medium, prior to the conclusion of the contract, since this will obviously also satisfy the other requirement as to provision prior to the conclusion of the contract.

The reference to 'writing, or in another durable medium which is available and accessible to the consumer' would extend to printable or downloadable terms and conditions.

Other terms and conditions C4.13

The foregoing represent the terms and conditions made mandatory by the *Consumer Protection (Distance Selling) Regulations 2000 (SI 2000/2334)*. Other terms can be added by the supplier to provide the appropriate safeguards.

Restrictions on copying C4.14

'This software is supplied solely for your use. It must not in any circumstances be copied, other than by way of providing a back-up copy, nor may copies be supplied, whether free of charge or for a payment, to any third party.'

The obvious intent with this example is to safeguard the supplier's intellectual property rights, in particular his copyright in the software.

Virus warning C4.15

'Although we make every effort to ensure that no form of virus is transmitted to you in the course of your downloading this software, no guarantee can be offered. YOU ARE THEREFORE STRONGLY ADVISED TO ENSURE THAT YOU HAVE UP TO DATE ANTI-VIRUS SOFTWARE INSTALLED. If you do not, then we cannot be held responsible for the effects or consequences, no matter what they be, of any virus which you might download.'

The supplier of the software cannot be liable for the effects of any virus which might already be present on the consumer's system. It may be, however, that there is a virus in the software being downloaded. The warning in this case is given in clear and unequivocal terms and, while it can be challenged under both the *UCTA 1977*, and the *Unfair Terms in Consumer Contracts Regulations 1999 (SI 1999/2083)*, there is always a chance that it will survive challenge.

Technical support   **C4.16**

The following can be used to provide technical support.

'The following technical support services are available to you. You can visit our website at www _____ or you can visit our support services website at www _____.

You can also e mail us at advice@ _____ and enter [supplier to insert heading] as the subject of your E-mail to obtain the index of our documents. You can also call us on [012345678] on our fax back service and request document number [123456] for our index of documents. Technical support is also available during normal working hours from [012345678].

You can also visit the online forums by typing [XXXX] into your search engine. Online volunteers and forum managers offer advice on our products when issues are posted on bulletin boards. If any issues or problems are uncovered, they will be posted on our website.'

System requirements   **C4.17**

The following can be used as an example.

'It is your sole responsibility to ensure that you are operating a system which can support the software downloaded by you.'

Installation issues   **C4.18**

In terms of installation issues, the following can be used as an example.

'If there is a failure at any point in the installation of the software, a complete uninstall will then be performed. It is therefore important not to close the installation prematurely by clicking on the "close" button. No liability can be accepted if there is any such premature closing, whether by deliberate action or by some extraneous event beyond our control, such as a failure in the public electricity supply system.'

General exclusion of liability   **C4.19**

The following is an example of a general exclusion of liability.

'The supplier accepts no liability of whatsoever nature for any failures of whatever kind in the capacity and performance of the software supplied. Without prejudice to the generality of the foregoing, the supplier cannot accept liability for any damage which may have been caused to any data stored on the customer's drives. The customer also agrees that, in selecting and downloading this software, he relied entirely on his own skill and judgement.'

Controls on such clauses

Since the contract is for the supply of a service, the supplier has relative freedom to exclude or limit the obligations implied by the *SGSA 1982*, to provide the service with reasonable care and skill, and to exclude any implied obligations as to the quality of the service provided. Such an exclusion clause will, though, have to survive challenge under the *UCTA 1977* and the *Unfair Terms in Consumer Contracts Regulations 1999* (*SI 1999/2083*).

A Two Tier clause

Since such a clause as the foregoing could well fail to such challenge, the following should be added:

'Should the foregoing be held unreasonable or unfair by any court or arbitrator, the supplier will accept liability for any failures as above described in an amount not exceeding the contract price.' This too, of course, will be subject to scrutiny under the Act and Regulations.

Checklist   **C4.20**

- Are you fully aware of the applicability of the *Consumer Protection (Distance Selling) Regulations 2000* (*SI 2000/2334*) and the *Electronic Commerce (EC Directive) Regulations 2002* (*SI 2002/2013*) and what they require?

- Are you also aware of the fact that normal contract law also applies, in particular the rules as to offer and acceptance?

- Are you aware of what information is made mandatory by the Regulations?

- Have you given proper thought to how the delivery charges will be calculated?

- Has there been a clear indication as to the right to cancel and how this right can be lost?

- Has there been a clear statement as to the duration of the offer?

- Has a proper geographical address been given for complaints?

- Has proper thought been given to protecting minors?

- Have any requirements as to data protection been observed?

- Are you sure you have complied with the requirements as to the time by which and the manner in which the mandatory information is to be provided?

- Have you given proper regard as to where this information is located?

- Have you complied with the requirements to material being in written or other durable information?

- Have you considered the use of terms and conditions beyond those required by the Regulations?

- In particular, have you thought of adding such terms as clearly prevent unauthorised copying, virus warnings or setting up helplines?

- Has proper use been made of exclusion or limitation clauses?

Table of Cases

Table of Statutes

353

Table of Statutory Instruments

Index